On Liberty

T0386363

CURZON JEWISH PHILOSOPHY SERIES
Series Editor: Oliver Leaman

It is the aim of this series to publish books in the general area of Jewish philosophy. A broad interpretation will be taken of what Jewish philosophy comprises, and the series will be interested in receiving proposals which involve a philosophical treatment of a Jewish thinker or topic, or which look at some aspect of Jewish cultural life from a philosophical perspective.

MEDIEVAL JEWISH PHILOSOPHY
An Introduction
Dan Cohn-Sherbok

FACING THE OTHER
The Ethics of Emmanuel Levinas
Edited by Seán Hand

MOSES MAIMONIDES
Oliver Leaman

A USER'S GUIDE TO FRANZ ROSENZWEIG'S
STAR OF REDEMPTION
Norbert M. Samuelson

ON LIBERTY
Jewish Philosophical Perspectives
Edited by Daniel H. Frank

On Liberty

Jewish Philosophical Perspectives

Edited by

Daniel H. Frank

Routledge
Taylor & Francis Group

LONDON AND NEW YORK

First published 1999 by Curzon Press

2 Park Square, Milton Park, Abingdon, Oxfordshire OX14 4RN
52 Vanderbilt Avenue, New York, NY 10017

Routledge is an imprint of the Taylor & Francis Group, an informa business

First issued in paperback 2019

British Library Cataloguing in Publication Data
A catalogue record of this book is available from the British Library

Library of Congress Cataloguing in Publication Data
A catalog record for this book has been requested

Typeset in New Century Schoolbook by
LaserScript Ltd, Mitcham, Surrey

ISBN 13: 978-0-7007-1144-4 (hbk)
ISBN 13: 978-0-415-59255-0 (pbk)

Dedicated to the Memory of

Madeleine Goodman and Ze'ev Falk

Colleagues
Scholars
Friends

Contents

PART TWO
LIBERTY AND AUTHORITY IN JEWISH POLITICAL THOUGHT

Contributors

Aryeh Botwinick is Professor of Political Science at Temple University, USA

Ze'ev W. Falk was Rector and Professor of Jewish Law at the Seminary of Judaic Studies (Jerusalem) and Berman Professor of Law at the Hebrew University of Jerusalem, Israel

Daniel H. Frank is Professor of Philosophy and Director of the Judaic Studies Program at the University of Kentucky, USA

Lenn E. Goodman is Professor of Philosophy at Vanderbilt University, USA

Peter J. Haas is Associate Professor of Jewish Thought and Literature at Vanderbilt University, USA

Edward Halper is Professor of Philosophy at the University of Georgia, USA

Jonathan Jacobs is Associate Professor of Philosophy at Colgate University, USA

Oliver Leaman is Professor of Philosophy at Liverpool John Moores University, UK

Daniel Statman is Associate Professor of Philosophy at Bar-Ilan University, Israel

Introduction

With its theocentric focus and emphasis on communal law
and regulation, Judaism and traditional Jewish thought
would seem to ill consort with the modern (post-Lockean), liberal
political sensibility and its focus upon rights, personal autonomy, and a studied values neutrality with respect to the human
good. From this angle the central issue of this collection devoted
to political liberty appears to be the commensurability (or
incommensurability) of tradition and modernity. And in a
general way, this is the problematic here. But the reader will
be in for a surprise I think, for the starting point, the very
presumption of the debate is here reversed. Invariably it is
presumed that it is tradition (or religion), in this case Judaism,
that must play catch-up. It is Judaism that must reform itself in
some fashion, so as to take full part in modern life and the liberal
state. There is no thought that it is the liberal state, indeed
modernity itself and what it stands for, that is lagging behind
and in need of reform. But it is just this possibility that many of
the chapters in this volume, especially in the first part, address.

This volume in its own way joins company with the chorus of
those urging a revisioning of liberalism, at least in the form
championed by Locke and Mill. A number of the chapters
(Goodman, Halper, Jacobs) display the kind of discomfort that
contemporary communitarian critics of liberalism (Sandel,
MacIntyre, Taylor, Walzer) have felt with both the premises
and the political agenda of modern liberalism, its atomistic
(asocial) view of the individual, its values neutrality with respect
to the human good, and its commitment to a very wide values
pluralism to underwrite its neutral stand. This communitarian

response to liberalism, evocative of much pre-modern, classical political thought and its molecular view of the individual and 'thick' conception of the good, places traditional religion in general and Judaism in particular in a very powerful position to *lead* the discussion concerning the reconceptualization of the modern political sensibility. Whether religion and its norms and values should play this role is of course another question. Goodman, Halper, and Jacobs, each in his own way, certainly think so, and they argue for a (liberal) agenda not at odds with a strong normative stand, indeed prescriptive of those extra-political values that Judaism entails. For them, the philosophically interesting problem becomes that of finding common ground between Judaism and the liberal state that goes beyond mere accommodation.

But classical liberalism is not dead and the last three chapters in the first part (Frank, Falk, Statman) provide differing responses to the communitarian critique. As noted, the un-spoken presumption underlying the debate between tradition and modernity, between religion and the liberal state, has been that it is tradition and religion that must be modernized (and depoliticized), rather than that modernity and the liberal state be infused with extra-political, religious norms. This regnant assumption, created out of the crucible of post-Reformation religious intolerance, demanded of religion(s) a time-out period, a time of restraint, at least until a set of extra-religious norms could be fixed. Some sort of separation of church and state followed in all liberal democracies. This legacy, often written into law, continues in the (classical) liberal agenda with its manifest lack of enthusiasm on the political level to impose or prescribe any particular set of values, save those of a (negative) non-interventionist sort catering to the pluralism and the commitment to personal autonomy undergirding the modernist pro-gram. While such non-interventionism is anathema to the communitarian prescriptivist, the non-communitarian liberal, ever mindful of the (not so distant) past, rests content with the strict separation of church and state and the correlative privatization of religion. For the liberal, religion is still the culprit with its imperialistic tendencies, and for the liberal living as a Jew in an overwhelmingly Christian country such as the United States, the strict separation of church and state makes perfect sense.

In Israel too a debate continues between and over religious and secular powers and authority. Since the promulgation of the Basic Laws in 1992, which explicitly defines Israel as 'a Jewish and democratic state,' the debate has been especially vigorous. Is it possible to be both a Jewish *and* a democratic state? Or as Falk puts it: 'Can Judaism Incorporate Human Rights, Democracy, and Personal Autonomy?' With the Palestinian uprising and the ever increasing power of the *charedi* the issue is joined, and the challenge for the Jewish state is to retain its identity while guaranteeing the rights of all living within its boundaries. While communitarians in long-established secular, liberal democracies such as the United States and Great Britain may long for a religious sensibility to begin to pervade and transform the political culture, in the existentially-charged environment that is Israel (mere) accommodation between the various factions may be all that one may reasonably hope for. I think that Statman in his chapter argues tacitly to the same conclusion. In vigorously defending traditional halakhic Judaism against the charge of complicity in reactionary politics and the assassination of Yitzhak Rabin, he signals agreement with Falk, that traditional Judaism and democratic institutions need not be in conflict. Again, it will be noted that from the Israeli perspective lack of conflict, not positive interaction between the religious and secular camps, is the practical goal – a cold peace.

The second part of the volume includes chapters that are more historically focused, but similarly revisionist. As axiomatic as the aforementioned presumption that modernity requires the reform and depoliticization of religion is the supposition that before the modern period no liberal ('modern') ideas are to be found, in particular, notions of personal autonomy, rights, and (what Isaiah Berlin has dubbed) 'negative' freedom or liberty. As Goodman, Halper, and Jacobs found reason to question the former presumption, so Leaman and Botwinick find reason to question the latter assumption. Their chapters focus on the medieval period and point out that such dichotomous thinking as would render incomprehensible such liberal (modern) notions as negative freedom (freedom from interference and from another's will) and (voluntary) contractual obligation cannot be sustained with respect to the pre-modern period. Leaman points out that the very logic of freedom and liberty entails that freedom to act in a certain way requires freedom from interference by others. Even if the medieval period constrained choice by presuming a rather monolithic conception of the good – in the Jewish Middle Ages an unbending commitment to halakha – nevertheless unencumbered choice is vouchsafed. A recurring theme found in medieval authors from Saadia on is why God gave us the law, given that it was open to him to change us miraculously. And as Leaman points out, the answer in large part presumes divine respect for human beings and their autonomy as well as a correlative notion of negative freedom or non-interference in the sense that it is part of the divine plan that we perfect ourselves *by ourselves*, without interference.

The final two chapters by Botwinick and Haas are an interesting contrast in the variety of interpretations of medieval Jewish political thought. Writing on the notions of liberty, authority, and consent in Maimonides' magnum opus, *Guide of the Perplexed*, Botwinick emphasizes the contractual nature of the Sinaitic revelation and the (proto-Hobbesian) voluntarism that is there instantiated. For Botwinick, the relationship between authority and consent present at Sinai is 'a harbinger of modern liberalism.' If Botwinick's claim stands, one will be forced to revise the simple-minded medieval-modern distinction. Meanwhile, Haas takes a close look at two of the most renowned rabbis of early European Judaism, Meir of Rothenburg and Solomon ben Adret (Rasba), and makes clear that for them personal liberty may be limited, sometimes quite severely, by communal authority. This may perhaps be considered the standard view of Jewish life and thought in medieval times, giving way to greater freedom in the modern period. But, as Haas points out, the deployment of Jewish communal authority in the modern period is real, and must be, even considering the voluntary nature of Jewish community involvement today, and he illustrates this authority by considering how a contemporary Reform responsa deals with the issue of personal liberty and communal authority.

This, then, is a rather controversial collection, calling into question some sacred cows, the avant garde nature of modernity and liberalism, the backwardness of religion and religious norms and values, and the illiberal nature of medieval life and thought. It may appear to the casual reader that much of this volume subserves a traditional, conservative agenda, one wedded to a revivifying of the past. But upon closer consideration it may just turn out that those extra-political norms so praised by Plato, Aristotle, and their followers in the monotheistic religious traditions are, if not timeless, not yet passe.

———

The seventeenth annual conference of the Academy for Jewish Philosophy provided the occasion for the initial presentation of the chapters in this volume, except for those by Jonathan Jacobs and Daniel Statman, which were invited by the editor. The Academy conference, 'On Liberty,' was held June 2–3, 1996, in Nashville at Vanderbilt University. In light of the discussions at the meetings, the essays first presented there have been revised, and only Lenn Goodman's and Oliver Leaman's chapters have been published earlier, the former in his *Judaism, Human Rights, and Human Values* (Oxford University Press, 1998, pp. 98–136) and the latter, in abbreviated form, in *Rivista di Storia della Filosofia*, LII, 1, 1997, pp. 141–51.

The editor and all the participants at the conference owe a debt of gratitude to Lenn Goodman for organizing the conference and to Vanderbilt for the excellent facilities that were provided. Two other debts, sadly, cannot be repaid, at least now. One is owed to Madeleine Goodman, who, as Dean of the College of Arts and Science at Vanderbilt, welcomed us at the opening of the conference. Madeleine Goodman was a gifted scholar and administrator, as well as a loving mother and wife. The other debt is owed to Ze'ev Falk, one of the contributors to this volume. Ze'ev Falk was a preeminent scholar of Jewish law and a warm and friendly interlocutor. It is entirely fitting that this volume, focusing in large measure on the role that Judaism and Jewish values can play in an understanding and reconceptualization of the modern liberal state, be dedicated to their memory.

PART ONE

JUDAISM AND THE LIBERAL STATE

CHAPTER ONE

On Liberty Reconsidered

Lenn E. Goodman

Timelessness is the signature of revelation in Judaism. Thus an ancient gloss on the *Amidah's* striking phrase *Attah gibbor le-'olam*, 'Thou art mighty eternally,' explains that God's voice does not dwindle over time. One way for the Mosaic canon to make good its revelatory claims and for the rabbinic tradition to validate its grasp on an inspired continuity with Mosaic revelation is by demonstrating its timeless relevance.

The values of the Judaic tradition and the principles articulated in its canon stand proudly among the ancestors of modern liberal humanism. They offer striking early support to the idea of the consent of the governed (Exod. 24:7; Deut. 27:9–26), for example. But they also offer a purchase point that can aid us in teasing out some of the problems liberalism faces today. In this paper I offer a critique of Mill's formulation of the liberal idea. Critiques running in the opposite direction, from Mill's princi-ples to the various traditions of religious and naturalistic virtue ethics, have been familiar for a century or more. But my object here is not to seek proof-texts in the Jewish canon to be urged in turn against Mill. Rather, the critique is in part internal. I see the liberal tradition as a legitimate outgrowth of Jewish, Christian and classical values,and I treasure Bergson's evolutionary interpretation of liberalism, in the ideal of the Open Society. I do think that a more coherent liberalism than Mill's in *On Liberty* can be elicited from the fuller, classic repertoire, which does not pull quite so clear as Mill does from the traditions of natural and revealed law that gave birth to liberalism. But there is little point in simply confronting one text with another – biblical communalism, rabbinic humanism, or

3

medieval pietism, against Mill's liberal utilitarianism. The outcome would simply confirm the already ingrown prejudice (enunciated long ago by Cynic philosophers like Lucian) to the effect that philosophies are marketplace commodities,[1] paradigms or worldviews that one can – at will, paradoxically enough – buy into or leave alone.

I find argument more compelling, and compelling in ways that marketing is not. The tenor of my argument is not that liberalism is mistaken but that liberals have erred in holding Mill's now canonical recension of the liberal idea at the core of the humane and tolerant tradition they espouse. I find Mill's formulae in *On Liberty* ill-grounded and, partly for that reason, skewed and pinched. Further, Mill's formulations have been abused – extended by interests he had no intention of serving onto turf he never envisioned defending. I find support for a broader idea of liberty than Mill's utilitarianism affords, in the humanism that grows from the Mosaic tradition. Jewish philosophical thinking today, I think, can, by developing those humanistic values, continue to make distinctive contributions to the general political, moral and social discourse in which the Mosaic canon has long been a formative influence.

1. Mill's Liberty

In laying out the basic principles of liberty, Mill tells us, he has no intention of appealing to any notion of absolute rights: 'It is proper to state, that I forego any advantage which could be derived to my argument from the idea of abstract right, as a thing independent of utility.' (*On Liberty*, p. 74). The disavowal is a deep obeisance to Bentham's scorn for the very idea of rights, and to the variety of naturalism underlying that scorn. Whether Mill remains true to his decision to disavow all appeal to rights is a matter for discussion. For clearly, in the end, Mill does espouse an absolute right of free opinion and free expression of opinion. He mounts on the very stilts that Bentham meant to have hidden away for good.[2] But beyond that difficulty, Mill's decision to derive an absolute right solely from its utility means that all liberties are made contingent; at the same time, the scope of the liberty the argument will support is drastically narrowed.

4

Mill's account opens with the broad affirmation of a universal sounding liberty, grounded in the 'one very simple principle' that Mill finds adequate 'to govern absolutely the dealings of society with the individual, whether the means used be physical force in the form of legal penalties or the moral coercion of public opinion,' namely: 'that the sole end for which mankind are warranted, individually or collectively in interfering with the liberty of action of any of their number, is self-protection. That the only purpose for which power can be rightfully exercised over any member of a civilized community, against his will, is to prevent harm to others' (p. 72). Mill's target, of course, is the oppressive substitution of judgment that we call paternalism (see Sartorius, ed., 1983). But the liberties called for by Mill's standard here are just three:

(1) The freedom to harm oneself[3] – or fail to improve oneself: One 'cannot rightfully be compelled [by force, *or even public opinion*] to do or forbear because it will be better for him to do so, because it will make him happier, because, in the opinion of others, to do so would be wise, or even right' (73). Mill himself deduced, as applications of his rule, the inappropriateness of restricting the sale of alcohol, or poisons, or any commodity whatever. He specified the importation of opium into China as one of the liberties his doctrine would protect (*On Liberty*, p. 151).

Strictly applied, Mill's standard means that if we could determine, say, that a given narcotic, quack cure, sadistic practice, meretricious or exploitative relationship were harmful only to adults who freely choose it, the state would have no authority to oppose it – even on utilitarian grounds! The argument would be that there is a greater utility in preventing paternalism than in restricting the offending harm. Even the familiar passing of responsibility to social and educational agencies, churches, schools, neighborhoods, families, or pressure groups would be normatively unwarrantable. No free society could give even passive support or tacit legitimation to such efforts. Rather, the laws would have to restrict such efforts as repressive of undeniable human liberties.[4] The sale of opium, then, could actually be enforced – as it was to be in the full flowering of British imperialism.

(2) The freedom willingly to submit to the will of others.

It is hard to specify exactly what Mill should mean by this. Yet he does qualify his limitation of the abuse of power with the phrase, 'against his will.' He might mean to allow, say, acceptance of the authority of a government, or the conditions of gainful employment on terms mutually agreed. But even if this is all Mill means he sharply departs from the Lockean assumption that such 'submissions' are no more than expressions of one's own will and so cannot be construed as a surrender of one's interests to the arbitrary will of another. And if he means what he seems to say, he knocks the imagination sprawling among thoughts about frightful regimes that tolerate or legitimate (voluntary) slavery, mind control by cults, and penal institutions that demand control or reconstitution of the convict's will. On the most charitable construction, Mill here has simply failed to distinguish free employment from slavery or free citizenship from subjection to a totalitarian regime, since he construes each of these as a surrender of the subject's will, rather than its voluntary adoption of another's goals (in the case of employment) or its acceptance of shared goals (in the case of government and community).

(3) The freedom to hold, express, and disseminate what views one pleases, without regard to the opinion of others, and, least of all, the pleasure of the state or common opinion, on all sorts of issues, especially those regarding the nature of the world in general and matters moral, religious, or political in particular.

Like Hobbes, Mill trusts in human nature with an abiding faith in the rational pursuit of self-interest. He knows that there is no better – or, at least, no charier – judge of that interest than ego. So he is not concerned that the liberty to harm oneself or surrender one's very liberty will be abused or misapplied. The paradoxical liberties of harm to self and self-surrender are, it seems, foregone conclusions, or trivial consequences, of the rational egoism that anchors Mill's larger scheme. They are matters of private judgment, rightly left to individual discretion, in no special need of caveat or qualification. The benefits to be gained by debarring substitutions of judgment, Mill assumes, will far outweigh the costs incurred by the occasional irrational private decision.

Besides, there are institutions that can step in to protect the interests of the mentally infirm, just as there are parents to protect the interests of children. As for societies that are not, or not yet, 'civilized,' they too can be aided, by colonial powers like Mill's own East India Company, which can provide the necessary steering – the value system and the policy decisions about its implementation – that will use paternalism where it belongs, for those who lack the faculties, individually or civilizationally, to exercise discretion in their own behalf. Thus Mill writes, still speaking of his simple principle:

> It is, perhaps, hardly necessary to say that this doctrine is meant to apply only to human beings in the maturity of their faculties. We are not now speaking of children, or of young persons below the age which the law may fix as that of manhood or of womanhood. Those who are still in a state to require being taken care of by others, must be protected against their own actions as well as against external injury. For the same reason, we may leave out of consideration those backward states of society in which the race itself may be considered as in its nonage. (73).

When Mill does consider such 'backward states of society,' he warrants a quasi-benevolent despotism in their behalf (*Representative Government*, chapter 18) – a despotism whose benevolence must be qualified by realism, and which Mill thus models on the regimes of Akbar or Charlemagne: 'Despotism is a legitimate mode of government in dealing with barbarians, provided the end be their improvement, and the means justified by actually effecting that end.' (*On Liberty*, p. 73). Aristotle said as much regarding ends in his justification of slavery.

Mill's consequentialism here is complete. He insists that actual betterment flow from a paternalistic regime, but he draws no constitutional restraint on the intrinsic character of the means deployed to that end. He cannot, without appeal to absolute rights. The anomaly is heightened when Mill assigns what look like absolute rights to those whose societies he does deem civilized. For now we have societies, living side by side, and in relations of trade or even colonial – or mercantile – dependency (see Frankel, 1949, 1960), where the denizens of one are denied rights available to the citizens of the other. The question naturally arises whether the absolute guarantees available so freely here are not purchased at the expense of their denial there.

I mention all this not to score points ad hominem from Mill's employment at the East India Company,[5] but because the anomaly persists. Under the guise of an easy relativism, some would be liberals still hold civil rights, human rights, to be a European, bourgeois notion not readily accommodated to the values and cultures of African or Asian societies. The racism implicit in such varieties of relativism will be evident.[6] When questions of profit from cheap goods are considered, the matter of dependency, of the parasitism potentially concealed within the rights we hold so proud and dear, returns with a vengeance. Mill at least believed that India was being governed in its own interest. But the post-colonial free marketeer has left the Third World in free fall. Today's political relativists are liberal as can be about the regimes that others – including a billion Chinese – may toil under, as long as cheap goods are available in quantity at Wal-Mart and Kmart.

Confident that self-harm and the surrender of liberty itself to the will of another will be rare in what he is pleased to identify as civilized societies – notably Britain and the United States (*On Liberty*, pp. 127–29, 167) – Mill focuses on the object of his most immediate concern, freedom of thought and expression. In the end – although we parse the liberty of his title generically, as Mill's rhetorical posture expects and demands – the liberty he singles out as his cynosure is in fact just one, freedom of mind. Even the individualism that he makes the great theme of his third and fourth chapters is instrumentalized in the service of intellectual liberty.

Further, Mill's preoccupation with intellectual freedom and its corollary, the freedom to communicate, strongly color his anti-paternalist thoughts. For when he speaks ingenuously about the opinions of others as to my true interests and warms to the topic of my right not to pursue those interests, should I so choose, it is not suicide or mind control, tattooing, euthanasia, or even self-neglect that comes to the fore, but the presumptive interest of the soul in its salvation, which do-gooders among Mill's contemporaries (or our own) might seek to protect by restricting skeptical, heretical, or anti-religious speech. Mill's formulation may be general, but his concern is very topical and particular. The core of that concern, as the unfolding of his argument makes crystal clear (*On Liberty*, p. 91), is with the expression of moral, religious and political ideas. Self-harm is envisioned, as if in scare-quotes, as failure to go to church or pay lipservice to pious verities. That is why it can be safely left to the self-help of individuals.

The demands of great corporations for our labor and that of our children, at ruinous or exploitative wages or in unsafe or unwholesome surroundings are not uppermost in Mill's mind when he chooses the words to be emblazoned on his broad, libertarian banner. Nor is the liberty to assume environmental and other risks in exchange for economic benefits. Free trade is protected, on the vague grounds that it is a 'social act.' More pointedly, it is defended on the grounds that when economic transactions are left 'perfectly free,' we have learned, 'both the cheapness and the good quality of the commodities are most effectually provided for' (*On Liberty*, pp. 150–51)[7] So the potential harm of alcohol, narcotics, or tobacco, if these can be sold to us, simply does not weigh in the balance. Thought and speech stand paramount among the goods to be protected. And even the protections of our right to harm ourselves (or arm ourselves?) or to surrender our will to that of another are couched as protections of thought and speech. They come down to us still framed and hemmed in by Mill's rationale – as if our sole concern for the human person were with the right to refuse to pray and the right to welcome or turn away the missionary at the door.

2. Mill's Argument

Mill's defense of the utility of freedom of thought and expression is grounded in his famous trichotomy: Speech, he argues, must be either true or false, or some mixture of the two. But, (1) if true, even the most unpopular or seemingly outlandish theory should surely be allowed to win men's minds. Only dogmatic pretensions of infallibility could provide the necessary assurance to those who would suppress a claim. (2) Even ideas or claims that are in fact false still have the value of keeping familiar truths from becoming dead and dormant, losing the living edge that only the honing of criticism can impart. And (3) if, as is most often the case, new and old ideas involve some mixture of truth with ignorance and confusion, the marketplace of ideas should be left free to sort out what is of lasting value from what deserves to be forgotten or discarded.

(1) Mill's argument, in the case of presumptive truths, parallels the claim of some environmental advocates that we must not destroy, say, the rainforest, since no one knows what genetic treasures it might hold – not least, perhaps, the cure for AIDS or cancer. To apply such argumentation here, one needs to know that the ideas that are unwelcome are indeed at risk of suppression that is permanent, in the way that extinction is permanent. One needs to know also that ideas, like creatures in the rainforest, cannot be harmful (unless, of course, disturbed).

Mill's consequentialism here does not serve him well. It does not, for example, forestall the oppression or persecution of persons who hold unorthodox or unaccepted ideas, so long as those who do the persecuting are unlikely to succeed in utterly uprooting the ideas (or obliterating the expressions) of which they disapprove. An employer could dismiss an employee for holding certain views, as long as it seemed likely that the views themselves would survive unimpaired. Not appealing to any notion of rights, Mill's argument does not distinguish between censoring a newspaper and stifling a thought; it does not distinguish between burning a book and burning the author. Further, the charge of dogmatism is misplaced. A perfect fallibilist can act to suppress an idea, as perhaps Pilate tried to do, while making no claims to know what the truth is, let alone claims to infallibility.

(2) If an idea is false, Mill argues, it should still be allowed its day in court – not for any absolutist reasons involving fairness to human beings, but because the challenge of argument will clarify and strengthen the correct view. But it is hard to see how any ideas can be useful or beneficial unless some can be harmful. The assumption that thought must always be held harmless trivializes the work and power of ideas, even while the presumption that bad ideas are the catalysts of good ones romanticizes that work and power.

Jewish experience vividly bears the memory of a kind of speech that can hurt, and unleash the dogs of war, and the jackals of genocide. The experience, tragically, is not unique. It puts in question Mill's very premise that civilization has made some nations safe for the liberties he defined. Industrial democracies are vulnerable to the poisons of misappropriated speech, like the countries of the Third World. The experience of Bosnia is no different in kind from that of Rwanda and Burundi, or Cambodia. Education was no bar to membership in the SS. On the contrary, the Nazi officer corps drew heavily from the intellectual elite of Germany. Ideas can be a vehicle of destruction as well as of creation. The pattern runs back to the Corcyran massacre and beyond, to the Egyptian slavery and attempted genocide of ancient Israel (Exod. 1:16). Once a population has been marked notionally as pestilent or subhuman, wholesale destruction awaits only the opportunity and the means.

The inference I would draw from the fact that there is dangerous and destructive speech is not to a rationale for suppressing unpopular or unwelcome views. Rather, I would find here a warrant and a need for the encouragement of critical and constructive thinking. But such encouragement has costs. It involves positive rights, rather than the negative ones Mill's essay deems sufficient. The partial outcome, for all who have faith in the power of understanding, is a warrant for the creation and support of libraries, schools, museums, orchestras, educational media and opportunities – the diffusion of books, and (in our time) computer access, informational and educational broadcasting. But beyond that, there is a warrant and a mandate for all human beings, individually and conjointly, to attend to the tenor of the ethos and the ideas that inspire it. For no mere medium guarantees that love and generosity, or even tolerance, will be its message.

My own inference bears with it a problematic, the very problematic of orthodoxy that was exercising Mill at the dawn of the information age. And linked to that is the related problem of vulgarity that also surfaced in Mill's time and was an object of concern in his earlier thought – the loss of depth, complexity, and critical edge in the materials intended to convey and diffuse the ideas that make critical thinking possible. For the broader the diffusion of an idea the greater the risk of a loss of subtlety and the greater the liability of blurring argument into authority, and of blunting or even reversing the idea's nisus.

This difficulty was recognized by Plato and addressed by him with the expedient of enlisting that class of human beings whom he called the poets in the cause of truth and justice. Plato's hope was that the beliefs and attitudes that creative works have the power to instill would coalesce in an ethos that aims at truth and fairness, rather than serve one or another passional or appetitive master. His fear was that the appeals of human passions and appetites, wrapped in the rhetoric of freedom, would be used to enslave the populace politically or exploit their desires commercially, to their own detriment.

Religion is the name we now give to Plato's answer to the problem he confronted. As a human institution religion itself is susceptible to corruption. It suffers not only from the dynamic of vulgarity that Plato hoped it would surmount, but also from the original passional and appetitive illnesses that he hoped it would treat. Epicurus, whose egoist hedonism lies at the root of liberalism and laissez faire, and whose individualist credentials are far stronger than Mill's, preferred to deny the problem Plato addressed, rather than confront it. So in Epicureanism no natural passion or appetite was admitted to be dangerous, if only we keep our heads and moderate our desires. The notion of a problem about the vulgarizing of knowledge was dismissed as elitist and confining. No moral truth relevant to all could possibly lie beyond the reach of all. Religion, the poetry that Plato had hoped would weave a ladder from the light of the stars to the unseen majesty beyond, seemed now to be no more than a tangle of anxieties, entrapping the unwary in their own unreasoning fear of death.

The conflict that ensued between followers of Plato and followers of his heretical successor Epicurus is too large to be more than noted here. It sharply defines two rival ideas of knowledge and of liberty. I mention it only to make clear that dismissal (as elitist) of the problem of vulgarity, in and beyond religion, is itself just one of the stratagems in the deep and ongoing warfare between rival ideas of human freedom – and to remark that the idea that no truth relevant to the masses can possibly be inaccessible to them poses a dilemma for those who adhere to it: Either they must acknowledge and adopt a kind of know-nothingism that ill befits their democratic pretensions, as familiar as it may be in populist rhetoric, and relegate the masses in whose interest they profess to speak to the sheer role of consumers, a flock or herd to be fed and fleeced or milked, but not enlarged or intellectually enriched. Or they must commit themselves to the great project of universal education, to the fullest potential of each individual. In that case, they must part company in some measure with the intellectual laissez faire of liberals from Epicurus to Mill and join hands, in some fashion, with the reformism of Plato, shouldering some of the burden entailed by hopes for universal enlightenment like those voiced in the Mosaic Torah and the prophetic tradition that takes up its discourse and ideals.

(3) In the commonest case, Mill points out, still dwelling on his typified polarity of heresy and orthodoxy, 'the conflicting doctrines, instead of being one true and the other false, share the truth between them; and the non-conforming doctrine is needed to supply the remainder of the truth, of which the received doctrine embodies only a part.' What happens most often, in matters of controversy, Mill urges, is that the rival views (one new, unaccepted, perhaps untested; the other, established, perhaps unquestioned – but both already channelized into schools of thought) each contain a mixture of truth and falsity, and suppression leads to loss: 'even in revolutions of opinion, one part of the truth usually sets while another rises. Even progress, which ought to superadd, for the most part only substitutes one partial and incomplete truth for another' (*On Liberty*, 105–6). For that very reason, the vigorous dialectic of open debate is surely the best arena for the threshing and winnowing that will separate the intellectual wheat from the chaff.

I have always been suspicious of Mill's easy slide from the black and white of truth or falsity to the grey tones of his third alternative. Not that I doubt the prominence of half-truths in ours or any culture, nor that I disparage the acuteness of Mill's tragic sense that something is always lost even as new insights are gained. But the relativism Mill flirts with in this third and favored member of his trichotomy (and even in the first, when he charges the intolerant with dogmatism and assumes they must be infallible to claim prudence in suppressing a view they deem dangerous or unhelpful) does not, in my opinion, sit well with the objectivism of the first two members, by which the utility of the entire process (and thus of liberty itself) is to be weighed on Mill's account.

If even progress seems to lose ground as it advances, discarding opinions that are as valuable or useful, potentially, as those that replace them, then the entire dialectic of progress that Mill invokes in behalf of intellectual liberty becomes

13

problematic. If tribal societies are as right as urban ones – and indeed much *is* lost when we leave the savannah or the Mato Grosso for the village or the metropolis – and if no one can say conclusively that there has been a net gain, or that we have not lost more by leaving the rain forest than we might have gained by staying behind, then what exactly is the payoff we are promised for the protection of dissent? The truth here is problematized by Mill in a way that makes it insufficient warrant for the bearing of any social costs, let alone the potentially heavy costs of absolute non-interference with the devising and dissemination of new (or old) ideas.

3. An Alternative Basis for Liberty

If we are to free Salman Rushdie from the threat of death, I do not think we need to find a kernel of truth in his *Satanic Verses*. Nor do I think we need to resort to the flimsy rationales of rule utilitarianism urging that the world would be a better place if authors were allowed to say and print what they like. That may be so. But I think it's a big a mistake to rest intellectual freedom on heuristic grounds – as it is to rest freedom of labor on appeals to efficiency, or civil rights on good or 'productive' citizenship. For, in all these cases, the assurance given is contingent and conditional. But the right we need to anchor is categorical. It must be so in some way, to make it proof against the peremptory claims of church and state – and of private exigency and bias, even when they use higher sounding names like 'global competition,' or tradition.

Why not offer absolute protections of our intellectual freedoms, on the grounds that these involve our very humanity, which includes the freedom to be in error. Our right to think and to express our thoughts, I argue, is not conditioned on the contribution its exercise might make to general human knowledge and understanding. If so, there would be more value in the effective utterance of a half-truth than in the demanding and perhaps faltering articulation of a fuller one. That way lies the paradox of the Grand Inquisitor. For a half truth consciously promulgated is more than half a lie.

Grounding our intellectual liberties in the deserts of personhood avoids making a basic human right contingent. And it

14

affords broader scope than Mill does to our liberty of mind. For it accords us a right to think, even if we do not broadcast, teach, or promote our ideas. It allows them to be private, if we wish, since it does not predicate freedom of thought on the usefulness of one's thoughts to others. Further, it allows liberty to fictions and artistic ideas, including fantasies that make no truth claims at all. Such ideas and fantasies might be expressed for their sheer aesthetic interest, or in play, for profit or for fun, or as objects of intrinsic interest. They need not be instrumentalized in the service of truth, or progress, or any other goal extrinsic to their own.

With these thoughts in mind, I ground our intellectual freedoms in our humanity and in the ideal of human flourishing, for I do not believe that persons can flourish without thought. Thinking is as vital to humanity as breathing, and more distinctive to our natures, as Aristotle would add. Clearly, expression and communicative interactions are of the essence in cultivating thought, allowing it to move beyond daydreaming, zoning, or mental doodling, to the articulation of larger ideas. But an idea need not be put to work to be of value. Some ideas do prove of instrumental worth, but some should be valued intrinsically. For surely, if the measure of worth is the reach of a being, the measure of a human is his dreams. And not every dream need be acquisitive.

This core thesis of mine, that intellectual liberty should grow not from utility but from the intrinsic worth of our humanity, is rooted in Jewish ideas of human deserts and dignity in the same way that Mill's approach is rooted in British ideas of self-interest, rational choice, and the integrity of the human will. Intellectual freedom here is clearly a special case, albeit an important one, of our general liberties – all of which rest in the idea of human flourishing, which rests in turn on the ontological approach to value and personhood that I have championed philosophically and elicited textually from the Jewish sources, in *On Justice* (1991) and *God of Abraham* (1996).

The timelessness that imparts a claim to inspiration to the Jewish approach to deserts, including intellectual liberties, derives not from the antiquity of the canon or the historic continuity of its elaboration, but from the precious idea of personhood itself. It is the clarity and constancy of that idea in the tradition, lying at the root of that ancient continuity itself, that allows intellectual freedom to be taken for granted, built into the norms of the Torah and of rabbinic discourse, and not placed at the center of the biblical problematic of freedom, as it is at the center of Mill's idea of liberty.

One of the strengths of the biblical standpoint for us here comes simply from the fact that its historical and cultural roots are distinct from those of Mill and Locke, whose ideas were framed against the backdrop of ideological, ultimately credal disputes. The Torah imparts the guidance that gives the meaning to its name not by inculcating dogmas or making demands upon our will to believe, but by stamping the impress of its symbols on our lives. The Sabbath, overlaid upon the work and struggles of our days, becomes the living symbol of the liberating Creator's presence in our lives. The words of the law and the epithet of its author inscribed on our lintels, and his expectations held up before our eyes become the everpresent reminder of the standard set before us, binding our hands to strengthen and restrain them and advertising to our neighbors the standard of perfection to whose holiness we aspire. The seal of the covenant, stamped in our flesh, as the liturgy tells us, signifies an intension that cannot be imposed but can only be imparted, aspired after, and appropriated as one's own. The mind is free to make of all this what it can.

We are commanded to love God – to love his goodness, his holiness, and the wisdom of his creation. We are not commanded to believe. Belief and trust, faith and confidence are products of the understanding that grows from the Torah's way of life. They are not its foundations. Just as we are commanded not to test God, not to try his patience or put him to experiment, so God does not test us like a suspicious lover, demanding constant feats of faith, as proof of our fidelity.

Are not the ordeals of our history trials imposed by a jealous God? In a sense they are; but in a sense that Saadiah well understood they are not. For they have no determinate outcome, like that of an experiment or a trial by ordeal. God's jealousy, as Maimonides shows, is his demand for exclusivity (*Guide* I 54; cf. I 23; II 47); and our fidelity is loyalty to his ways – a moral, not a credal commitment. With numerous fallings away, it is a commitment that the people of Israel have borne, through centuries of suffering, with miraculous and inspired good faith. Its reward is compact with acceptance of the Torah's way of life.

Its price in sufferings is balanced, even as it is paid, in the coin of authenticity, continuity, and righteousness. Thus, again, Maimonides is right in saying that the idea of a 'trial,' as an ordeal of arbitrarily imposed 'sufferings of love' is a notion antithetical to the biblical thematic (*Guide* III 24). For to make the reward of obedience to God's law extrinsic to the life of that law violates and vitiates all that the law itself has to say in painting its rewards as constitutive in that life. A saintly life is its own reward, just as a vicious life is its own retribution. The life or death of a martyr, after all, testifies not by bearing its reward as a consequence and presenting that reward before the eyes of some tribunal of doubters, but by affirming the intrinsic value of the ends the martyr chooses, even over undisturbed survival.[8]

What this means is that our life is not a trust-game, and our norms, unlike those of utilitarianism, are not experimental. Rather, our fidelity is in our way of life, grounded in the idea of goodness – our confidence and trust that only absolute goodness is worthy of recognition as divine. The faith of Israel, to give the word 'faith' the sense that it bears in the history and lives of the people of Israel, is a quiet, non-dogmatic security in the recognition of the goodness of being in general and of human being in particular. Because our faith is manifested in a way of life rather than a catechism, questions of heresy, orthodoxy, imposed intellectual authority, dogmatic coercion, and even social or societal pressure to intellectual conformity are alien to the Mosaic universe. The openness of our law is in the continuous reapplication of its core values and ideas, not in the contingency or dubitability of its principles.

Intolerance, intellectual chauvinism, sheer dogmatism, will be present, of course, in Jewish life, as in any other – just as theft or battery will, and for the same reason – because Jews are human and have egos, and ids too, like any other people. But no abiding and enforced norm of dogma will be found. The Torah contains social, moral, and spiritual commandments, but it does not shackle the mind. The celebrated case of Maimonides' thirteen articles is the seeming exception that proves the rule. For these elements of belief are offered by Maimonides to enable him to explain how it is possible, if the human intellectual affinity with the divine is the basis of immortality, for anyone other than a philosopher to attain what the Sages called 'a portion in the world to come.' Drawing upon Plato's distinction between knowledge and belief, Maimonides argues that for non-philosophers, beliefs such as those that the symbols and rituals of the law seek to impart, although on a lower epistemic plane than perfect knowledge, allow the minds of persons who are not conceptually adept to attain their own intellectual attachment to the divine and to realize their inner affinity to God. The so called articles of the Maimonidean creed, then, are not obligations of faith that are to be rewarded – in proportion to their counter-intuitive demands – with a ticket to Elysium. They are paradigmatic counterparts to the conceptual knowledge of the philosopher, allowing intellectual access to immortality, for all whose trust and practice bring them, by way of imagination and aspiration, within intellectual range of the transcendent.

The Rabbis liberate theology and release it to the free play of imagination by placing it within the realm of *aggadah* and by locating *aggadah* itself outside the realm of legal obligation. They can afford to exempt human reflection and speculation from the stringencies of praxis because the imagination they call upon as the vehicle of aggadah is disciplined by the life of the law and so can be counted on, critically, not to be perverse. Thus the abstemiousness of the midrashic *ke-ve-yakhol*, which can freely resort to the treasuries of the fabular without worry that God will be reduced to some mere super-demon. Rabbinic imagery constantly places the divine in the role of a human king, but never allows the condescension of that imagery to set a precedent or ground an inference that would degrade God's majesty to the plane of the merely human.

The realm of theory and speculation remains open to the creative play of imagination. I have glossed Philo's play on the playful name of Isaac in the same vein: Abraham was ready to sacrifice his laughter, but God returned it to him.[9] The laughter here, as Philo teaches, is moral and intellectual freedom. Thus Philo argues that every virtuous man is free, that liberty is the greatest of all human blessings and the fountain of all happiness, that if there is some pagan glory in dying for a sprig of parsley or an olive wreath in the arena, it is far greater glory to die for freedom, and that free speech is the birthright of the free man: 'To speak freely what is commanded by a clear conscience befits the noble soul' (*Quod Omnis Probus Liber Sit*, 1.15, 17; cf. 20). These remarks are not idle rhetoric on Philo's part. Recounting an incident at the theater where praises for the very name of freedom, embedded in a play of Euripides', brought the audience to their feet in a standing ovation (*Quod Omn.*, 141), Philo shows clearly how polyglot Alexandria, under Roman rule, yearned for a freedom it did not enjoy. The Greek poetry of an ancient bard, like the 'proclaim liberty throughout the land' of the still older Hebrew text (Lev. 25:10) kept the dream alive, and even the denial of liberty kept its taste fresh in the mouths of those who could not relish it fully.

Throughout the normative history of Jewish thought, intellectual liberty is presumed,[10] not asked for, except where foreign rule has imposed some rival scheme. Thus Josephus needs to explain that 'Everyone should worship God in accordance with the dictates of his own conscience, and not under constraint' (*Life*, 23). And we find Simeon ben Tzemach Duran (1361–1444) in his *Magen Avot* urging, 'God forbid that such a thing should occur in Israel as to condemn honest inquiries on account of their divergent views.' Spinoza continues the same tradition, which was under pressure in his times, from the internalization among Jews of Dutch Reform concerns for Protestant orthodoxy. He wrote the *Tractatus Theologico-Politicus* in an effort to extend to his European contemporaries the standards of intellectual freedom that his own community had not felt itself free to extend to him. On the title page of that work he wrote: 'Not only is freedom of thought and speech compatible with piety and the peace of the state, but it cannot be withheld without at the same time destroying both the peace of the state and piety itself.' And Moses Mendelssohn, defending his own religious tradition against the charge that its norms sought to bind the mind in the manner all too familiar to his adversaries from common Christian practice, was voicing the long established rabbinic standard when he wrote in the last two pages of *Jerusalem* (1783): 'Convert not into law any immutable truth, without which civil happiness may very well subsist . . . Leave thinking and speaking to us, just as it was given us, as an unalienable heirloom . . . as an unalterable right, by our universal Father.'[11] Underlying the centrality of intellectual freedom from a Judaic standpoint, I emphasize, is the recognition that to deny freedom to the mind and concomitant freedom of expression, is to negate the very humanity that the Torah seeks to foster and preserve. Intellectual freedom is not simply a concession made by Jewish norms. It is part of their purpose. No system that makes it instrumental guards it as well.

4. Mill and the Marketplace

Mill himself plays with doubts addressed to the assumption that the free flow of ideas will inevitably trend upwards and fulfill the human hope of intellectual progress. That hope, like the more general hope for progress and the betterment of the world, may indeed have some foundation, despite the doubts that afflict us as we reach the end of an especially bloody century. The assumption that there is progress in the realm of thought has certainly held true in some domains and for certain periods. But this contingent outcome can be judged a universal truth only when all history is finished, and then only when an adequate yardstick is found for comparing advances, losses, and retrenchments in diverse realms and for diverse individuals and communities. So, short of the millennium, the notion of universal progress seems far too feeble a stick to prop up an absolute right, one that we ask policemen to risk their lives to protect, juries to uphold, legislators to define and defend, and jurists to serve.

If the benefits in which Mill proposes to ground our rights are contingent, clearly they leave those rights subject to exception, defended, or enforced under the watchful eye of expediency. Implementation in a given case may look helpful or harmful, easy or difficult. Some rights may seem objectionable, say, to a great power like China or offensive to a paltry one like Myanmar, and policy will waver accordingly. Cicero, not at his best, advises his son that there are few services more highly valued than the eloquence of a skilled defense, but 'take care when you want to help one group not to offend another' (*De Officiis* II 68). We've already seen enough of the fruits of such an approach in international affairs to know very well the tenderness of the joint between the claims of utility and those of rights.

John Stuart Mill is hardly responsible for that melange of opportunism and rhetoric that is pleased to call itself pragmatism in politics. A liberal can be – *should be* – a strict constructionist when it comes to human rights and would, we have suggested, look silly at best proposing absolute rights for 'us' and not for 'them.' But liberals often seem strangely confident – especially those who are empiricists – when they claim that the preservation of intellectual freedoms will always (in the long run, or when followed as a rule) produce more good than harm.

We have to ask ourselves, when we see committed liberals holding firm on questions of rights, standing their ground on principle, is there not more behind their adamancy against the plaints of expediency than mere expectations of the greatest benefit? The certitude that committed liberals bring to bear on the expectation that the common good (in this case, public access to the truth) will be served by doing the right thing carries an assurance that is anything but empirical or fallibilist. The urgency of the claim that freedom of thought and expression must never be violated, regardless of the costs, because in the long run humanity will surely benefit, carries a moral, not an empiric nisus. The same is true in any defense of rights – civil rights, for example, like the rights of the accused. I see followers of Mill here playing a card that utilitarians have not dealt themselves and that Mill has explicitly declined.

Not every liberal, and still less every politician or decision maker, is so principled as are those followers of Mill who would rather risk the inconsistency of appealing to absolute ideas of right than surrender rights claims to the vagaries of history and political fortunes. I worry that resting absolute claims on mere utilities will too readily leave the absolute outweighed. But I also wonder about Mill's reliance on the assumption (which his own experience seems to call on him to qualify) that truth will always triumph in the end – if only given long enough! – in an open fight. If it will, of course, one can always say, as used to be said to Marxists, that an inevitable outcome surely needs no practical support, and still less the the bearing of risks or sufferings in its behalf.

But I also feel uncomfortable here for the same sort of reasons that make me uncomfortable with Mill's assumption that individuals are the sole and sufficient guardians of their own best interests. Who, after all, guides *this* invisible hand? And how, if not by means that Mill's principles forbid, is his secular apocalypse to be achieved: the gradual emergence of the truth? How do we achieve the social closure that Mill holds out to us as the payoff of our tolerance – without falling into new orthodoxies, or relying on the force of public opinion. For surely tolerance alone does not produce conformity and acquiescence. What is to become of skeptical, heretical, or non-conforming opinion when human understanding becomes as universal as Mill hopes and expects and promises it will be? Do idiosyncratic opinions persist? Or does the triumph of truth simply bathe away in the light of understanding the rustic and rusticated views of the unwashed?

Polytheism, we must note, did not die without a fight. It was not simply refuted. It was marginalized, relegated to country places, as the name 'pagan' reminds us. The dress of the Elizabethan courtier becomes the old fashioned costume of the country bumpkin, so ridiculed as a clown that the very iconography of foolishness still wears his ruff. Hippies, now also often relegated to country places, have begun to become caricatures of themselves. The words that might have voiced the Elizabethan clown's antiquated views are silenced in his modern counterpart, but not by argument. Erasmus and Montaigne beat scholasticism not by reasoning but by laughter; and the Threadneedle Street group secured their reforms and put others in motion far beyond what they had sought, not by argument but by voting and more pragmatic means. Not that argument is irrelevant or even ineffectual, but argument does not secure a social or ideational foothold without struggles of the sort that Mill seems eager to disapprove – if not necessarily to disavow.

The problem is not that discourse or intelligent conversation is impossible, still less that there is no such thing as a dialectically informed change of heart. What troubles me is the idea of unanimity or consensus to be achieved by way of persuasion. The promise of such an outcome seems to me to play on a form of false consciousness. Those who have made intellectual conformity their goal rarely stop at rational argument as their means of winning souls.

Mill today seems naive or disingenuous when he leans on nineteenth century visions of progress to make the pragmatic, Baconian rewards of tolerance seem winnable. To begin with there is the matter of rhetoric, for that is where at least a great deal of public discourse is conducted. Eugene Garver seems right to me in suggesting that in a rhetorical contest it is dubious that truths will be the product or the outcome of the dispute – let alone new truths. For rhetoric, by its nature, as Aristotle saw and showed us, pivots on accepted opinions. It does not make opinions, not out of the whole cloth. It uses them. If its discourse results in changes of heart or mind, those usually spring from the already constituted common ground that a speaker or persuader seeks to discover and solicit or exploit. The point is not that rhetoric cannot convince anyone of anything, or even that such persuading cannot be legitimate, for assuredly it can. But the discovery of truths is not what rhetoric is about.

Eliciting a line of thought from Aristotle's analysis of rhetoric and the springs of public responsiveness to it, Garver shows why this is so:

> While scientific principles hook up to reality throughout a demonstration, the topics in rhetoric function in situations where such a possibility is rare . . . . In each of the three kinds of rhetoric, Aristotle will begin with the political or ethical parent of rhetoric, and move toward its logical progenitor. Each kind starts with the need for the orator to know what he is talking about, to be responsible to, and reflective of, the nature of the *polis* and its laws . . . . That order is not reversible: Aristotle gives us no reason to think that starting from the free competition of ideas, one can eventually hit up against truth and reality . . . . rhetorical competition works in a good polis; it does not produce a good polis. Given a grounding in a knowledge of the state's aspirations, needs, resources, and laws, an advocate can argue for policies and judgments too specific to be laid down in advance by the laws, but there is no corresponding license to begin with advocacy and end with truth. (Garver 1994, pp. 82–83).

The marketplace of ideas is an oxymoron. Ideas are understood or seen through, not bought and sold. And what is bought and sold is not ideas.

Mill was long aware of this fact, as Himmelfarb has shown (1974, pp. 47–48). In an 1833 letter to Carlyle he wrote: 'I have not any great notion of the advantage of the "free discussion" men call the "collision of opinions," it being my creed that Truth is *sown* and germinates in the mind itself, and is not to be struck *out* suddenly like fire from a flint by knocking another hard body against it' (Mill, *The Earlier Letters*, ed. Mineka, vol. 1, p. 153).

Mill's *Autobiography* (1873), papers over the contradiction between his early doubts and later faith in the promised fruits of the free flow of ideas. There and in his essay on Coleridge, he locates the real benefit of intellectual freedom in the emergence of a small number of advanced social thinkers who will win over the rest of humanity to their views.[12] Like Plato, then, Mill tries to contain and harness elitism by enlisting the intellectuals in a metaphysically charged educational project. But he reverses the polarities of the metaphysical charge, for he uncouples from the idealism of Plato and puts in its place the positivism of Comte – if not a blander and seemingly more tolerant relativism and agnosticism. Covering his tracks, as Himmelfarb showed, by suppressing some of his earlier writings and simplifying his argument, in what Victorians called an 'economy,' the Mill of *On Liberty* rests his hopes on the marketplace of ideas. Free competition in the realm of thought will work the same magic that was expected of it in the world of commerce. One wonders, then, how it is possible that homeopathic medicines are still sold that contain scarcely a molecule of active ingredient and that are blended and compounded in accordance with theories that even a self-respecting alchemist would have held up to doubt.

We have the benefit of hindsight in judging Mill's accuracy as a prophet. But to assay his position adequately, we must consider a realm of expression that was quite marginal to his thought, although it lies at the juncture between free expression and free trade, that is, advertising. Rhetoric makes its public appeal through a quest for shared ideas of the common good, but advertising does not confine its appeals to ideas. The textbook appeals are Food, Sex, Babies, Animals, Color/Design, Snobbery, Fear, and Humor. Lately we observe Envy, Guilt, Anxiety, even Horror. The nexus of any appeal to a purchase (or voting) decision is largely per accidens. What is bought or chosen has slight if any natural or rational connection to the promptings that led to its being bought or chosen. Indeed, the trend in advertising in recent years has been away from an appeal in the now classic sense to the building of a mood or image, pre-selling a product, service, candidate, or idea. Where rhetoric uses creativity to seek a common ground or common interest, advertising uses creativity to invent or forge an adventitious nexus between act and attitude. What does advertising experience tell us about Mill's confidence in the triumph of truth in the marketplace of ideas?

The American public has had the truth about cigarettes for decades now. In recent years that truth has been printed on each pack. There aren't many truths clear enough and simple enough to be printed legibly in a space that size. Yet the information has not cured Americans of their smoking habit. A few years ago we read that new deaths attributable to increased smoking among women had wiped out all the gains against cancer mortality made by research in the war against cancer. The appeal used to sell cigarettes to women has often been Style. But one brand, Virginia Slims, has compounded that affront with an appeal to Women's Independence and Self-Reliance, forging a brand identity about as focused as the notion that Joe Camel is Cool – and about as relevant to decisions that might cause cancer and other diseases leading to early death. Do people have a right to smoke themselves, their coworkers, and family members to death – and does liberty of self-expression serve that right?

If would-be followers of Mill are true to his desire to list all the possibilities, then surely we should expand his typology beyond the views and visions that are true, or false, or both, and add those that are neither. If we have learned anything of public debate since Mill published *On Liberty* in 1859, it is something of the power of such debate – and the cloud of advocacy that surrounds it – to obfuscate and oversimplify. It does not simply tease out the subtle shadings of partial truths. As Todd Gitlin puts it (1992, p. 37), 'In the country of the sound bite, the one liner is king.'

What complicates the issue is that not every expression is a self-expression and not every vision is a theory, or even an opinion. Does it not rankle, just a bit, to hear from the lawyer hired to keep a strip joint open that the poor dancers employed there would be denied their right to self-expression if the place were closed, or denied a liquor license? Is self-expression what the dancers are there for, and is Mill's quest for truth sufficient warrant for a court's decision in cases on such a matter?

Cass Sunstein has sought to rationalize our practice of bringing peep shows, pornography (and the $3 billion industry they represent) under the broad skirts of the First Amendment. 'Sexually explicit works,' he urges, 'can be highly relevant to the development of individual capacities. For many, it is an important vehicle for self-discovery and self-definition' (Sunstein 1993, pp. 18–21; cf. 215). The 'it' here is pornography, and the

JUDAISM AND THE LIBERAL STATE

self that is discovered or defined is one that pornography can discover to us or help us to define. Sunstein hedges his bets when he says 'can be.' He backs away from a categorical endorsement of pornography when he confronts, say, the life and work of Larry Flynt, the publisher of *Hustler*, a magazine whose snickering celebrations of molestation and mutilation do not readily comport with the sunny images of pornography as a form of education. Sunstein balks at press reports that treat Flynt as 'kind of a hero of the First Amendment.'[13] But when Milos Forman put his formidable directorial talents to work in a film for Oliver Stone, *The People vs Larry Flynt*, based on a screenplay by Larry Karaszewski, which goes far out of its way to whitewash the nexus between Flynt's viciously abusive and exploitative lifestyle and the expressive values of his magazine and to make Flynt the poster child of First Amend- ment freedoms, the American Civil Liberties Union felt called upon to rebut the complaints of Gloria Steinem and others, by buying an advertisement in *Variety* that acclaimed Forman as a 'First Amendment advocate and an artist of unsurpassed creativity, ability, and courage.'[14]

Sunstein's arguments for the social value of pornography, like my own arguments against it, appeal to the ideal of self- development, in which I have found intellectual freedom constitutive, and to which he finds it, once again, instrumental. I find his rationale somewhat disingenuous. He objects to anyone's setting a standard for the self whose development the state is called upon to protect or promote.[15] But what is served, then, is not personal growth but the sovereignty of impulse – the same impulse that the marketplace seeks the liberty to cultivate and, if profitable, corrupt. The notion is that a free society (still bearing in mind Mill's strictures against social pressures) should have and foster no substantive notion of self-development. Self- development, when pled as a rhetorical appeal, still carries with it a secular glimmer of the aura that once surrounded the idea of working out one's own salvation. In its humanistic form it is made to sound like Confucian self-cultivation. But when it comes to the directions individuals pursue, such expectations, having been aroused, are dismissed. Society, we now learn, must be wholly neutral to the modes of expression and symbolization that might cultivate the imagination of a John Gacy, or a Mother Theresa.

A state or society as morally bankrupt as that, one might respond pragmatically, will not long endure. But perhaps it is more relevant to say that such a state or society does not deserve to endure and is not worthy of the name or the trust that we humans pose in human institutions – not for the sake of their many inconveniences but for the sake of promulgating a shareable vision of human potentialities and creating the conditions in which a wide variety of lives that realize diverse versions of such a vision are made possible.

If it troubles us to see pornography placed in the nurturant role that Socrates once assigned to dialectic and the love of wisdom, Sunstein reminds us that 'the system of deliberative democracy is not supposed simply to implement existing desires.' With the aid of this appeal to the dialectic of desires, the entire package is wrapped in a flag that Sunstein does not blush to call 'Madisonian' (1993, pp. 10–11). Citing Sunstein's arguments, Collins and Skover argue tellingly that a kind of Gresham's law is at work by which the idioms and images of mass marketed pornography are in fact eroding the very possibility of public discourse, by undermining its language and undercutting its mood:

> As long as the First Amendment is rooted in Madisonian soil, the ideal of a democratic state inevitably entails reasoned political discourse . . . . the traditional First Amendment would be unrecognizable without some meaningful dedication to the political function of public reason. A well-informed and active citizenry might best maintain a stable and just society through an open exchange of ideas rationally related to the public good. This, at bottom, is the premise typically invoked by jurists and scholars to legitimate American constitutional government . . . .
>
> However pornography is understood, there are troubling consequences for the Madisonian ideal when the pornographic experience is coupled with public expression. In this regime, is it any longer possible to differentiate Madisonian self-realization from pornutopian self-gratification? Is it any longer possible for rational logic to trump erotic logic? . . . . will this regime tend to collapse the First Amendment theory of reasoned discourse into a principle of pleasure? (Collins and Skover 1996, pp. 149–50)

That, of course, is where Mill came in, urging a regime that places higher pleasures above lower ones and that pursues and provides for the education rather than mere the servicing of desires – lest sheer hedonism lead us to a porcine life that would never be choiceworthy. (*Utilitarianism*, 8–9; *Bentham*, 95–96).

The difficulty is that once mass marketers, in their role as civilizational movers, have found the pleasure centers, and other motivational centers, in the brain of the body politic, reason, or even public discourse altogether, has begun to appear irrelevant in their sights. Political, or erotic, or hedonic decisions (choices, at any rate) can be made quite readily without reliance on that already widely questioned counselor.

Public discourse, to be sure, is not the only free speech value. We have named others already. But if the argument stays on Mill's grounds, that is, if the appeal in behalf of pornography rests on the cause of truth, and pornography is conceded to be a form of truth, regardless of its other motives, the question remains, and it is a question that must be put pointedly to followers of Mill's doctrine: Is this form of truth worth what society will pay for it? If truth is the object in question, are truths of the kind that strip joints traffic in to be the highest values recognized by the law? Does the dignity of women, or of the sexes, or the human body, as a repository of intrinsic and semeiotic value, have no standing? Are the image and the dignity of women, or the human body – whether of the dancers in this strip joint, or of other women whom their art may typify in the minds of sundry viewers, and thereby implicate in its semeiotic web – are these values too intangible to hold a place alongside commercial interests or the appeal those interests make in the name of artistic liberty, or the sheer idea of truth itself?

When the doctrine free of thought and expression was formulated, against the backdrop of the religious wars of the sixteenth and seventeenth centuries and their settlement at Utrecht, or in the Peace of Westphalia, or the Glorious Revolution, the liberties championed by all friends of human enlightenment did concern opinion – the right to form opinions for ourselves, to teach them to our children, to argue them with one another, and print them on paper. The claim of the persecutors had been, in the days of the Inquisition or when

William Tyndale, the author of so much of the noble language that we now know in the King James Bible, was garrotted and burnt, that heretics or unbelievers were being saved not merely from themselves but from Hellfire. Mill could rightly hide a smile at the archaism of such a thought – although, truth be told, the Spanish Inquisition did not cease its operations until 1834.

Mill's writing is full of hope that human progress would soon expose to all the fatuity of believing that a person needs to be saved from his or her own false belief – meaning, sotto voce, damnable unbelief. But unbelievers were still shunned or ostracized, or denied their civil rights, even at the time of Mill's writing. Here, in three such cases that he cites, is the still visible irritant of Mill's essay. The conscientious refusal of principled men to swear a Bible oath is the paradigm case of an act that Mill defends (*On Liberty*, pp. 90–91). But Mill's formulation, being politic and philosophical, is not pointed but general, and thus abstract. And the resultant model is faulty.

Philosophers, at least since Hume, have been saying that opinions are not what move or motivate human beings at all. That claim, in fact, underwrites Mill's intuitive confidence that opinions must be held harmless – although Hume's cynicism about the efficacy of truth tends also to undermine the trust Mill asks us to place in the practical value of truth's disclosure. Why, we might ask, do the annals and apologetics of intellectual liberty not register in their archive of cherished truths Hume's claim that opinions do not move men? But beyond that issue, why is expression still so quaintly equated with ideas?

Advertisers have long assumed that facts are not what move product. The motto is 'Don't sell the steak, sell the sizzle!' But would-be followers of Mill are slow to orient their theories towards recognition of the fact that choices or decisions, including many bad ones, are made, not just by the marginal few but by the populace of great (and soi disant civilized) nations, not on the basis of reasoned argument but in response to all sorts of illocutionary acts and the appetites and instincts that those acts arouse, flatter, direct, manipulate, and, yes, discover and help to define.

The image of Edward R. Murrow, looking and sounding thoughtful, cigarette in hand, sold far more cigarettes than any argument in praise of smoking or evidence in its defense. As the electronic media have begun to mature, image and mood rather than any factual claim at all are relied upon increasingly for sales. The approach is typified, as Collins and Skover note, by 'An Advertising photo of a riderless horse grazing in a snow-covered graveyard, with the caption "Marlboro Country"' (Skover and Collins, p. 116) No verbal claim at all is made, but the Marlboro Country campaign, over the years, turned Marlboro from a lackluster brand to an industry leader.

As Skover and Collins explain, reflecting on the cultural impact of the media themselves: 'Marketers exploited the possibilities of photography by intensifying the symbolic association between goods and the consumer's self-image.' Informational advertising, they add – although the notion is still used in the apologetics for extending First Amendment protection to what is ingenuously called commercial speech – is 'an idea that's gone the way of the Remington typewriter' (p. 74). Mill, strikingly, does not put his associative psychology to work on the matter of market decisions but presumes an earnest, Victorian consumer, whose standards are those of reason.[16] It would be unfair, of course, to expect Mill to anticipate the saturated marketplace and supersaturated marketeering of the present age. But, by the same token, we must ask ourselves how appropriate Mill's ideas of persuasion can be in an age when mass marketing has far outstripped the patterns Mill knew best.

How many persons were turned on to drugs in the 1960s by the maunderings of Aldous Huxley in *The Doors of Perception*, proposing that psychedelic chemicals might open new avenues of consciousness and creativity (a suggestion that Mill's formulation would protect on the grounds that when it had been widely enough discussed and tested the truth would out), or even by the experimental reports of Leary and Alpert (whose experiments on unsuspecting human subjects could and did appeal not simply to the experimentalism of Dewey but to the empiricism of Mill), compared to those who turned to drugs because of the promotional activity and attitudinizing of the Beatles? Or are we prepared to say that the crude but sly allusion to LSD in a lyric about 'Lucy in the Sky with Diamonds' was in fact a propositional claim – a claim about the truth?

How many followers of the Reverend Moon were convinced of his divinity by argument? Is it not bizarre to protect under the mantle of free intellectual exploration cults whose chief techniques and methods of operation – specifically, a cynical exploitation of the basic mechanisms of human sociality and socialization – negate the very capability of forming independent opinions? Or have we here a case of the inalienable freedom of the individual to alienate the will?[17]

I am not speaking here of the frightful denouements that set the taste of horror in the very names of Jonestown, David Koresh, the Temple of the Sun, Aum Shinrikyo, or Heaven's Gate. I am speaking of the means such figures and groups use to gain the trust and loyalty that can bring their members to kill or die in their behalf, to lead men to give up their wives to the appetites of cult leaders, their bodies to self-castration, or their children to beatings and abuse, or drafts of cyanide-laced Kool-Aid. The means to such an end do not rest on the free exchange of ideas. But they are protected legally, constitutionally, by principles that were devised to defend the free exchange of ideas.

What opinions, whole or partial truths, are conveyed by sado-masochistic materials on the Internet, by the use of gore as a token penalty or reward in video-games like *Mortal Kombat*, or by the crude humor of video chess games that include the graphically represented rape of the Queen when her piece is taken? What exactly is the ideational content that advocates seek to shelter under the cloak of Mill's ardent defense of intellectual freedom when they champion rock music that promotes suicide, parricide, racial violence, rape, violence against police officers – not by enunciating a doctrine but by mere suggestion, celebration, and innuendo? Is it possible that Mill's conclusions are being applied where his arguments do not reach, and where they were never intended to apply?

Some students of mine in Hawaii were given an audience with a celebrated Eastern saint. On their return, each of them was wearing a small string around his neck, bestowed by the visiting eminence. I asked them what the holy man had said, naively assuming that the occasion had involved a lecture or a sermon. They seemed surprised at the question. He didn't say anything, they told me. It was just that he was there. Now these were graduate students in philosophy, who knew what argument is. Many of them still wear the little string. Their lives were changed. I can't say whether for better or for worse, but the notion that opinions were involved is, shall we say, simplistic. Opinions changed, but not as a result of the communication of opinions.

The Eveready people use a pink plush mechanical bunny to tag the idea of endurance to their product. Other battery companies use other animated figures to make a similar claim. But people like the bunny and identify with its repeated triumphs over adversity. The campaign works, not because customers have been shown that Eveready batteries actually last longer than the competition, or because they are convinced that batteries are more economically or environmentally friendly than electricity from the mains, but because the advertising links good feelings to product image. My point is not that this is wicked, but just what we all know, that what we communicate is only in part matter of propositional content, let alone news and views about the world.

Advertising uses identification and association along with Appetite, Fear, Shame, Libido, Parental Emotion, Envy, Familial Tensions, Guilt, Anxieties, and Longings of all sorts to move or sell. The tugs it exerts are rarely propositional, let alone claims about what is true, or what truth is. Association is the key tool: auto (or electric paint sprayer) with authority, fun with immortality, lipstick with charisma, charisma with orgasm, perfume with mystery, and mystery with power. Much of the manipulation is relatively innocent, but not all of it is. Budweiser's frogs, the Absolut bottle, the Michael Jordan pitch for McDonald's have all scored high with a youth audience – as did Joe Camel. Youth alcohol consumption, early habituation to smoking, and a high fat diet are more than casual consequences of such mass campaigns. The makers of moral, religious and political opinion and commitment long ago discovered that they can play the same game and work the same magic. In some respects, as Plato has it, they invented it. And, we also know, whether we consider the peculations of the latest televangelist, the mind control of Dianetics, Muktananda, and the Reverend Moon, or the sinister plots of Shoko Asahara to gas innocent subway commuters or spread the Ebola virus in urban settings, there is no guarantee of purity in the motives of such manipulators. Still less can we be certain of the powers of sheer clarity to counteract their messages when they become un-wholesome.

5. Mill Abused

What is unwholesome, it might be said, is a matter of opinion. Here again we slide from a utilitarian objectivism that puts a cash value on truth to the relativism that can find no truth about values. I vividly recall the days when we were told that LSD was a drug with no side effects; and later, when cocaine was promoted, not just on the street but in mainstream national magazines, as a harmless and non-addictive thrill. How many minds must be blown, how many Jonestowns must we witness, how many addicts must die, and how many infants must be born addicted to crack and infected with AIDS, before we are ready to acknowledge that harm has been done; and some of it by what we classify as speech? We rightly shun government intervention against every sly innuendo. Still we must ask, of the mass marketing of drugs in the 1960s and '70s, where were the protests and boycotts? Where was the Fourth Estate?

I see no difference here between, say, the labeling of impure rapeseed oil as good food (although it can cause blindness and death) and the promulgation of stereotypes that degrade, dehumanize, and nurse violence, or rock videos that tout narcotics – least of all do I see a difference measurable in utilitarian terms. Mill's argument, I am saying, does not shield the mislabeling, or the misleading. It does not protect hate speech or narcotics promotion or the marketing of homicide or suicide, any more than it protects fraudulent sales of tainted foods or unsafe pharmaceuticals.

True, the magazine publishers who, long after the counter-culture psychodelicatessen had closed, ran features on the virtues of cocaine and LSD were not the actual drug dealers. And the purveyors of virulent racial and sexual stereotypes, or potent mixtures of the two, say, in rap music, videos, and performances were not usually the actual skinheads, klansmen, militiamen, or gang thugs who perpetrated violent acts of racial, ethnic, or sectarian hatred. But apologues couched in such terms ignore the ways in which magazine articles are placed and popular music sold.

Mill's argument does not differ from my own in condemning what is dangerous. It does not support the weight of degradation, exploitation, or manipulation that masquerades as expression of ideas and shelters under the banner of the pursuit of truth. But it is not my humanism but rather Mill's version of liberalism that is pled in behalf of the violence of pornography and the commercial promotion of violence as an end in itself. The disingenuous equation of pornography not with degradation but with personal or political revolution is sugared with promises of freedom – self-expression for the purveyors and the exploited actors, models, and dancers, self-discovery for the leering audience. Such fictions and pretensions make Mill the apologist of degradations that he did not remotely envision. We can see how disingenuous such pleadings are if we hew closely to the values to which they appeal. If our earnest desire is indeed for the development and expression of human potential, we should not shy away from envisioning that potential in all its creative varieties. Appeals in behalf of intellectual freedom, in that case, would look not to the presumptive fruits of freedom but to its intrinsic value as a constituent of human fulfillment and the good life.

When we value intellectual freedom for its capacity to foster creativity, if we understand creativity not in empty, formal terms but in a substantive and life-affirming vision of humanity, then the ideal of intellectual freedom will not sustain just any form of expression that might work as a poison to personhood and a source of dehumanizing violence or abasement of the human spirit. Nor will it protect modes of action that deaden the very freedom that is pled in their behalf. Still less will it warrant state sustenance of modes of expression and social relation that are destructive of the very capacity to form ideas or sustain relationships.

Those who urge ingenuously that ultimately the truth will out – that people will learn to avoid what they know is harmful and to ignore the poisons bred in words and images – are neglecting at least two facts: First, by the time such lessons have sunk in, the damage, sometimes irreparable, may be done, and the actual purveyors, whether of thalidomide, asbestos, impure rapeseed oil, cigarettes, cocaine, or racial or religious or gender hatred, will be vanished into the shadows, their profits secured or their agendas served. The world may learn, perhaps. But, when the world learns in this way, it learns as victims learn about confidence games, after their bank accounts are emptied. Such learning is always temporary. For, as grifters and stand-up comedians say, there's always the younger generation, who haven't yet heard the joke or smelled the strange fruit of ethnic cleansing. Meanwhile, those who have done the damage, sold the goods, gotten the store burned down, altered the rates of marriage or divorce, suicide or matricide, are safe behind a screen of anonymity or corporate inviolability, well along with their next assault, their anonymity and latitude of action well protected by academic hired guns, journalists, and highly principled lawyers and politicians, whose job it is to ensure that rising generations of the populace do not learn from the experience and the errors of their elders.

The second fact often forgotten by those who take comfort in the hope that truth, like murder, will out, is that there are impulses toward death. So, even when the condom people, say, have sold the television audience on the proposition that indiscriminate sexual activity can be fatal, there are those who will be drawn to that very fatality.[18] They are drawn not simply by an exuberant libido but by morbid fascination, transformed by various social and psychological dynamics into an obsession that may be linked adventitiously to the impulses of libido itself.

But quaintly, I say again, we who cherish liberty, and intellectual liberty in particular, still labor with a hundred fifty year old theory based on a popular, topical essay[19] embodying the assumptions *i)* that speech is the heart of liberty, *ii)* that speech is a matter of opinions, *iii)* that opinions and thus speech cannot be harmful in any critical measure, and *iv)* that neither the government nor the public has any rightful interest in the harm individuals may choose to do themselves, or the good they might have done instead.

The impact of these four assumptions of Mill's account of liberty is exacerbated by the overextension of the conclusions to which he intended them to lead. So that even for a private person, a college community, or a moral critic, journalist, or minister of religion to object to tasteless racial or gender humor or monitory speech on the grounds of its destructiveness, or to call pornography by its rightful name, is widely deemed censorious and rejected on grounds adduced from Mill. Ultimately, in effect, the claim is that human knowledge and understanding depend for their advance on the freedom of every stand-up comedian to portray the Poles or the Portuguese as stupid, the license of every pub owner with a cabaret permit to degrade women for the edification of paying customers, the liberty of every klansman to paint the ethnic or credal other as a racial blight or moral threat, and the freedom of Al Sharpton, Louis Farrakhan, and every other streetcorner Hitler who can arrange a subsidy from the Saddam Husseins and Muammar Khadafys of the world (or a marriage of convenience with our mainstream politicians) to represent Jews collectively as bloodsuckers, and all whites as oppressors.

6. Beyond Mill

I want to take issue with each of the four assumptions I have listed, and with the overextension to which they are linked. I am seeking to lay out a conception of liberty that is broader but also more perspicuous than Mill's. I think it high time we had one. We have learned too much to be able to rest our idea of liberty, its scope and boundaries, on Mill's arguments alone. His categories are hemmed in by the limits of his concerns and hidebound by his assumptions and those of his age about human motives. Indeed, they are hamstrung even by Mill's capacity to rely on the civilizing pressures of the very conventions whose engines in public opinion he was seeking to restrain. Yet we still cling to Mill's argument as though it gave us the only theory capable of protecting the liberties we rightly cherish. Mill's essay itself has become a shibboleth, a mandala, and a shrine. Many liberals are more willing to see the burning of the flag than the challenging of Mill's arguments.

I think there is more, much more, to liberty than freedom of speech and thought, that there is more to speech than the expression of opinions and thus that Mill's utilitarian reliance on the emergence of truth as the warrant of freedom is neither necessary nor sufficient. I think that there are kinds of speech that can be harmful and indeed poisonous – not by enunciating 'heretical' opinions (rosily envisioned by Mill as potentially too advanced for those who first hear them), but by diminishing or degrading the humanity of individuals or abasing the social standing of entire races, peoples, cultures, or genders. All of which is to say nothing of the dissemination, say, on the Internet, of instructions for making pipe bombs, polluting the water supply, constructing computer viruses, or sabotaging the power grid – information that can be gotten, in some cases, from diligent research in the library, but that yields a world more damage when freely and graphically accessed and topically organized on the home computer.

I want to argue that society has a rightful interest, through public expressions of indignation and through concerted actions that give force to public disapproval, sometimes including organized communal responses and programmatic undertakings by government, acting as the agency of society, to uphold interests that are degraded and to sustain the worth and dignity of the human person. I would argue further that the public airwaves and the ethernet are no more free for the appropriation of every molester and purveyor of images and instructions that foster violence and molestation than are the public roads and sidewalks.

Willmoore Kendall (1960, pp. 972–79) makes some valuable points about the bankruptcy of the notion that the state should be wholly neutral in the realm of ideas. He raises legitimate worries about the impact of making freedom of thought and speech the paramount social good. Indeed, had Mill held consistent to the utilitarian principle he announced at the outset, all goods would be interchangeable in utilitarian coin and none would be placed on a plinth high enough to demand the steady sacrifice of any other. But how can we accept Kendall's efforts to hedge the freedoms Mill does protect, in the interest of what Kendall calls 'a public truth'? This smacks too much of dogma. And I worry about the disutility of ham-handed attempts to curb offensive expression, since we know very well that there are places, and not just overseas, where what is offensive is the sight of a woman's arm or ankle, or her face, or the sound of a questioning or cynical voice, or the presence of a black child or a Jew.

I propose to address the dilemmas that Mill faced and poses not by narrowing but by broadening Mill's idea of liberty. I do believe that society has an interest, a public interest, in promoting individual discoveries of the truth and not merely in clearing the ground for them. Yet I think that many liberties intertwine inseparably with freedom of expression and can never therefore be rightfully sacrificed to it – still less to any eidolon puffed up about its name. The problem with the ideal of intellectual freedom is not in making our liberty of thought and speech uncompromisable, but in construing the reference class of actions protected by these liberties so broadly and indiscriminately as to force conflicts among the deserts that we legitimately treat as rights. Complementarity is the key to accommodation, that is, to the avoidance of conflicts among rights. This means that for practical as well as conceptual reasons we must inform our idea of free speech by the idea personhood, on which it is founded. We should regard destructive and anti-human expressions not as exercises of liberty but as abuses of it. For, as Locke made clear, what is self-destructive is not a power or liberty at all. If Mill and his followers erred in privileging expressive liberties, the wise and prudent response is not to cast about for some other shibboleth or icon to set up in their place but to study the modes of expression that are compatible with the preservation of all our liberties and vigorously to pursue the protection of these.

Mill faces his followers with hard choices – conflicts of right and obligation (and of rights with obligations) – that hark back, beyond the moral empiricism of Epicurus, to the value relativism of the Sophists. He vigorously enunciates his respect for liberties other than those of speech when he warms to the cultivation of individuality in the third and fourth chapters of *On Liberty*. But he subordinates these liberties to those of expression, by making the advance of thought the goal and aim of human development and by failing to find any circumstance that would curtail liberties of expression in the interest of human fulfillment. He clearly did not foresee the threat to human individuality, personhood, and personality that would arise from overextension of liberties that parody the ones he zealously protected. And, by comparison with thinkers of both earlier and later periods, he worked with a much diminished idea of the need and obligation to foster human growth and individuality. This was no mere accident or casual outcome of his views on political economy and the market – his worries about public education or his sometimes faltering support of free trade. Mill's prejudice against (and willingness to take for granted) the concerted cultural and religious systems that have traditionally addressed the fostering human individuality made him gunshy of any effort by church or state to guide humanity in the quest for its potentials.

Mill was attracted to the humanism and even the teleology of human nature that he found in Humboldt's idea of human development. But he eschewed any form of essentialism and thus could describe the goals of human development only in terms of maximal diversity, even eccentricity, in modes of life and 'experiments of living.' Reacting against dour Calvinist notions of humanity's sinful nature, he was prepared to valorize all manner of desires and impulses, but could not impart a similar legitimacy to human nature itself, as rendered canonical, say, in the Aristotelian eudaimonistic tradition. The ability to integrate competing impulses through the notion or ideal of an organically integrated self (whether that self is construed as a given of nature or as an achievement of cultural investment and individual effort) therefore eluded him. Nor did his knowledge of educational methods and practices make him sanguine about the impact of the broad efforts of humanity and humanism, over time, to foster and refine human nature, or its social face, through the mediation of culture and tradition.

The practical impact of Mill's preference for an absolute and formal notion of the liberties of expression has not been the removal of the sort of restraints he abhorred. Rather, where and to the extent that Mill's preferences are heeded, it has led to the delegitimation of such restraints generically and to the relative deracination of the individuals and the individuality to which Mill was so dedicated. Mill himself, to his credit, strikingly anticipated the extent to which individuals would be unable fruitfully to define for themselves the liberties he urged for them. His response, once again, was elitist: All was for the sake of a few emergent geniuses, whose worth would be redeemed by their teaching. Yet it remains in doubt whether experiments in living like those found in any in city tenderloin have any helpful relation to the production of genius; and it remains unclear as well how Mill's idiosyncratic geniuses can be expected to teach, or what benefit (if others popularize their ideas and lifestyles) can be expected to arise from the practice of their precepts. Experiments in living even a fraction as wide ranging as those that Mill notionally urges will, of course, have their victims. The benefits of even one social experiment – say, no fault divorce – can come to seem rather problematic, relative to its costs. And the idea that lifestyle experimentalism and eccentricity of lifestyles, pursued as intrinsic goods and equated with individuality and human development, must inevitably produce more good than harm seems not only counter-intuitive but remarkably a priori by utilitarian, empiricist, or pragmatist standards.

Yet the outcome of Mill's abdication of the philosopher's role in speaking normatively about human nature and the human good is neither the anarchy that Willmoore Kendall feared nor the Edenic efflorescence of individuality for which Mill hoped. Rather, it has been the invasion of individual imagination by commercial, sectarian, and other interests that do not respect Mill's standards any more than they respect the individuals whose minds they seek to manipulate. Clearly Mill is not responsible for acts that violate the standards he enunciated. But the fact remains that Mill did not reckon with the vulnerability of individuals, including adults, to manipulation and exploitation. The openness that Mill's standards intend to preserve becomes an invitation to parasites; and those standards themselves, enacted into law or enshrined as constitutional principles, become a sword and shield to the manipulators of public consciousness, the exploiters of human weakness, and the would be enslavers of the human mind and spirit.

Guidance is no less problematic for being made a social or a public responsibility. A group or culture can err at least as catastrophically as an individual can. But neither is the sanctity or sovereignty of the individual adequately protected once all responsible social agencies – whether communal or societal – have left the individual to his own devices. If history teaches us anything, it is that the individual needs and deserves all the help he can get; and if the study of politics and society teaches us anything, it is that it is for the sake of such help that social agencies, from the family to the state, are legitimately formed, fostered, and tolerated.

My argument in defense of human liberty rests on an expanded conception of the human person, assigning a penumbra of deserts to the human name and image, enlarging the sphere of protections beyond what Mill had in mind when he spoke of harm. But my argument goes beyond Mill in another way as well, since it assigns positive deserts to human personhood, including a desert of honest information, fair labeling, and indeed liberal education of a kind that will enable its recipients to rise somewhat above the human vulnerability to invidious and manipulative appeals and to scorn them with the same sort of scorn, although far better justified, that Bentham applied to the idea of rights.

i. Liberties that go beyond self-expression. A central plea of this paper is that we need broader gauge conceptions of our human rights than those afforded in *On Liberty.* I derive these broader rights not simply by stretching Mill's argument or making positive rights the precondition or concomitant of negative rights but by appeal to the idea of self-perfection. Rights, and deserts of all kinds, including the right of free inquiry, free thought and free expression, derive from personhood. For it is personhood that is thwarted, vitally, when thought is curtailed or expression is denied. But the function of law is the protection and furtherance of personhood, not the protection of persons for the sake of what they might have to say, nor the protection of personal sovereignty for the sake of a diversity or experimentalism that will in turn, on occasion, yield interesting or fruitful statements.

The function of the law, and more broadly of the social ethos, is not to keep the world safe for science, or for discourse, or even for conversation over coffee. The life of the mind is not in that sense the paramount good or goal, although such a life does have intrinsic and not merely instrumental value. The substance of liberty is not confined to the freedom of the mind to roam at will. Rather, the substance of liberty is the freedom of the whole person to act and grow, to forge relationships and friendships – to learn and discover, but also to be nourished physically, to flourish in sensibilities, to raise children and enjoy grandchildren in intact and integrated families, neighborhoods, and communities.

To focus the rights of humanity in one, paramount negative freedom, the freedom of the mind and mouth, pen and keyboard, is the same as supposing that a city can get by with libraries and does not need hospitals, playgrounds, and parks. Indeed, it is worse, since sheer non-interference with expression, as a merely negative liberty, robs minds and mouths and pens of much that they might think or speak or say, and leaves the channels of communication open to whatever combination of commercially promoted content might stimulate a demand and whatever melange of politically motivated messages might make one.

The laissez-faire approach to intellectual liberty will generate clutter, and in time, a glut, as any bulletin board or newsgroup where access is anonymous and free will demonstrate. For, in the Information Age, as in any age of affluence, the Tragedy of the Commons is not neglect but pollution. The information superhighway is already clogged with roadkill; and the ether is infested with viruses that did not spring up by spontaneous generation but were artfully devised by the anonymous Schadenfreude of the alienated.

The same considerations that expand the idea of rights to the sphere of health care, or that spread out the safety net by which a humane society husbands and invests its resources (that is, the energies of its members) for the sustenance and education of all those whom it can aid effectually, also describe for us the limits of free speech – just as they help us to delineate what is actually help and what is not. For the orienting principle of all rights is in the projects of persons, and there is no right of self-destruction or of fostering or facilitating destructiveness.

ii. Speech that is not about opinions. I have clearly sought to narrow the reference class of the presumed liberties that are commonly sheltered under Mill's defense of intellectual freedom. Commercial speech is not here my major concern. But we need to note not just its presence but its methods, which are often subtle and indirect. And we need to note the nisus embedded in the dynamic of those methods, not only in undermining discourse (which is serious enough), but also in all sorts of social impacts and pathologies that advertisers and opinion makers shelter under the aegis of free speech. Society and society's children, to mention just one example, have paid and continue to pay a social cost from the promotion of free love or sexual revolution. But for the promoters of, say, steroid contraceptives, such costs are as irrelevant (or as necessary to suppress and remove from the realm of choice making) as are the claims that a given product heightens the risks of uterine or breast cancer.[20]

Leafing through a women's magazine at the supermarket checkout counter, I am not surprised to see this month's formulaic article on extra-marital affairs, tucked in among the contra-ceptive ads. It opens with a lead about the need for planning: One might imagine that spontaneity and passion are the issue, we are told. But an affair requires preparation and expense – from leg waxes to lingerie. Lifestyles are marketing clusters, and indirec-tion in marketing need not be subtle: The reader has not gone beyond 200 words before she has been given a shopping list.

Perhaps commercial speech needs clearer labeling. And if it has consequences for public policy and public welfare, perhaps the makers of public policy and the servants of public welfare, whether state funded or privately sustained, should at least be aware of what they are facing and find a voice and venue to respond. They will need more than their usual subtlety, if they are to be effective, or even to be heard.

Let me be very concrete about this. If there is a link between extra-marital affairs and the vicious abuse or murder of spouses by their outraged mates, that linkage should be established in the minds that matter, and not just in the methods of the police. Yet this is not the sort of linkage that campaigns appealing to anger over the abuse and murder of spouses have singled out for attention. In fact, such campaigns tend to treat the very mention of such a nexus as part of the abuse, or as an apologetic in its behalf.[21] Nor is such a linkage a matter that the purveyors of the lifestyle goods listed in a checklist feature article are likely to want prominently discussed among the presumptive pros and cons thoughtfully, titillatingly, lovingly dwelt upon in the pages between the advertisements for the hair dyes, hideaways, and shampoos that feature in the shopping list of indiscretion.

I have argued that Mill's intentions and, more critically, his argument do not extend to the protection of violent or violative pornography, racist caricature, incitements to violence against the members of a class, a race, sex, ethnic group – or humanity at large. They do not protect representations that dehumanize persons or inculcate cruelty or destructiveness as values, and they should not. Nor should they be allowed to protect the dissemination of technical instructions for the implementation of mass violence, teleplunder, arson in the cities or the forests, or other sorts of depersonalized destructiveness.

Once we get past the initial phase of denial, that is, the denial that such incitements take place, that destructive caricatures are drawn, that there is anyone at all who would be influenced by such portrayals, or who would instigate such acts of vandalism, theft, invasion of privacy, sabotage, or fraud, we encounter a subtler form of denial, the claim that regulation of information flow is too sensitive a matter for public concern, that even the critique of representations of any sort is too subjective a business to be a concern of social response, let alone of legislation. Pornography is not presented as an assault on the human image, an assault whose frisson derives from the differential between dignities degraded and the levels to which they are abased. Rather, it is described in terms of the graphic or explicit portrayal of various anatomical parts and physiological acts, whose representation may or may not be offensive to some.

This characterization is naive, or disingenuous, in the extreme. It is stunning to see philosophers in particular, who long ago abandoned the 'picture' theory of language and expression still clinging to it when they speak of pornography in terms of the 'graphic' or 'explicit.' Representation is always the portrayal of X *as* φ. The response of a viewer, especially the affective response, is attained not by some 'willing suspension of disbelief' but as a byproduct of the recognition of what is represented. When a human individual is represented as degraded, the immediate emotive impact is one of dehumanization. That response can be suppressed or rejected, leading to pity on the one hand or cruelty on the other, by a dialectic that Spinoza brilliantly described (*Ethics*, Definitions of the Emotions, 38). But, when the affect is made a goal of gratification, we have not merely cruelty or its portrayal but the roots of sadism.

Once the affect is a matter of gratification, a hedonic goal, there is a corresponding appetite to be addressed; the act of degradation itself, or its imagery, which is itself a degradation, can be marketed, made an object of prurient but also hedonic interest, and a source of artifactual value. At this point not only the dignity of the initial object is degraded, but so is that of others who are assimilated to her image by the psychology of association. Permissions are extended by the very publicity of the degradation. And, since we are social creatures and the dynamic of cruelty began with identification, the degradation of the object generates a concomitant degrading of the outlook and character of the viewer or participant.

At issue here is not the merely symptomatic question of what an unreflective bystander might find offensive, say in the portrayal of the human form, but the core of the ethos that is a society's lifeblood. It is the colorations of a culture's ethos that are the clearest markers of decadence or morbidity in a society, the clearest indications of the regard or contempt that we hold toward one another and one another's sensibilities. Is there a proper moral concern with such outcomes? Clearly there is. The tenor of our human character is the very subject of morals, for the ethos is what informs our actions. Is there a proper social concern? Once again there is, for cultures and the vehicles of culture are the seedbeds of the ethos that expresses and perpetuates the mores and the traits of character by which we live with one another, amicably or desperately, peaceably or in the anxious anomie of alienation. Is there a proper legal concern? There can be. Jeffrey Dahmers are made, not born.

The objection to a legal or programmatic concern on the part of government or other social agencies with violative pornography is that such efforts inevitably involve attempts to legislate or coerce morality. Morality, it is assumed, is a private matter. But the first premise, about coercion, is false; and the second is equivocal. Law need not mean the police, and character is never wholly a private concern. Of course there is a sphere of private morality. The open ended cultivation of the virtues is too long, too arduous, and too many-branched a path to be specified by the exigent and sanctioned imperatives of the law, or even the neighborhood – although, in my view, the machinery of the law and the standards and atmosphere of the neighborhood should be used to make that path and its byways more open and accessible.

But if the notion is that laws and social pressures can and should have nothing to say about the framing of an ethos, that notion is far more problematic – certainly not a question to be begged by appeal to an equivocation on the familiar private sense of the idea of morality. I think the claim is false, precisely because culture is the vehicle of morality and culture is a social, not a personal creation. Consider the alternative: If morality is not legislated, even indirectly, then what will be the subtext of our laws? Some arbitrary construction that has, *per hypothesi*, no relation to right and wrong? And if moral standards are not made expectations, not even by the pressures of public manners and opinion, what motivational standards will hold the field? Those of commercial, sectarian, partisan, and factional interests that care nothing for Mill's standards, or any other than their own?

Accepting the keystone of liberalism, that laws must be minimal, to allow maximal scope to human freedom, we still reach the view (well stated in Islamic jurisprudence) that laws legislate to sustain what is right and good and restrain what is wrong and evil. As a liberal, I must add – especially with the images of embattled Algiers and prostrate Kabul vividly in mind – the laws must not attempt to do so in every case conceivable – not because there are no objectifiable standards of right and wrong, but because the human condition is too complex and delicate and the realm of human action too vast and ramified to permit a simple rule, let alone a government agency to enter and act without violating the freedom and individuality that laws exist to protect and sustain. Typically, laws focus, as they should, on wrongs that are palpable and indisputable, extreme in consequence, significance, or extent. The goods that laws pursue must, similarly, bear a social interest that reaches the threshold of public concern. And the laws themselves must cross even that threshold equitably, gingerly, and with respect. The goods that laws serve must not only stimulate or demand legislative attention but raise issues deep enough to foster and warrant public acceptance of the costs and inconveniences of legislative intervention and governmental engagement. Even then there are principles not to be violated, trusts not to be broken – the first of which is the trust reposed in government as the champion and not the bully of human individuality, creativity, and personality.

Taking pornography as a test case, the defining issue is not offensiveness, a standard that is subjective not only in its measure and scope but also in its ictus. Individuals vary in what offends them and in the extent to which they are offended by a given act or expression, or say they are. But, beyond that, when I speak of the ictus of the act I mean that the affront itself is subjective, a blow to the sensibilities, not the body or the pocketbook. For that very reason legal authorities are rightly chary of intervention; and they often treat such affronts, nominal or notional as they are, slightingly. Yet we do not hesitate to condemn and restrain acts of libel, where the ictus again (or much of it) is in the mind. We rightly restrict pandering and sexual soliciting, incest and child pornography. These do not differ in the locus of the damage from several types of commercialized demoralization that are not at present restricted or that are defended as commercial avenues to a special kind of enlightenment. Assaults to sensibilities may deserve legal attention. But, in the case of pornography, we need not and should not rest our case or repose our legislative attention on the subjective dimensions of the offense, where able advocates, who wish to classify pornography simply as a special case of free speech, speech that might offend, have knowingly located it. What arouses legislative concern that goes beyond the issues of sensibility and privacy is the potential in pornography for palpable, indeed wholesale harm. Here the question we must ask ourselves, as we scrutinize the principles on which we legislate, especially against the backdrop of Mill's liberal manifesto, is when does the utility principle, on which all of Mill's legal interventions rest, reenter the picture, so that data can be evaluated and impacts assessed?

Clearly a critical test for expressive acts is the likelihood of their producing violence. Leering or tasteless representations on the order of 'What the butler saw' might, for example, be deemed morally objectionable, as acts of violation, in that they debase the human image and sour the ethos of intimacy, even if they do not reach the threshold of legal response. But some representations so degrade the human image and abase human dignity as to amount to clear and present dangers – even though their impact may be diffuse or delayed. For a time bomb is no less a clear and present danger because its impact is delayed or because its victims are an indeterminate number of a somewhat ill-defined class – e.g., subway riders.

If a jury finds that a given representation or source of representations is harmful or dangerous to humanity, say, by its degradation of the human image, or its dehumanization or demonization of an individual or a group, there may be grounds for a legislative response. The principle, like any legal principle, can be abused. But it won't do to say that the judgment called for is too vague or arbitrary to be fairly made. Judgments about such matters are no more problematic than judgments about malice aforethought or *mens rea* in the realm of intention, or about restraint of trade or environmental pollution in the realm of consequences. Legal tests and standards of evidence are precisely what laws and courts are called upon to devise and marshall. And the basic standard of potential for harm, demarcating what is morally noxious in a grave enough way to become an object of public concern, is less arbitrary and problematic than the presently used vague and concertedly flimsy notion of offensiveness by community standards.

iii. Harmful speech. What, then, of harm? I do not concede that physical or fiscal harm is the only harm that matters, or that victims of a crime or tort must be named or nameable individuals. I have in fact urged that society has a legitimate and vital interest in protecting the ethos that gives definition to its project and that underlies the possibility and value of its survival, let alone its self-integration and advance. But I agree that most of what concerns the ethos, as a moral matter, is beyond the purview of the law – not because laws have no business with morals, but because most moral adjustments and concerns do not reach the threshold of significance that warrants legal intervention and because most are too delicate for the clumsy operations of the public apparatus to address case by case. For this reason, it is not improper for laws to focus on utilitarian standards, since these are the most palpable and least controvertible. It is here that liberals must face the music and submit their empirical claims to empirical tests.

Exponents of media interests are fond of saying that media violence is a safety valve allowing the harmless release or sublimation of energies, anxieties, hostilities, and aggressions that might, if frustrated or pent, cause real damage. Evidence has been mounting in recent years that with certain kinds of representations and expressions this brand of denial or defense simply will not wash. The backup claim that television, movies, and sensate literature are the mere passive mirrors of (a decadent or violent) society – rather than the active instruments or megaphones, permission givers, or popularizers[22] of standards sensationalized from the ambient extremes – is particularly disingenuous. It assumes that the makers and users of cultural artifacts simply do not know what they are doing. But many of them, especially the most effective, know exactly what they are doing.

Dashiell Hammett *intended* to produce sensate literature to feed the unwholesome appetites of what he viewed as a decadent society, and thus to accelerate its fall.[23] Steven King could not be as effective as he is if he did not know what he is doing, or understand the emotional impact of his work on its audience. Television people research such questions with the same care that the cigarette industry used in researching the addictive properties of nicotine. When the small screen repeatedly shows the rape scene through the eyes of the rapist, the images projected in our homes are as attuned to the sensibilities of the viewing audience as was O'Brien's choice of rats in the final torment and temptation that will break the spirit of Winston in *1984*.

The standard I am proposing with regard to symbolic or representational violence is similarly an empiric one. If the issue is to be one of utilities and not of arbitrary privilege for politically potent interests, let the studies be done and the damage assessed. The techniques of measurement are in place, and the great strength of utilitarianism is that the harms and benefits on which it concentrates are measurable. So let us see, without special pleading, whether certain forms of expression that are not in fact expressions of opinion, or that express opinions only or largely as a vehicle for venting hatred or fomenting resentment have, as part of their effect, an impact that heightens the level of violence in our society, against persons in general, against women, against persons of one or another racial, ethnic, or religious background, against homosexuals – for no one should be beaten senseless or murdered for his sexual orientation.

Let us investigate, impartially, and without the kind of back room lobbying that allows newspapers to exempt themselves from the child-labor laws or broadcasters to monopolize the airwaves at no cost, whether sado-masochistic expressions, drug or suicide or parricide promotion, or apocalyptic racism have palpable negative effects on our society. Then, let us regulate and restrict those expressive acts that are shown to do damage. The V-chip is not the answer, but simply a standard buck-passing appeal to our protectiveness of children – an advertising gimmick: Child appeal linked to a bait and switch. The damage and the danger we confront are not confined to children; and the idea that the fare provided by the World Wrestling Federation could not foster sadism anywhere, or that the TV programming that any indulgent parent might permit, or ignore, or use for baby sitting is *eo ipso* perfectly acceptable for children is no longer acceptable on a priori grounds but must stand up to empirical test and refutation.

In a market driven society, audience is the court of last resort for any mode of amusement or communication. Why not some effort at educating more critical and discriminating audiences, instead of the assumption that all reading, all opera, all art, music, or poetry is worthwhile – and all, created equal? Some followers of Mill object to the mobilizing of social disapproval, say, in group boycotts of the broadcasters or sponsors of materials or representations that a community finds repugnant. They see here the very pressures against which Mill spoke out. But consumer sovereignty is as much a reality as are the market forces that feed and are fed by, say, rap music and videos, or combat-videogames – the market forces to which the purveyors make their ultimate appeal. *Seventeen* Magazine has avoided religious topics for years, not because the subject is uninterest-ing to adolescent girls, but because it is a focus of anxiety to potential boycotters who do not think *Seventeen* the proper vehicle for religious discourse. The motives of the boycotters may be as unsound as those of the publishers, but the effectiveness of the threat demonstrates an avenue of response that could be more judiciously explored, if thinking rather than raw prejudice and fear were enlisted, and thinking were not hamstrung by the notion that no one but the market makers has any business having views about what teenagers are reading.

What is critical, if the market is to act wisely, is education, including the education of taste and judgment – not indoctrina-tion, which does nothing to contain prurience, but the growth of sophistication and discrimination. Caution is needed, since education is so often the politician's counterpart to the football punt. Intractable social problems are laid at the schoolhouse door, as though schools, rather than parents and peers, were our chief role models. But schools help. To name just one problem area, that of our human diversity in a pluralistic, multicultural society: Schools can provide a primer, as it were, in tolerance; so can the military and other forms of national service, at a very experiential level. America has made some halting steps away from normativizing an artificial, whitebread amalgam identified proudly in the 1950s under the rubric of conformity – perhaps, the last vestige of Zangwill's melting pot idea. We have not yet wholly given up the notion that the chief function of the public schools is to serve as the crucible of conformity, or of whatever newer standards of political correctness may be offered to replace it. Thus intellectual interests are neglected, and the vulgarization and politicization of the idea of diversity, for example, has rendered it down to a celebration of stereotypic identity markers, while attaching to the pluralistic ideal the same repressive anxieties that long accompanied the conformist paradigm. Deeper and more sensitively guided study of literature, of history, of biology would be far more to the point than painful role playing exercises and noisy sloganeering. The more cognitive path is always harder than lipservice. But it produces results that are more lasting and more real, because it preserves the content and not just the name of education.

Ideally, insofar as it serves an integrative function, education will plumb the complexities of group identity and individual diversity; it will not merely celebrate differences but provoke understanding, in part by projecting individual and communal experiences against a background of literature and history. But the task is a subtle one. I recall my daughter's experience at a fine private school that prided itself on the rainbow of its student population and on its multicultural curriculum. When the English class was busy with the mandatory, and then brand new, *Woman Warrior*, Maxine Hong Kingston's portrayal of Chinese immigrant experience, a Chinese-American classmate asked Allegra to explain all this to him. She was known as a literary person, and all this stuff about Chinese women was something her classmate confessed he just could not relate to.

In addressing the negativities in the media, however, the immediate task is simpler than the long term one of educating the taste and analytical sophistication that frustrate prejudice. Why not start with full disclosure of the sources of income that support any published or broadcast communication? That certainly is no panacea, but I suspect that the policy, if implemented, would have powerful effects. We can get some idea of its prospective impact by the hue and cry that echoes even suggestions of any form of media regulation, which is labeled 'chilling' by those whose practices it might affect. But I have trouble understanding in Madisonian terms the notion that political influence, or media exposure, can legitimately be bought and sold through a junket, an emolument, or a lunch. Perhaps the nexus lies closer to Madison Avenue. And if such practices really are perfectly sound, there should be no objection to public knowledge of them, just like the published scores of health department inspections of restaurant kitchens.

iv. The public, the ethos, and harm to self. Rights are a species of desert, and deserts are the claims of beings. Deserts, prima facie, are the program or project that a being defines and develops in the affirmation of an identity. It is because all deserts are ontically affirmative at base that there are no rights to harm the self – no right of suicide or self-mutilation, self-degradation or self-destruction, although heroism and martyrdom, when they affirm the dignity of personhood and uphold humane values, are another matter entirely.

I take it to be an authentically Jewish view that it is paradoxical to urge a right to harm one's own genuine interests, and I locate the metaphysics underlying the exposure of that paradox in the positive valuation that the Jewish tradition places on being – not because it is the handiwork of God, but rather as the warrant of our inference that being is God's handiwork and expressive act. To apply the relevant insight concretely: It would be absurd, say, to make a right of sado-masochism, even among consenting adults. Indeed, I link sadism and masochism here not only because they are linked clinically, but because the moral standpoint (despite the commonplace confusion of morals with altruism) regards the interests of ego as no less worthy of consideration than those of the other.

Kant might imagine, along with others in the liberal tradition – Mill, Locke, and surely Hobbes, who was no liberal but laid out the ground on which liberalism pitches its tents – that self-interest can take care of itself, and that self-serving cannot be moral, since it would not naturally be praised. But we know enough of the perils of internalized resentment, of ambient hatred and rejection, and of the struggles of personal integration, to know that the constitution of an integrated personality and plan are achievements indeed and well worthy of praise. Further, we can hardly presume that self-interest will be adequately understood, let alone effectually pursued, without social support, in infancy and childhood, or beyond.

Where social and economic pressures militate in behalf of euthanasia or infanticide, the task of society is to combat them. This means not simply and crudely opposing such practices politically but providing the kind of sustenance to human life, health, and well being that will make the hard choices rare and that will diffuse at the source the pressures that prompt the demand for such choices. Again, if there are social and cultural currents, including ideational currents, that disrupt the environment in which individuals can discover their own identity and devise their own life plan, it is the task of society to channel those currents more constructively, to foster the emergence of selves – not to form them, but to free them and

52

nurture them, allowing them to discover their own paths of growth.

Many of the social pathologies that traditional religions and moral systems frown on, it is said, should not be restricted or even disapproved, since they harm no one, or no one other than their willing participants. But there is no victimless crime, and that for two reasons: First, because all the members of a society are interlinked with one another, so that the motorcyclist who rides without a helmet will almost certainly share the heavy cost of his cranial injuries not only with family members, but also with the coinsured, and the taxpayers who must mend and heal him. Second, because the status of victim does not exclude the freely consenting adult. The alcoholic or compulsive gambler – or the impulsive gambler, for that matter, who gambles and loses what he cannot afford – shares his habit or his lapse, and his loses, with his family; and, in a lesser degree, with coworkers and society at large. But he is himself, by many measures, the most damaged victim of his own behavior.

Prostitution and drug addiction, similarly, have multiple victims – the family of the john or user, whose trust is violated, whose hopes are hazarded or dashed, and who are exposed, among other detriments, to AIDS. These victims include even the unborn, who may contract AIDS and other diseases in the birth canal. But hardly negligible among the victims is the individual prostitute or drug abuser, who perhaps freely chose a course that jeopardizes every chance of human fulfillment. If the libertarian slogan is mooted at this point, urging that my body is my property, to do with as I like, we must ask the very Jewish question, when did the self become property? and doesn't even property demand responsibility?

The work of society and of culture, their sole task, is the fostering of identities and nurturance of the circumstances in which identities can self-define and flourish. Despite the appeals of many advocates to the contrary, I have suggested, pornography is not quite the best starting point or vehicle in this task of self-definition. I say this advisedly, even bearing in mind the mixed results I know of in one or two cases where something like that did occur. I am not at all sure that the casualties and occupational hazards of the industry are worth that payoff. But in a positive vein, there are many fruitful avenues to be developed and explored. Legally, institutionally, societally, the task is one of richly endowing the moral environment with the models and materials that will allow and promote human self-definition. It is certainly and centrally the task of the family to provide such nurturance. Communal agencies like churches and synagogues, Y-s and Jewish Centers, neighborhood groups and clubs, sports teams, exercise groups, dance clubs, and community bands and orchestras can help individuals to give definition to their personalities and foster the emergence of more developed identities, not only in the young. By such means, communal enterprises can not only build self-esteem, but help to give it grounds. In the process they combat anomie and demoralization.

Government lacks primary expertise here, and we tend to prefer that these tasks be undertaken privately. We rightly worry that when this kind of work, moral work, is done by societal rather than communal agencies it will be done badly. Not that governments do all things badly. But a certain crudeness of touch and blandness of taste naturally result from seeking a lowest common denominator. We are rightly chary of slighting individuality, and of the adverse reactions that impersonality can provoke. These are among the reasons, surely, why we do not, if we can help it, prefer to have our children raised by others, but would rather keep this onerous task (or, at least, control of it) to ourselves, within the family and in institutions that are as close as we can manage to the oversight of the family.

Even when we pursue activities that seek to integrate our communities more broadly than the family or the neighborhood can, we see increasingly the need for sensitivity to interests, outlooks, and sensibilities that are 'sectional' as Mill might phrase it – ethnic, regional, gender and generational identities. Every folksong and piece of teenage slang is founded on the notion that 'We alone know what sex is' – or what life or death are. The exclusivity of that 'we' is naive and potentially dangerous. But it should not be too rudely awakened. It rests on the negation and exclusion of what is seen as alien or exotic, old fashioned or simply old hat. This is a negation that we all must learn to grow beyond, by coming to see our social identities in positive rather than negative terms. Granted it is not an exclusivity that everyone, in the best case, is simply jolted out of; there is a public interest in the forging of larger than local identities. National service is a good vehicle for such efforts, because it draws energies and attentions away from locality and idiosyncrasy and toward a common goal and task. Regardless of the vehicle, there is a public responsibility to foster deeper, sounder, larger and at the same time more individual conceptualizations of the self and its project than would typically emerge in, say, a neighborhood playground or ethnically homogeneous recreation program. Clearly there are cross-pressures between the public responsibility for fostering personhood and the dangers of standardization, with its relatively empty secular and minimalist notions of 'good citizenship.' In acknowledgement of those cross-pressures, pluralistic societies seek means of sustaining highly varied approaches to the formulation of ideals and the forging of identities.

The tax deductibility of philanthropic contributions to educational, social, recreational, religious, and cultural bodies is one rather successful means. It provides both an index and a suitably pluralistic medium for the valuing of all sorts of programmatic efforts. By proportioning state support to articulated communal interest, and by offering that support obliquely, through tax forgiveness, it preserves a high degree of independence in each particular effort and permits self-defined communities to formulate their own objectives, devise their own means of pursuing them. Programs grow, change, and disappear according to the effectiveness of their message and the appeal of their goals. But no private agency is sufficient to attain all the social goods that lie in the public charge. And none is so infallible, we might say, with Mill in mind, as to be left to define its goals without let or restraint. Critically, for example, why should we condone the abuse of indirect public subsidies by abdicating the responsibility to ensure that they are not appropriated by hate groups, criminal gangs, or mind controlling cults?

Public education, at least in recent years, has sagged under the weight of its responsibilities, and has not, as effectively as might be wished, promoted the emergence of personal, communal, or national identities. Public libraries, public broadcasting, arts and cultural programming, although less frequently and less presumptively criticized, have produced even more mixed results vis-à-vis the ethos. For here, despite the mingled hand-wringing and self-congratulation, there is often not even lipservice to the shallow and minimal educational ideal of good citizenship. Indeed, the mere suggestion that there is a public responsibility for the public ethos is likely to be met with charges of big-brotherism or Pavlovian conditioning. The idea that public (or even private) expenditures on art or music should aim to enlarge the sensibilities of the public is rhetorically conflated with Socialist realism or fascist kitsch. And the idea that music (or fiction) is an important public institution, a realm in which identities form and spirits grow, a vehicle through which, as Aristotle suggested (*Politics* VIII 5, 1340a11–29), our moral experience can be enlarged, is liable to be conflated with a Stalinist arts policy. Yet the ethos that is thus left to the intense and highly focused vagaries of commercial and political manipulation is counted on in every public institution and presumed upon in the most elementary of our notionally private acts.

My final proposal here is a modest one: that we should regard and treat our cultural institutions as if they matter – since they do – not merely to the welfare and survival of our society, but to the worth and credibility of its claims upon existence. If Little League and Pop Warner are really where characters are forged – if these are really the places where boys become men and learn the meaning of teamwork and cooperation, not to mention masculinity – then we ought to reflect on the rules we play by and study the lessons actually taken home from the playing field. If the arts are as important to us as we say they are and as the attendance at arts events testifies – for it outdistances the attendance at all sports events – then we ought to consider what our arts are saying about us and what we are saying through them about our visions of ourselves and one another. Ballet says as much about us as baseball, and if ballet is decadent, that is as serious a problem in our culture and mode of education as is the corruption of our sports.

The reflection I am calling for is something we need to do publicly and deliberatively, through the boards and committees of our arts and sports and other cultural institutions, not surreptitiously, through manipulation of the media, and not triumphally, with a view to imposing uniformity or conformity to some preestablished standard of minimal (or maximal) acceptability. Reaching beyond the invidious display of the symbolisms of wealth and power that attach themselves to art and sport and all cultural institutions, we should deliberate with a view to the enrichment of the human experience, pronouncing to ourselves, through our institutions, in all their diversity, who it is that we think we are. It is in this way that we can escape the trap of merely paying lipservice, when fund raising time rolls around, to the notion that our cultural expressions are the vehicle of our communal memory, social identity, and civilizational future.

Notes

1 Lucian, *The Sale of the Philosophers*.
2 What Bentham wrote: 'reasons for wishing there were such things as rights, are not rights . . . want is not supply – hunger is not bread. That which has no existence cannot be destroyed – that which cannot be destroyed cannot require anything to preserve it from destruction. *Natural rights* is simple nonsense: natural and imprescriptible rights, rhetorical nonsense, – nonsense upon stilts.' *Anarchical Fallacies*, Bowring, ed. vol. 2, p. 501. Bentham speaks sagely when he goes on to urge us to specificity, not jumbling legislative proposals in 'an undistinguishable heap . . . under any such vague general terms as property, liberty, and the like.' But the danger of his approach becomes evident when he argues, in the same paragraph, 'as there is no *right* which ought not to be maintained so long as it is upon the whole advantageous to the society that it should be maintained, so there is no right which, when the abolition of it is advantageous to society, should not be abolished.' Cf. Bowring, vol. 3, pp. 217–19; vol. 8, pp. 242–53, 327–8; and see the texts and discussions in Ogden 1932.
3 Feinberg 1986.
4 A paradox naturally emerges here, since some social pressures might naturally take the form of expressions of opinion. The tension is not merely theoretical. The dialectic of political correctness is one expression of its power: Some forms of speech and action, deemed, say, progressively heretical, are privileged as such; their criticism is presumed censorious – at least in social contexts governed by fairly homogeneous norms – while other forms of social criticism are suppressed, under rationales drawn from Mill's own arguments.
  The closest Mill comes to addressing the difficulty is in acknowledging that it 'is neither possible nor desirable' to expect no one's feelings towards another to remain uninfluenced by the other's personal deficiencies, say, of taste, good sense, or character. Mill counsels sensibly that we should caution our acquaintances about the estrangement which their foolish attitudes or offensive behavior might engender. This parallels the biblical obligation of reproof (Lev. 19:17). But that mild obligation of fellowship (*re'ut*) does not endorse a right or responsibility of bringing concerted social disapproval to bear, and Mill's counsels, similarly, do not extend to public actions undertaken with a view to altering behaviors that seem,

say, self-destructive – or repressive. Mill writes, simply, 'What I contend for is, that the inconveniences which are strictly inseparable from the unfavorable judgment of others are the only ones to which a person should ever be subjected for that portion of his conduct and character which concerns his own good, but which does not affect the interest of others in their relations with him' (*On Liberty*, pp. 134–35).

5   For the philosophical import of Mill's 35 years at the East India Company, see Zastoupil 1994.

6   Himmelfarb (1974, p. 21) seems to write apologetically when she stresses that Mill's examples of justified despotism come from the distant past. His strictures against Chinese culture (*On Liberty*, pp. 129–30) and against the French and Spanish peoples of his own day (*Representative Govern-ment*, p. 213) show how contemporary and near to hand were the applications of his view that some peoples and cultures are simply not ready for liberal government. The very arguments in which Mill links liberalism with progress are mired in a chauvinism that broadcasts disapproval from the ancient civilizations of China and India to the nearby opposite shore of the English Channel. Social criticism of traditionalist societies is always in order – although the old Tory response to Whiggery stands by: that exploitative capitalism can carry individualism too far when it battles against long established traditions. But beyond the niceties of that debate, the fact remains that colonialist paternalism or neo-mercantilist benign neglect sits a little too cozily with a willingness to write off the traditionalism or communalism of, say, the entire Third World as mere Asiatic or African backwardness, tropical or sub-tropical torpor – leaving the shrewd dealer of the industrial world not only with the profits but also with the comfort of moral superiority in the collectively claimed virtues of vigor, individualism, and ambition. Mill does not voice colonial or imperial designs against France or Spain. He turns his argument in the direction of a vague hope that the energy and industry of individuals from these European nations (and trading partners) will, with the aid of institutions like those that he commends, lead to the gradual reforms that will make liberal institutions possible – or palatable in new locales. But aiming to hold up even *these* foreigners as an object lesson and a foil before the jingoism of his audience, he does not shrink from dismissing the French at large as 'essentially a southern people' for whom 'the double education of despotism and Catholicism has, in spite of their impulsive temperament, made submission and endurance the common character' – any more than he balks at remarking (on the same page, 213) that 'the most envious of all mankind are the Orientals.' The fascination of the exotic and the practices of opium exportation and full scale imperialism help to explain how global dismissals of entire cultures can be turned from a hope and expectation of progress in Europe to a weary denial that it will begin any time soon in Asia. But mediating between civil (or cousin-like) disdain and mercantile or colonial contempt is always the chance of war, in which stereotypes like those that Mill freely indulges become as much a part of the armamentum as canon balls and powder. For the history and dialectic of environmental racism in general and the notion of a 'southern' temperament in particular, see Goodman and Goodman 1989.

7 The warrant for free trade, Mill urges, 'rests on grounds different from, though equally solid with, the principle of individual liberty asserted in this Essay.' The trouble here is not Mill's argument for the utility of free trade but the absoluteness of his faith in its efficacy and – as with free speech – his unwillingness to consider values that might count against it. In classic utilitarian fashion, Mill is more than willing to sacrifice varied interests to what his Benthamite calculus expects to be the general good: 'In many cases an individual, in pursuing a legitimate object, necessarily and therefore legitimately causes pain or loss to others, or intercepts a good which they had reasonable hope of obtaining . . .' The inability of Mill's standards to differentiate cases of this kind which require regulation or remediation from those which do not – except where 'fraud, treachery, and force' may be in play – is one good reason for preferring the Mosaic attempt to integrate law and morals over the secularist assumption that the two should be held apart. Monopoly, nepotism, and usury are just a few examples of unfair practices that do not involve fraud, force, or treachery.

8 Thus, in the Hebrew idiom, one can live as well as die 'for the sanctification of God's name' – and the former is by far preferable, where the choice is possible.

9 Philo, *De Abrahamo* 36.201–4; see Goodman 1996, pp. 23–24. And cf. Philo's treatment of play in *Questions on Genesis* 4.188.

10 See *God of Abraham*, pp. 84, 97–98, 123, 140, 182–4.

11 *Jerusalem* (1783), ii, tr. Samuels, p. 171. In the same last two pages, Mendelssohn writes: 'Brothers, if you care for true piety, let us not feign agreement where diversity is evidently the plan and purpose of Providence . . . . Why should we make ourselves unrecognizable to each other in the most important concerns of our life by masquerading, since God has stamped everyone, not without reason, with his own facial features? . . . Reward and punish no doctrine, tempt and bribe no one to adopt any religious opinion! Let everyone be permitted to speak as he thinks, to invoke God after his own manner, or that of his fathers . . . . Let no one in your states be a searcher of hearts and a judge of thoughts; let no one assume a right that the Omniscient has reserved to himself alone' (tr. Arkush, pp. 138–39).

12 See Mill, *Autobiography*, ed. Coss, 1924, pp. 116–17; compare the more open elitism of *The Early Draft*, ed. Stillinger (1961, p. 139), and the 'rejected leaves,' pp. 188–89; see Himmelfarb 1974, pp. 52–55.

13 New York Times, December 22, 1996, Section 2, p. 1.

14 New York Times, February 21, 1997, p. B–3. For the misrepresentations of fact in *The People vs Larry Flynt*, see Matt Labash, 'The Truth vs Larry Flynt,' *The Weekly Standard*, February 17, 1997, pp. 19–26.

15 Indeed, the claim is made, widely, that it is censorship for the state to decline to offer public support for the production and display of pornographic art.

16 I owe this last thought to my colleague Elijah Millgram.

17 Locke's naturalism reserved to the individual the freedom to act and choose; Rawls's argument from virtual consent does the same. It was the Hobbesian idea that no rational chooser would give up the right to chose in

matters affecting his own life and ultimate welfare that led Locke to the
ideas of inalienable rights and limited sovereignty, and Rawls to the
notion that no rational subject would surrender the right to choose. But in
the present context Rawls's reassurance has only the force of a tautology.
Meanwhile, Mill's anxieties about paternalism and his confidence in the
Hobbesian rational ego allow his formulations to extend our liberties into
a freedom to negate our rights and surrender our reason, undermining not
only the rights themselves but their Lockean rationale.

18 See Jesse Green, *New York Times Magazine*, September 15, 1996,
pp. 38–45, 54–5, 84–5.

19 Mill's essay was intended to be popular and topical, but it was not a mere
occasional piece. As Himmelfarb has shown (1974, especially pp. xv-xviii),
it was a carefully crafted and painstakingly revised essay, in the light of
which Mill made critical publication decisions affecting the balance of his
oeuvre.

20 For the nexus linking the family planning movement, Zero Population
Growth, eugenics, and the contraceptives industry, see Greer 1984.

21 Note the disparity here with the public relations posture of public health
campaigns. Adolescent sexual activity, drug abuse, unwelcome pregnan-
cies, and other disapproved acts are described as inevitable when access to
condoms, needle exchanges, or abortions are in question. Such access, we
are assured, is not to be construed as social condonement. But the very
mention of the hypothesis that spousal murder or abuse may be part of a
larger pathology that might or should be socially addressed is branded,
from a public relations standpoint, as blaming the victim.

22 *Hustler* used to run a regular cartoon feature, 'Chester the Molester,'
designed to facilitate the judgment that violent and violative behaviors,
including some pretty gory fantasies, were not only amusing or funny but
also commonplace, and in that sense ordinary, normal, and acceptable.

23 Philip Durham (1968) explains how Dashiell Hammett set 'the violence-is-
fun technique' at the core of his fiction: 'The Continental Op soon became
physically and personally involved in violence, getting smashed up
thoroughly in "One Hour." It was not long, as in "Women, Politics, and
Murder," before he thought violence was sheer pleasure, "I began to throw
my right fist into him. I liked that. His belly was flabby, and it got softer
every time I hit it. I hit it often." And the mood continued in "Dead Yellow
Women" where the Op observed Dummy Uhl, who with "all the middle of
him gone – slid down to the floor and made more of a puddle than a pile
there." As the Op continued down a hall, "cracking everything" that got in
his way and being "cracked" back, he began to enjoy the violence, which
was technically accentuated by one sentence paragraphs. "When he
crouched above me I let him have it./ My bullet cut the gullet out of him./ I
patted his face with my gun as he tumbled down past me."' We even see in
Hammett's sensate writing the birth of the climactic scene of *Prizzi's
Honor*: 'Gooseneck fired at Kewpie at the moment she threw a knife at
him. Kewpie spun back across the room – hammered back by the bullets
that tore through her chest . . . . Gooseneck was in similar trouble as he
stopped shooting and tried to speak, while the haft of the girl's knife
protruded from his throat. He couldn't get the words past the blade.'

(pp. 62–63) That last irony, about trying to get words past a knife blade, is meant to be funny as well as sensate. It educates a sadistic taste by overlaying laughter onto horror. For the nexus of Hammett's topics and technique to his politics, see Grebstein 1968, p. 35.

References

Bentham, J. 1838–43. *Anarchical Fallacies*, originally published in E. Dumont, *Tactique des Assemblées legislatives* (1816) and collected in J. Bowring (ed.), *The Works of Jeremy Bentham* (London, 1843)

Collins, R. K. L. and D.M. Skover. 1996. *The Death of Discourse*. Boulder: Westview

Durham, P. 1968. 'The *Black Mask* School,' in D. Madden (ed.), *Tough Guy Writers of the Thirties*. Carbondale: Southern Illinois University Press, pp. 51–79

Feinberg, J. 1986. *Harm to Self: The Moral Limits of the Criminal Law*. New York: Oxford University Press

Frankel, S. H. 1949. 'The Concept of Colonization,' inaugural lecture, Oxford University, 9 June, 1949. Oxford: Clarendon Press

——. 1960. 'The Tyranny of Economic Paternalism in Africa: A Study of Frontier Mentality, 1860–1960'. *Optima* (supplement). Johannesburg

Garver, E. 1994. *Aristotle's* Rhetoric: *An Art of Character*. Chicago: University of Chicago Press

Gitlin, T. 1992. *The Murder of Albert Einstein*. New York: Farrar, Strauss and Giroux

Goodman, L. E. 1991. *On Justice: An Essay in Jewish Philosophy*. New Haven. Yale University Press

——. 1996. *God of Abraham*. New York and Oxford: Oxford University Press

Goodman L. E. and M. J. Goodman. 1989. "Particularly Amongst the Sunburnt Nations . . .' – The Persistence of Sexual Stereotypes of Race in Bio-Science.' *International Journal of Group Tensions* 19, pp. 221–43, 365–84

Grebstein, S. 1968. 'The Tough Hemingway and his Hardboiled Children,' in D. Madden (ed.), *Tough Guy Writers of the Thirties*. Carbondale: Southern Illinois University Press, pp. 18–41

Green, J. 1996. *New York Times Magazine*, September 15, 1996, pp. 38–45, 54–5, 84–5

Greer, G. 1984. *Sex and Destiny: The Politics of Human Fertility*. New York: Harper and Row

Himmelfarb, G. 1974. *On Liberty and Liberalism: The Case of John Stuart Mill*. New York: Alfred Knopf

Kendall, W. 1960. 'The "Open Society" and its Fallacies.' *American Political Science Review* 54, pp. 972–79

Lucian. (2nd century C.E.). *The Sale of the Philosophers*, translated by P. Turner as 'Philosophies Going Cheap,' in *Lucian: Satirical Sketches*. Baltimore: Penguin, 1968

Mill, J. S. 1831. 'On the Spirit of the Age,' in G. Himmelfarb (ed.), *Mill: Essays on Politics and Culture*. New York: Doubleday, 1963

——. *The Earlier Letters . . . 1812–1848*, edited by F. E. Mineka. Toronto, 1963
——. 1838. *Bentham*, in *John Stuart Mill on Bentham and Coleridge*. New York: Harper and Brothers, 1950; 1962
——. 1859. *On Liberty*, in H. B. Acton (ed.), *J. S. Mill: Utilitarianism, On Liberty and Considerations on Representative Government*. London: Dent, 1972
——. 1861a. *Utilitarianism*
——. 1861b. *Considerations on Representative Government*
——. 1873. *Autobiography*, edited by J. J. Coss. New York: Columbia University Press, 1924; and *The Earlier Draft of John Stuart Mill's Autobiography*, edited by J. Stillinger. Urbana: University of Illinois Press, 1961
Ogden, C. K. 1932. *Bentham's Theory of Fictions*. Paterson, N.J.: Littlefield Adams. Reprinted, 1959
Sartorius, R. (ed.), 1983. *Paternalism*. Minneapolis: University of Minnesota Press
Sunstein, C. 1993. *Democracy and the Problem of Free Speech*. New York: Free Press
Zastoupil, L. 1994. *John Stuart Mill and India*. Stanford: Stanford University Press

CHAPTER TWO

Judaism
and the Liberal State

Edward Halper

N o political system has been more beneficial for Jews than
the liberal state,[1] for it removed barriers to political
participation and allowed, at least in principle, all citizens the
opportunity to pursue their personal interests and economic
advantage. Nevertheless, it has often proven difficult for Jews to
maintain Judaism in liberal states. The reason, I shall argue, is
that the values of the liberal state are intrinsically at odds with
the values of Judaism. Ironically, it is just the feature of the
liberal state that has been the chief source of its benefit to Jews,
its liberality, as it were, that works ultimately to undermine
Jewish values. The two reasonable responses to the conflict in
values define two modes of political participation – and these are
precisely the two primary modes of Jewish political participation. The liberal state undermines not only Judaism but all
individual pursuits, and this is a serious limitation because its
theorists conceive its purpose to be the *promotion* of such
pursuits. Rather than molding Judaism to liberal values, we
should, I propose, take our cue from Jewish values and begin, in
the broadest possible terms, to reconceive the modern state.

1. Judaism and Community

Now to explain. The liberal state is based upon the idea that the
role of the state is to prevent people from infringing upon the
activities of other individuals.[2] So long as what I do concerns
only myself and poses no threat to others, the state has no
justification for interfering with my activities; its role is rather to

63

insure that I can pursue my individual interests unobstructed. To be sure, this simple notion needs manifold qualifications, for only someone who is sound in mind and body makes free choices. Thus, liberal political theory can sanction any action of the state that seeks to ban what obstructs free choice (e.g., drugs) or to promote what enhances choice (e.g., education). Nevertheless, the role of the liberal state is primarily negative; happiness remains the prerogative of the individual. In other words, the liberal state exists to facilitate the individual's pursuit of happiness. The state has no ends of its own.

In contrast, Judaism, as articulated in the Chumash and later writings, has an end: holiness (Lev. 19:2). The study of Torah is both means to this end and part of it. The Torah commands Jews to 'love God with all your heart, all your soul, and all your might' (Deut. 6:5). As Maimonides explains, a person cannot have feelings on command; the injunction must be to learn the ways of God that one would love Him.[3] Learning is just one of the mitzvot, but it is essential for all the others for the obvious reason that it is impossible to do them without knowledge of how they are to be done. Learning by itself is not sufficient for holiness; it must be accompanied by the performance of the mitzvot that it makes possible. However, the presumption is that learning will inevitably lead to the performance of mitzvot. So learning and performing mitzvot constitute the two dimensions of holiness.

Both are essentially communal. Learning is not a solitary activity; it is done, minimally, with another person and ideally in a center of learning, a school or yeshiva. And it is clear that the Chumash envisions a society where the commandments are communal and, consequently, the end of holiness is attained in common. Thus, sacrificial services requires a class of priests who are sustained materially by the community and who in turn offer communal, as well as individual, sacrifices. Further, repentance is made for the entire community by the high priest. The land is distributed in a way that prevents the development of gross inequities, for every fifty years it reverts to the descendants of its original possessors. Moreover, the reward for the observance of the commandments, abundant agricultural produce, is received by the community – note the use of plural verbs at Deut. 11:13–21 – as is the punishment for non-observance.

The communal character of Judaism is even more apparent in Rabbinic Judaism. Sacrifice is replaced with communal prayers that require a quorum and are incumbent upon all men; complicated issues of law make a communally sponsored rabbinic authority necessary; strictures on foods and utensils knit Jews into an economic unit; and the obligation to tithe becomes a duty to give charity. Jewish literature and lore record at least two tokens of the communal expression of religion. One is the ubiquitous *schnorrer* who demands charity (or justice, as *tzedakah* could also be rendered) on the ground that he makes it possible for the well-off to fulfill their obligations. The other is the idea that it is the most righteous of a community who are most likely to be forced to commit *kiddush ha-Shem* because they are, to some degree, responsible for the failings of the others.

In short, holiness is to be realized communally. If the notion of an end realized in common seems alien, we have only to think of the players on a football team: the individual effort of each member contributes to the victory sought and enjoyed by all. Analogously, the end of the practice of Judaism is to be a holy people.

There is a certain resonance between Judaism and contemporary 'communitarian' theories.[4] However, there are still more striking similarities between Judaism and Greek political philosophy. To be sure, happiness, not holiness, is identified as the end of the state by Plato and Aristotle, but happiness turns out, on close consideration, to be something unexpected: philosophical contemplation or acts of virtue. These latter are nearly the same as the ideals of Torah study and mitzvot; so what the Greeks call 'happiness' turns out to be much the same as being holy. Most importantly, Plato and Aristotle take happiness to be realizable in the collective activities of citizens. Thus, Plato thinks that the proper functioning of all parts of the state makes it possible for some people in the state to engage in philosophical thinking; Aristotle maintains that the people realize virtue by performing the assigned jobs, particularly that of rule, that are necessary for the operation of the state. That is, the state is not simply the sphere *in which* happiness is realized; its functions – performed by its citizens – *constitute* the happiness of its citizens. Moreover, each endorses land distribution schemes comparable to those of the Chumash, schemes that

65

serve to preserve moderate wealth in all citizens.[5] Whereas Plato and Aristotle limit wealth by statute, the Chumash establishes the hereditary possession of land that must revert to its original owners or their descendants every fifty years (Lev. 25:10–16; Num. 36:7). Because land could not be sold permanently, it was impossible to lose all wealth. Possession of land remains a common heritage.

Of course, I am passing over large and important differences here, both the well known differences between Plato's and Aristotle's accounts of the state and the differences between them and the theocracy described in the Chumash. For my purposes, what are striking here are the shared presumptions that the state has a positive end and that that end is realized in common by its citizens.

I need to acknowledge here some rather large qualifications in my thesis of communal ends. With the rise of Chasidism, the relation of the individual to God comes into prominence. Martin Buber calls this the 'I-Thou' relation. It is strikingly at odds with the first person plural forms that are pervasive in the prayer service, a relation better termed 'We-Thou.' With this increased emphasis on the individual, it comes to be important that certain individuals are holier than others. Thus, the end of holiness is no longer strictly communal. To recall my earlier analogy, holiness has come to be less like the victory of a football team, where the same victory is shared by all, and more like victory in a track meet: the team wins because of high scores attained by different individuals in different events. Ironically, though, this development in the realization of holiness served to strengthen certain aspects of Jewish communal life, for the holier individuals (the Rebbes) attracted a following and thus became the core of new communities. In contrast, the Reform movement emphasizes the universal dimension of Judaism. It judges as irrational those practices that make the Jewish community particular – it is the *chuqqim* that by and large have this function – and ignores or rejects them. Hence, it is left with a community-based social ethic, and no real community upon which to exercise it.

Whether holiness is or is not realized communally, it constitutes, from the perspective of the liberal state, a private end, one of many whose realization the state aims to make possible. To the extent that a liberal state allows its citizens to pursue their own notions of happiness, such a state seems thoroughly compatible with Judaism. Certainly, it is possible to be a Jew in a liberal state. However, I contend that the very openness of the liberal state to all individual pursuits works to undermine the importance of these pursuits. My central argument is that in making Jewish ends and, indeed, all other individual ends merely personal preferences, the liberal state relegates individual ends to relative unimportance. Just because personal preferences matter little to the state, those preferences tend to seem insignificant to its citizens. Though the liberal state makes possible diverse individual pursuits, it tends to replace the diverse ends with a kind of secular religion.

Before I proceed to present this argument let me note the peculiar modality of my claim: the liberal state *tends* to undermine individual ends. A tendency does not manifest itself all at once – indeed, given sufficiently strong counteracting factors, it may never manifest itself. How, then, can a tendency's existence be proven? Not empirically, I contend. First it would be hard if not impossible to measure the strength of individual ends and harder still to determine if they have been undermined. Second, even if we could somehow measure the strength of commitment to Jewish ends and determine that it is diminishing, there are so many potential factors involved that any trend could be explained in many different ways. (This is often the stuff of political campaigns.) So any empirical evidence for or against my claim that individual values are undermined by the state would be inconclusive. I must, then, resist the temptation to say that the withering away of Jewish values in liberal states can be seen historically in America. It is controversial whether this is true, and even if it is, it could have had any number of causes. No empirical facts could, by themselves, establish that Jewish values have withered because of the liberal state; nor would my claim be necessarily weakened by showing that those values were thriving in liberal states. On the contrary, my claim about a tendency stems from the concept of the liberal state: my argument is conceptual.

Now for the argument: A liberal state by definition does not endorse any particular end; it remains neutral and so particular, individual ends are matters of indifference to it, provided only that the ends not conflict with the legitimate private interests of others in the state. At the same time, the individual ends depend for their existence on the state; without a state that allows individual pursuits, the pursuit of Jewish values by a minority would be impossible. By virtue of this dependence, an absolute non-contingent value, holiness, depends upon something else: what should be absolute becomes contingent. To put the argument differently, because the pursuit of an absolute value depends upon the state's sanctioning such activity, the value itself depends upon the state and ceases to be absolute. Thus, the citizen grasps that Jewish value is but one of many possible individual pursuits, that his pursuit of this or any other value is a matter of indifference to the state, indeed, a matter totally arbitrary to it. This is the psychological dimension. More objectively, the absoluteness of the holy is truly diminished precisely by its appearance with other possible values and its dependence upon the state. Making pursuit of holiness possible, the state is not itself subject to the holy, a sign of the holy's failure to be all encompassing. In other words, insofar as the pursuit of the holy is not a matter of holiness itself, insofar as it depends on various extrinsic factors, there is something that falls outside the scope of the holy, something that is apparently not subject to *its* authority. Thus, Jewish value not only seems diminished when set against other possible values equally sanctioned by the state; it is genuinely diminished because it depends upon something that is outside of its authority. Ironically, the very liberality of the liberal state, its universal tolerance, threatens Judaism.

Does this argument apply only to liberal states? The practice of Judaism depends to some extent on something alien to it whenever Jews find themselves in states other than that envisioned in the Chumash or the Mishnah – which is to say that the practice of Judaism is and, mostly, was always dependent on outside factors. But the liberal state is different. Other states existed for the sake of the happiness of their citizens or their rulers; Jews did not share in their end because they were an alien population that happened to be living within the state's confines.[6] Whether or not Judaism was tolerated, it played no role in the life of the state. Consequently, attaining Jewish ends did not depend directly on the state; it required only that the state not interfere. The liberal state, on the other hand, accepted Jews within it; Judaism is one of those individual values that it aims to protect. (Indeed, the presence of Judaism in a state can be welcomed as a mark of its liberality.) Just to the extent that Jews are citizens of the liberal state and full participants in its life, their practice of Judaism depends upon the liberal state in a way that Jewish practice did not depend upon other types of states. Because the liberal state *aims* to make possible its citizen's pursuit of Jewish values among other personal values, attaining holiness within it comes to depend upon the state. If my argument is correct, then this dependence tends to undermine the absolute authority of holiness as a value.

I call this a 'tendency' to diminish Jewish values because it remains possible for any individual in a liberal state to insist that Judaism – or any other individual value, for that matter – stands above the state. That, of course, is the wonderful thing about liberal states; they make it possible for anyone to say and do most anything. But one who would deny the authority of the state must ignore the real benefit that derives from living in the liberal state; he must close his eyes to his genuine dependence on the state's allowing him to pursue the values of his choice. That is to say, the liberal state does not force its citizens to acknowledge its authority, but it retains its authority nonetheless. To fail to acknowledge it requires deliberate effort of will.

My claim could also be supported by relying on a point that Aristotle makes about states. He claims that the state's end is the highest end of human activities; that is, that the state is architectonic over other endeavors.[7] The idea is that any act that I engage in must be done either for some other end or be final. Some activities might seem to be final because they are apparently done for their own sakes, such as enjoying music or other arts and engaging in philosophical reflection; but these are all parts of a whole life and derive their value to some degree from the contribution that they make to life. Hence, the only truly final end is the happiness that belongs to the whole of life. Importantly, though, Aristotle assumes the activities that constitute a happy life are activities that are engaged in together with others. Just as a tennis game requires two players, political activity, philosophical pursuits, and other constituents of happy lives are activities that can only be fully realized together with other people engaged in the same pursuits. It follows that the happiness of an individual is only realized together with the happiness of others. But the proper end of a state is just the happiness of its citizens, a happiness to be realized in jointly pursued activities such as politics itself. Hence, the ultimate end of any individual is the end of the state, and the former cannot be attained without the latter.

To put this more concretely, any decision that I might wish to make about how to spend my time both depends upon the state and serves (or ought to serve) the ends of the state. It is only because of the process of intellectual, cultural, and moral development that I have received from the society in which I was raised that I can participate in that society, and my continued efforts to develop my own potential in these areas must inevitably further the interests of the state by enhancing its intellectual, cultural, and moral life. Indeed, all the activities that the state sanctions from individuals are precisely those that advance its own ends, while those that it proscribes, such as crime, obstruct those ends. Even what seems to be selfishly in my interest furthers the interest of the state insofar as it allows me to realize a potential that is only realized jointly with others; and my pursuit depends on the state's sanction. Hence, the ends of the state govern the ends of individuals in the state.

This conclusion serves as a premise in another argument for my claim that the liberal state undermines Jewish values. If the state does indeed govern ends of the individuals, then the liberal state is quite odd. Like all states, it would organize individual activities for its own ends; but it has no ends of its own other than the promotion of conditions favorable to the pursuit of individual ends. Thus, it would be charged with the task of insuring that the activities of its citizens promote the end of making conditions favorable to individual pursuits, and the citizens would need to recognize this end as the ultimate end of their actions. But any individual choice that I make would not, by itself, promote the end of free choice: on the contrary, my choice is an affirmation of what I personally take to be valuable. My personal choices will differ from that of another and would not promote other choices, unless I could somehow regard my choice as arbitrary, personal, and insignificant. Conversely, if the state's end of promoting free choice is the end of the individual, then he or she *must* regard his personal ends as arbitrary and insignificant. So if the argument that the state is architectonic over individual pursuits is correct, then the purposeless of the state must infect the lives of its citizens. They come to see their choices as mere choices, as arbitrary and personal. The liberal state is not just without its own purposes; it is actively purposeless and thereby undermines the personal ends it claims to promote.

Consequently, the pursuit of holiness through Judaism in the liberal state comes to be infected with the purposeless of the state. Judaism comes to be seen as one choice among many possibilities, a choice that is merely personal and to some degree the result of happening to be born into a certain cultural milieu. It should go without saying that such an attitude toward Judaism is antithetical to its precepts. If the state is indeed architectonic, then the liberal state must pervert the aims of Judaism.

Advocates of liberal states deny that the state is architectonic in this way. Rather than the aims of individuals taking their cue from the end of the state, they insist that the function of the state is parasitic on the aims of its citizens. The dispute turns on the autonomy of the individual; in particular, whether it is possible for an individual to realize his ends individually or whether realization requires a society. The classical view is that human beings are properly social. The view of philosophers in the 'modern' period is that man can realize his ends individually (in a state of nature), and that he enters a social contract only for ease in attaining certain ends. This is an issue that I can only broach here, but it is worth noting that the Torah lines up with the classical view. For all their greatness the forefathers' lives suffered from lack of society, a deficiency remedied with the formation of the Jewish people. As noted earlier, many Torah mitzvot are observed by individual priests acting on behalf of the community. Self-subsistent individual existence is only possible in the Garden of Eden where needs are met divinely; in the absence of the Garden, life must be social. Natural law theorists consciously inverted the Garden of Eden: all physical needs could be met individually in nature, but insofar as society can meet these needs better, it must be grafted on to autonomous individuals. Thus, leaving Eden becomes a means for improvement rather than a fall. This is not the place to pursue questions of human nature more deeply; suffice it to say that the conception of human nature embraced by the intellectual founders of the liberal state is incompatible with that of the Torah.

2. Jewish Political Participation

Thus far, I have been arguing that the liberal state is incompatible with Judaism and tends to undermine it because for the liberal state what Judaism holds to be absolute is arbitrary, personal, and subjective and because Jewish observance depends upon the sanction of the state. In this section I offer two brief observations on how this philosophical conflict sets the parameters of Jewish political participation.

First, if the preceding analysis is correct, assimilation is simply a consequence of the liberal state. Assimilation is typically treated as a social or historical problem stemming from a lack of commitment or some such moral failing. Instead, I have been arguing here that it is, ironically, the very liberality of a state that allows Jews to participate in it that *tends* to undermine Judaism. It is not impossible to resist this tendency, but to do so it would be necessary to fail somehow to see how Judaism in a liberal state depends on the state. Someone who could close his eyes to this relation would be less threatened by the state. In fact, those who choose to remain more observant often isolate themselves from the political mainstream. While this isolation may stem more explicitly from a perception of moral decadence than from disapproval of the liberal state, it extends also to the political process.

Those who have chosen observance have tended to be more politically 'conservative'; the more assimilated Jews are typically more 'liberal' or 'progressive.' The difference, I suggest, is not so much one of values but of who or what is responsible for attaining those values. Should Jewish communal values be realized by individual Jews or by the Jewish community? In either case, the government should drop from sight.[8] Or is the possibility of a community's realizing its own end within a neutral or even hostile state so remote that the government itself must take up this end as its own? In this case, we should look to the government to promote education and justice. Thus, the dichotomy between liberal and conservative Jews would seem to derive not from differences in values but from differences in who or what can and should pursue those values. Again, it is just because the liberal state *does* undermine individual ends that those ends seem attainable only by being incorporated into the state's ends. Or, alternatively, it is just because the liberal state undermines individual ends, that the best way to attain those ends is to remove the government, to the greatest extent possible, from the affairs of individuals.

Here I need to distinguish the liberal state from the complex of political positions that are generally designated 'liberal.' Nearly all Jewish thought comes under the latter head, and the probable reason is that the values of the Torah are communal. Again, the issue for Jews is not whether liberal, communal values are legitimate, but whether the government (the liberal state) should or should not realize these values; that is, whether they are political values or individual values. Jews who would deny the role of the government still look for the values to be realized by individuals and particular communities. So it is that Jewish conservatives, like Milton Friedman, will often speak of themselves as 'classical liberals.' And there is some justice in their claim that it is they who are most in harmony with the theory of the liberal state developed by its intellectual founders.

It is hardly novel to notice disputes over whether it is possible to participate in the mainstream and retain a Jewish identity or whether Jewish values are best attained through conservative or liberal agendas. My point is that the terms of these debates stem from the fundamental philosophical conflict between Judaism and the liberal state. This conflict sets the parameters of Jewish political participation. It is because the liberal state undermines Jewish values that Jews who have chosen not to isolate themselves have sought to find ways to affirm those values: ironically, they have done so both by looking to the government to achieve them and by seeking to prevent the government's interference with their being attained privately.

To be sure, plenty of other groups can be aligned along an axis by the degree of government activism they would endorse. But their different alignments stem from different values. Differently aligned Jews have much the same values, I am claiming, but differ on how to respond to what I have argued is a fundamental conflict between Judaism and the liberal state. This is not, of course, to suggest that Jews have posed the issue in these terms. Still, the philosophical conflict accounts for the positions. It also explains why they are so intractable.

Supporting the conceptual analysis offered here is the fact that politics in the state of Israel manifests, with one important exception, nearly the same spectrum of opinions. The secular

73

Jewish state is a liberal state with the same options for relation to communal and individual ends, and its existence as a secular state also undermines religious values, as much, if not more, than that of other secular states. The important difference is, of course, that as a Jewish state it has seemed to some in a position to put religious ends into practice; that is, there are movements that would have the Israeli state not be a liberal state. That this added dimension in Israeli politics threatens the continued existence of non-Jewish citizens and non-religious Jews in Israel indicates an important feature of the liberal state, the characteristic that has perhaps made it practically the only alternative taken seriously by political theorists, its capacity to accommodate diversity. Despite their nationalist rhetoric, nearly all modern states encompass ethnically diverse populations.

3. The Liberal State

So far I have focused on the effect of the liberal state on Judaism. In this section I shall propose that the conflicts explored thus far undermine the liberal state. My contention is that the purpose-lessness of the liberal state is not only antithetical to Judaism, but also works against the continued existence of the liberal state itself.

The liberal state undermines Judaism because to it all individual values are arbitrary. But, if this is the case, then what can we make of the liberal state's avowed goal of protecting individual choices? Insofar as the state apparently aims to protect individual choices that are arbitrary and meaningless, its own goal would seem to be arbitrary and meaningless. In undermining individual choices, the liberal state implicitly undermines itself. On this reasoning the liberal state is contra-dictory; it exists to attain something that it takes to be essentially unimportant.

We might try to resist this conclusion by maintaining that the state protects the freedom to choose, and that even if *what* an individual chooses is arbitrary and unimportant, the fact *that* he can choose is very important. But this response does not really solve the problem because it does not explain why choice should be important if all choices are arbitrary. It remains that the liberal state exists to protect something whose value it undermines.[9]

My argument differs from those that 'communitarians' have advanced against the liberal state. Against the liberal presumption that the basis of the state lies in individual choice, they have argued that in order to be capable of choice an individual must have undergone an intellectual and social development that depends upon the very state his choice would ground.[10] At first glance, this type of argument might seem quite plausible. But what happens when the state responsible for the individual's development is the liberal state – the state that, at least in principle, does *not* provide the network of communal institutions requisite for such a development? The communitarian argument presupposes a state that does *more* than the liberal state; the existence of a minimal liberal state would undermine it. I take it that communitarians think that any real state, even a so-called liberal one, would have to provide institutions that foster the intellectual development of its citizens, a development necessary for participation in the state. But many theorists of the liberal state have denied that such institutions are necessary. They have left education and other such activities to private hands – which means that they might not occur in a liberal state. Does the exercise of autonomy in such a state require a network of social and communal institutions? Or is it not that the degree of autonomy required in a minimal liberal state is so thin that its citizens could acquire the capacity for it on their own or from nature? Autonomy in a liberal state need only include acting on one's own personal preferences and not interfering with others. Autonomy, at least of this sort, would not require a *liberal* state. Moreover, the communitarian argument says nothing of the extensive argument developed by Rousseau in the *Émile* that the individual comes to be capable of social participation not through society but through his relation to nature. For these reasons, then, the standard communitarian argument against the primacy of the individual is not sound as it stands.

The problem with the liberal state is not that it presumes some other type of state, as this communitarian argument would have it, but, as I proposed, that the consequences the liberal state aims to bring about are arbitrary and intrinsically valueless. Again, the liberal state makes no judgments about which choices are better than others, provided only that they not interfere with the choices other people make. Even choices that would sustain the liberal state or improve its effectiveness in guaranteeing the continued possibility of individual choice are treated as on a par with choices of strictly personal value. Since all choices are personal choices and since the liberal state cannot favor one set of personal choices over another, it is unable to act in a way that will sustain itself. Indeed, insofar as it undermines the value of all individual choices, the liberal state works against even those choices that would sustain it. Hence, the liberal state actively works against itself. Its internal self-contradiction issues in a tendency toward self-destruction.

What has often sustained the liberal state are movements that have sought to add purpose to the lives of its citizens. The civil rights movement, the space program, and the global fight against communism have all provided a national sense of purpose. So, too, have more recent efforts to dismantle government programs, to criminalize abortion, and to preserve the so-called right to bear arms. Despite their great diversity, all these movements aim directly or indirectly at preserving the right of individual choice. They differ, sometimes dramatically, on whose choice to preserve and how to preserve it: whether, for example, it is the mother's choice or the fetus' potential choice that ought to count most. At bottom, though, each has a certain emptiness because it does not commit itself on most of the particular choices an individual ought to make. In seeking to preserve the goal of choice but not specifying what the choices ought to be, these movements pursue an end that is meaningless and empty. Freedom of choice comes to serve as a kind of secular religion: it provides purpose without specificity or content. It is most important to new immigrants who can identify it with opposition to the suppression of freedom they left behind. Its emptiness is more manifest to succeeding generations.

4. The Moral State

Conceptual problems with the liberal state should lead to its reevaluation. But this remains difficult because it alone seems able to accommodate the diverse and pluralistic populations that constitute current states.[11] We are witnessing in the former U.S.S.R. and Yugoslavia the disastrous results of trying to impose ethnically homogeneous states on regions with diverse populations. Previous policies of Kach and the PLO could have portended the same for Israel. A state that would impose its own values on its citizens seems more threatening than the liberal state.

It is clear, then, that we must tread carefully when we consider alternatives to the liberal state. And this is hardly the place to develop an entire political theory. Still, the preceding reflections suggest a direction to look in. The problem with the liberal state comes from its lack of ends. While the modern state should certainly not aim to foster holiness – there would be no end of fruitless discussion as to what holiness is – it can and should promote values that are essential to the existence of any state: education and justice. Education is essential to sustaining every state because a society without citizens capable of assuming leadership roles cannot endure. Education is also essential to sustaining industry. But most important education is valuable in its own right, *lishemah*, we might say. It used to be generally assumed that once human physical needs were met, people would devote themselves to developing their minds. It now seems that in the free market of entertainment possibilities, education has not fared particularly well. Why should it? No interest seeks to promote it, and there are at best very limited financial rewards for its providers and for its consumers. But a society that can readily meet the physical needs of its citizens does not need to satisfy commercial interests in all its activities. It should rather aim to develop its citizens, understanding development in its broadest sense.

Finally, the state should strive for justice. By 'justice' I mean the positive counterpart to 'liberty': where the latter refers to the absence of constraints on my will, the former refers to the positive capacity for moral acts. 'Moral' is a charged term that evokes heated controversy. As a philosopher, I think that it should. Nevertheless, the controversies tend to obscure the enormous amount of agreement there is about morality. A person who gives up his time or money to help those in need is recognized to have acted laudably; disagreement arises over who is needy, how they should be helped, and what ought to motivate the agent. Anyway, this is not the type of just behavior that a state ought to require. Rather, let us recognize that anyone who develops his own abilities will contribute to society. Thus, the person who has the ability to produce goods or services will, in honing his ability, be benefiting not only himself but others. And a person who develops his intellectual abilities will likewise benefit others by his writing or simply by his association. It is not the task of a state to provide for its citizens; its task is rather to let them provide for each other and this, I claim, is the broadest and most neutral notion of what it is to allow citizens to participate in justice. Thus, the state ought to find ways for citizens to contribute to society and to realize their potential. Instead of seeing the state's role as the removal of obstructions to individual autonomous action – a path that leads to emptiness – I suggest that the role of the state is to enable individuals to manifest their abilities in action, actions that are intrinsically valuable to the agents because through them agents realize their human nature.

In short, rather than maintaining Jewish values in a state that is both antithetical to them and self-contradictory, I have taken Jewish values and made them the basis for a reconceived state. In such a state Judaism could flourish and so could other religions, but in a rather different way from religious and ethnic groups in the liberal state. Judaism would not be a personal choice that is tolerated within a state along with all other personal choices that cause no harm. Rather, it would be one among several ways of realizing the values that the state aims to foster; it would be a species of the activities that come under the genus of the state. Torah and mitzvot constitute but one way of attaining the goals of education and justice. Obviously, there are other ways, and the state should not only allow all of them to exist; it should actively promote them as ways of attaining its own ends. The more diverse ways it can attain its ends, the more firmly these ends are likely to be established. To be sure, there are also activities that do not promote these ends, and the state would be justified in excluding them: this state will not be as inclusive as the liberal state. A distinction between activities that promote the state's ends and those that do not can be difficult to maintain, especially when there are so many differing notions about what constitutes education and what constitutes justice. This is a task for the institutions of this society. The details of how they might work cannot be addressed here. Let it suffice to say that they should be designed to facilitate action rather than to obstruct it. To tolerate diversity a society need not give up its own ends – as the liberal state does; it could be diverse by recognizing different ways of attaining the same or

parallel ends. Judaism is and will be a minority practice, even in
Israel, but its values are particular versions of general values
that ought to be the ends of all states.

Notes

1 By 'liberal state' I refer to the political system advocated by Mill in *On
  Liberty* and to the many variant political systems indebted to this work.
  Thus, I include the system set out in Rawls 1971 under the rubric 'liberal
  state,' though Rawls introduces different principles and accords a far
  greater role to government.
2 John Stuart Mill declares, 'The only purpose for which power can be
  rightfully exercised over any member of a civilized community, against his
  will, is to prevent harm to others,' *On Liberty* 1978, p. 9.
3 Maimonides writes:

    We are commanded to love God ... that is to say, to dwell upon and
    contemplate His Commandments, His injunctions, and His works,
    so that we may obtain a conception of Him, and in conceiving Him
    attain absolute joy. This constitutes the Love of God. *(The
    Commandments* 1984, vol. 1, p. 3.)

4 For a brief description of the contrast between liberal and communitarian
  theories, see Avineri and de-Shalit 1992, 'Introduction,' pp. 1–11.
5 For Plato, the pertinent discussion is in the *Laws* 744d–745a. He allows
  one person's wealth to be at most four times that of another. Discussing
  this work, Aristotle worries about the effect of increasing population when
  estates are indivisible (*Politics* II.6.1265b1–12). He himself maintains
  that the best practically attainable states (not the best in principle) are
  those with a large and powerful middle class (IV.11), and he endorses
  legislative restrictions on the accumulation of wealth (VI.4.1319a4–14).
6 On the different positions of Jews in the liberal and pre-liberal states of
  Europe, see Avineri 1981, pp. 5–13. Avineri argues that Zionism emerged
  in the nineteenth century as a response to the problem of Jewish identity
  in the liberal state. Though the liberal state was in principle universa-
  listic, with its emergence 'the religiously oriented self-perception of gentile
  society was not replaced by an undifferentiated, universalist fraternity
  but by a new identity distinguished by nationalism, ethnicity, a common
  language, and past history' (p. 10). Thus, Jews found themselves excluded
  from European states on ethnic grounds just at the time when religious
  barriers were removed. Zionism developed as a way of asserting a
  national, as opposed to a religious, identity; and, consonant with its rise in
  opposition to liberalism, it was more communal and socialist. Still, Avineri
  explains that this national identity was espoused not only by secular Jews
  but by, at least, some religious Jews (chaps. 2 & 4). In his final chapter
  Avineri claims that the state of Israel plays a normative role for worldwide Jewish identity, and he warns that it will be able to retain this role

only if it remains different from Jewish society in the Diaspora (pp. 222–27). Now, fifteen years after the publication of this book, the difference seems clearly to have all but disappeared: the Israeli state functions as a liberal state.

7 What follows in this paragraph is an interpretation of *Nicomachean Ethics* I.1–2,7 and the *Politics*. I have defended it elsewhere. Those who would dispute the interpretation are invited, for the present endeavor, to take the argument of this paragraph on its own terms.

8 In *Capitalism and Freedom* (1982, p. 21) Milton Friedman argues that Jews and other minorities would be better off without government interference. Friedman refers to his position as 'classical liberalism.'

9 Charles Frankel (1978) speaks of a recurrent tension between the procedural notion of justice in the liberal state and substantive moral ends (105–6). Though this conflict has led to the view that there is 'something inherently artificial and self-destructive in liberalism,' Frankel thinks liberalism provides a common sense way of avoiding greater evils.

10 Sandel (1984, pp. 91–95) claims that the liberal state presupposes an 'unencumbered self,' a pure agent of choice, and that such agency is embodied in a 'procedural republic'; but in order to preserve the conditions in which such agency can occur it is necessary to have a 'network of obligations and involvements,' a community. Hence, individual agency presupposes, and presumably is defined by, the community. Similarly, Charles Taylor argues that individual autonomy presupposes a state and social institutions in which an individual could develop his capacity for autonomy (in Avineri and de-Shalit 1992, pp. 29–50, esp. 49–50). Note the formal parallel between these arguments and my earlier argument that Jewish values are undermined by their dependence upon the liberal state: in both cases, some human activity is claimed to depend upon community. Whereas communitarians suppose that political activities depend on a richer communal network than the institutions of the liberal state, I claim that the practice of Judaism also requires a community. The point at issue is whether the actual community provided by the liberal state suffices for the activity that requires it. I do not think that communitarians consider sufficiently whether autonomy could depend upon a state that, at least in principle, does not provide the network of communal institutions requisite for freedom.

11 See Larmore 1984, p. 338; Gutmann 1985, pp. 313–14.

References

Avineri, S. and A. de-Shalit (eds.). 1992. *Communitarianism and Individualism*. New York: Oxford University Press
Avineri, S. 1981. *The Making of Modern Zionism: The Intellectual Origins of the Jewish State*. New York: Basic Books
Frankel, C. 1978. 'Does Liberalism Have a Future?' in *The Relevance of Liberalism*, edited by the Staff of the Research Institute on International Change, Columbia University. Boulder: Westview, pp. 97–134

Friedman, M. 1982. *Capitalism and Freedom.* Chicago: University of Chicago Press

Gutmann, A. 1985. 'Communitarian Critics of Liberalism.' *Philosophy and Public Affairs* 14, pp. 308–22

Larmore, C. 1984. 'Review of *Liberalism and the Limits of Justice.*' *The Journal of Philosophy* 81, pp. 336–43

Maimonides. 1984. *The Commandments*, 2 volumes, translated by Charles B. Chavel. London: The Soncino Press

Mill, J. S. 1978 [1859]. *On Liberty.* Indianapolis: Hackett

Rawls, J. 1971. *A Theory of Justice.* Cambridge, MA: Harvard University Press

Sandel, M. 1984. 'The Procedural Republic and the Unencumbered Self.' *Political Theory* 12, pp. 81–96

Taylor, C. 1992. 'Atomism,' in S. Avineri and A. de-Shalit (eds.), *Communitarianism and Individualism.* Oxford: Oxford University Press, pp. 29–50

CHAPTER THREE

Particularism, Pluralism, and Liberty

Jonathan Jacobs

I am going to be discussing particularism, pluralism, and liberty in a manner that uses some resources to be found in Maimonides. In many ways Maimonides' views are quite foreign to contemporary ones, and I do not mean to downplay the differences. On the other hand, his significance is not merely as a figure in the history of ideas, and I will be trying to indicate ways in which some of his insights and arguments can be importantly introduced into some current debates. One of the main claims here is that while it is true that liberty is a condition that makes room for religious particularism by requiring certain kinds of political and social tolerance, religious particularism can also make an important contribution to sustaining a social world that values liberty. An examination of some features of Maimonides' interpretation of religion and moral psychology will be the way of making this point. A second way in which Maimonides will figure here is that he makes a powerful case for the view that the excellences of moral and political life are valuable as conditions for a type of human perfection which is not moral or political. That is, as crucial as the political and moral order are to the possibility of a decent and flourishing life, there are goods for a human being that are not confined to the moral and political realms. They are not the most important things.

The reason for bringing this into the discussion is that it is a way of being reminded of how the goods of political life (and liberty among them) are not complete and perfect goods. It would be wrong not to attach great significance to them; but it would be a form of idolatry to elevate them to the level of first importance. That is reserved for knowledge, love, and imitation of God. Moral and political life can subserve that final end. Maimonides says, for example, 'The third kind of perfection is more closely connected with man himself than the second perfection [perfection of the body]. It includes moral perfection, the highest degree of excellence in man's character.'[1] 'The fourth kind of perfection is the true perfection of man; the possession of the highest intellectual faculties; the possession of such notions which lead to true metaphysical opinions as regards God. With this perfection man has obtained his final object, it gives him true human perfection; it remains to him alone; it gives him immortality, and on its account he is called man.'[2] Whether or not one agrees with Maimonides' interpretation of what is true human perfection, what he says makes the point that for the religiously serious, civil society and the form it takes are not the most important things. Still, the issue of liberty is significant because liberty is a condition for living a life in which what is most important can be most fully pursued. So, the main aim of the discussion is to present some considerations for the claim that from one important Jewish perspective liberty matters, but not more than everything else; and that in fact the particularism of the Jewish tradition can helpfully sustain liberty.

The problem that motivates the discussion is a familiar and extremely difficult one. It is the issue of how the particularism of a religious tradition or community is to be related to more general or universal ethical considerations, and what is the interface of these in the political arena. There is a sense in which liberalism might be regarded as having the resources to largely solve this problem, or at least to have the best chance of doing so. The reason for this is that a liberal state values tolerance and does not seek to impose or encourage any guiding conception of a good life on its citizens.[3] With respect to goods, it is in many senses both pluralistic and experimental. It is pluralistic in its not taking any conception of good to be dominant or required (except the goods that are necessary conditions for people living in a liberal state) and it is experimental in its tolerating individuals and groups seeking to fashion good lives through a process of attempt and discovery. 'According to the liberal vision of the proper relation of morality to politics, the politics of such a society–a religiously and morally pluralistic society–should aim to be neutral.'[4]

In a good deal of recent theorizing the understanding of liberty has been largely driven by the view that there are universally endorsable principles that are accessible to any rational agent. These principles determine some fixed limits on the ways people are to be treated and regarded and define the contours of some basic social institutions and strategies of conflict resolution.[5] It is a typical feature of theories of liberal society that agreement on these fundamental principles can be secured by each participant rationally considering them, and that they secure conditions of liberty in the basic sense that they allow for persons to pursue different conceptions of a good life.

Part of the distinctively modern dimension of these views is that individuals, as rational agents, will achieve unforced consensus on what these principles are; that is, as practical reasoners, persons will acknowledge certain requirements that supply the architecture of a just or rationally endorsable form of social and political life.[6] Within the bounds of this architecture, each is at liberty to undertake to furnish his or her own life with the goods that seem most choiceworthy. No one has an epistemic or moral monopoly on what is the best life or what is a good life, though all of the business of living is to be carried on in the terms of exchange that principles of liberty permit.

It is in that sense that it appears that liberal society creates and sustains the conditions of tolerance and respect that allow for different religious confessions, communities, and traditions. Without the boundary conditions supplied by practical reason uncommitted to any particular conception of a good or best life, there would not be (so the argument goes) the ethically agreed scope for different individuals and groups to be able to pursue their commitments about what matters most, and there would not be the consensual conditions for socially just resolutions of disagreements. The principles that would be agreed to by practical reasoners are the enabling conditions for the pursuit of different conceptions of good.

This sort of theorizing may be welcome to those who are religiously serious because of the way it has built into it permission for and respect for pluralism with respect to good.[7] One feature of the view that may appear to be one of its merits is that it is not grounded in or beholden to any tradition or any set of particular beliefs about human good. It is, as it were, a substrate in which different cultures of good can grow, but the substrate does not favor any of those cultures.[8] And for many, that is its great appeal.

The very idiom of the discussion so far may seem very remote from Maimonides, and in a number of ways it surely is. But there is also a way in which Maimonides' understanding of Judaism and moral psychology can be usefully brought to bear on the contemporary setting.

Maimonides shares with Aristotle the view that human nature and the excellences of human life are to be understood in terms of the telos of that nature. That is, he believes that given the constitutive capacities of human nature, there is a condition of complete actualization or perfection for a human being. What human perfection is does not depend upon an agent's choice, though the extent to which individuals perfect their nature depends upon voluntary activity. This normative notion of human nature, this idea of there being an intrinsic teleology of a human life is exactly what a great deal of modern theorizing is both skeptical of and attempts to displace. Notions of a human telos and of perfectionism are taken to be problematic at best and altogether untenable at worst. As Bernard Williams has put it

> Aristotle saw a certain kind of ethical, cultural and indeed political life as a harmonious culmination of human potentialities, recoverable from an absolute understanding of nature. We have no reason to believe in that.[9]

There are important differences between Maimonides' view and Aristotle's, but Williams's remarks are emblematic of a widely shared view, namely, that even if there are objective considerations of human good, they are not grounded in any sort of perfectionist interpretation of human nature.

For many, this sort of skepticism is virtually truistic. The difficulty has been to formulate a plausible conception of human personality, and in particular ethical personality, to replace the teleological understanding. One influential candidate who appears in a good deal of ethical and political theory is the (basically Kantian) rational agent without a teleological nature, or without a personal nature fundamentally constituted by cultural or historical dimensions of life. But this is hardly unproblematic.

One respect in which this is problematic is that it may well be that the ethical endorsements required by a great deal of liberal theory are not of the sort that one can make antecedent to a specific mode of engagement with the world, an engagement with contentful interests and aspirations. If we abstract those out, it may be that indeed there is no one for that agent to be, and nowhere for the agent to reflect and deliberate from.[10] The motivational traction and the valuational gravity of principles of justice, respect, and tolerance, that is, of principles of universal ethical validity are, as an empirical matter, grounded in particular commitments and contentful concerns. They arise from and are sustained by those. In order for the rational agent to make the sorts of recognitions that determine universal requirements, there needs to be some place from which the reflections and recognitions are made. What practical reason *can* do is to take over and generalize specific kinds of commitment and concern, and then recognize and formulate justifying grounds for their universal validity. Liberal theory often formally detaches certain sorts of principles from the commitments and aspirations that underwrite and make them effective. One can claim that a rational agent will of course come to certain conclusions about the nature of justice or what are fundamental rights, but such claims are based upon contentful assumptions about well-ordered moral personality; and the development in actual agents of a well-ordered moral personality occurs (when it occurs) in social and historical contexts, rich with their own texture.

Political theory may regard religious commitment as one of those options permissible in pursuit of a good life, as long as the mode of commitment satisfies the theory's criteria of legitimate activity. In that formal sense, religious commitment is in principle no different from sport, for example. But this way of seeing the issue gets things a bit backwards. Religious commitment can (importantly) be the originating source for the sorts of principles that abstract practical reasoning takes over and then claims as its own. The theory of the liberal state may claim as one of its merits that it is tolerant of different kinds of religious belief and practice, as long as particularism is not divisive and exclusive in a hostile manner. But it may well be that many of the basic ethical virtues and aspirations of the liberal state are in fact made part of living culture, made to be dimensions of the business of living, by (some forms of) religious particularism.

Jewish religion appreciates this, and in that respect its particularism is not a contraction of moral concern, but a manner of being engaged to a moral reality which is progressively articulated by the religious life and traditions of the Jewish people. The covenantal relationship with God *can* be interpreted as a ground of exclusivity, but it can *also* be interpreted as the basis of ethical aspiration that is of the widest scope. The law both commands ethical requirements, and demands an ongoing process of discovery and interpretation. What justice requires, or for that matter, *that* justice is required, has its ultimate ground in the relation between God and human beings, not, for example, in a social contract motivated by rational interest or (culturally neutral, a-historical) principles of practical reason. Moreover, the covenantal relationship is a motivating ground for sustained ethical aspiration. This is so not in the crude sense that punishment is feared: taking the covenant seriously is not a matter of prudential compliance. Rather, it is a ground for sustained ethical aspiration in the sense that the completion of one's nature, the actualization of one's self, is possible only through the determination to know and to be guided by ethical requirements that are not human constructions, though it is human work to interpret them and fulfill them in the human world. Striving for ethical perfection is a responsibility that one acknowledges in the deepest way as part of being a Jew.

Moreover, according to Maimonides, what is ethically required is also (at least in principle) rationally intelligible. The significance of this point is that Jewish particularism is not metaphysically or epistemically isolated. Moreover, in the Maimonidean view, reason's role in interpreting and applying the law is extensive and persistent. The law demands constant reflective and critical attention in order to be specified and articulated with intelligence.

On this understanding of Judaism, justice and righteousness are not originally proposed by reason, though they are fully endorsed by it. They are demanded of us by covenant, and reason is our capacity for fulfilling the covenant in a knowing way. Additionally, faith sustains the commitment to justice in the face of the many ways in which that commitment is tried by the world. And the particularism of tradition and a shared history is a way of belonging to a community (even if scattered) of shared commitment and ethical aspiration. While identification with a group or a tradition can be perverted into bigotry or conceit, there is a different manner for its expression. It can also be a dedication to the significance of maintaining conviction, and a way of reinforcing integrity and courage. This is an important point of moral psychology to which liberal theory pays inadequate attention. Particularism need not motivate or aggravate hostility or suspicion or alienation. It can be a mode of being trained in and valuing respect, when the self-respect it underwrites is not corrupted into arrogance. This is a way in which the particularism of a religious community or tradition can make possible the realization of values which are ethically universal, and a way in which dedication to a religiously particular form of life can contribute to a just and decent social world overall.

This participation in the historical dimension of ethical life can be an important motivational leavening for universal ethical concern. The particularism of a community or tradition can educate its members in excellence through the discipline of covenant and what that entails. Participation in the life of a particular religious community or tradition is a way for individuals to belong to the social world through shared senses of significance, mutual respect, and common pursuit of good. The distinctiveness of a particular community or tradition need not (though it may) alienate it from others by condescension or intolerance, but it may also (in a way which I think fits with Maimonides' thought) be a strategy for becoming an example of human excellence. It is part of Maimonides' understanding of our nature that ethical perfection is needed for the complete actualization and perfection of our nature. In that regard, deliberative excellence and excellence in moral judgment are demanded by Jewish particularism.

It is important to make clear here that I am arguing that certain sorts of religious particularism *can* motivate and sustain a liberal political order. The main focus here is on the way in which the moral psychology of Jewish particularism is of a sort that can reinforce rather than destabilize or conflict with some of the fundamental values of a liberal political order, values such as justice, respect for individual persons, equality of moral status, and the like. I am not arguing that as a matter of historical fact religious particularism has been the main impetus behind the modern aspiration to work out a tenable liberal political order. Still, there are important resources in Jewish particularism that can be, and I believe are, engaged in an important way in support of liberty in modern political life. It is not as though religious particularism is only a beneficiary of liberal politics, without the relation of support also going the other way.

Judaism can support a liberal polity, while at the same time sustaining commitments that it takes to be more important than liberty. Devotion to God through the law plainly is a kind of particularism, but it can be a kind of particularism the essence of which is to pursue *chesed* (loving-kindness), *mishpat* (judgment), and *tzedakah* (righteousness). This form of particularism is not a type of moral territoriality. It can be disfigured into it, but that is not a defect of the nature of the law; that is a human vice. There just is no easy, formulaic answer to questions about the relations of Jewish communities (or any religious groups) to secular political entities and institutions, and to questions about the relation of Jewish law to philosophical and conventional ethics. I am not trying to suggest an easy answer, though I think it is plain that practical reason cannot ascertain the architecture of all of this a priori. This is not a problem that can be solved by a rational formula that is arrived at outside of the interaction of communities and traditions and unmixed with the complex chemistry of social life. These just are some of the questions about the nature of ethical reality that human beings have to exercise themselves with constantly. And they are questions that one typically addresses from the standpoint of commitments and assumptions that are likely to have their provenance in the traditions and teachings of the religious or cultural communities with which one most strongly identifies. These identifications are not optional laminates, added onto a substratum of pure practical reason; they are more fundamentally constitutive than that.

Maimonides says in *Epistle to Yemen* 'It is imperative, my fellow Jews, that you make this great spectacle of the revelation appeal to the imagination of your children. Proclaim at public gatherings its nobility and its momentousness. For it is the pivot of our religion and the proof that demonstrates its veracity.'[11] In their discussion of the *Epistle* Halkin and Hartman write:

The source of hope in the *Epistle to Yemen* is the belief in the eternal normative force of the Torah rather than the memory of the miraculous liberation from Egypt. Maimonides believed that in order to survive the cruel vicissitudes of history, Jews must perennially reenact the dramatic story of Sinai so as to sustain their vital belief in the validity of Mosaic prophecy and in the eternity of God's covenant with Israel.[12]

They also write, 'Sinai creates a nation with a particular character. Apart from its doctrinal significance, this revelation inspires a people to uphold the Torah with courage and tenacity under all circumstances.'[13] One way in which this sort of particularist solidarity and identification is important is that it helps give individuals a rich sense of who they are and what matters, even when conditions of liberty and civic justice do not obtain. It grounds a kind of integrity of individual and group self-conception that the 'thin' notion of the self so often found in liberal theory lacks. There is an ideal to aspire to and there is a project of ethical and intellectual virtue that has a standing independent of the political order. While religious particularism is significantly helped by the tolerance that is a virtue of a liberal polity, the sustainability of a liberal polity depends upon persons having many of the virtues that Judaism requires of them, independent of the political order.

At the same time, we find in Maimonides the insistence that what makes a person a Jew is not something metaphysically particular. Jews are not, as it were, a distinct natural kind.[14] If it is one's deepest commitments concerning God that make one a Jew, and the most fundamental of these involve the resolve to understand the world and to be an excellent person in order to know God, then it is the teleology of ethical and rational perfection that is the animating principle of a Jewish life. That is to be taken quite literally in the sense that excellence is not ultimately a matter of observance and ritual, but a matter of being a living norm; observance and ritual are part of the discipline that sustains and encourages excellence.

The excellence that Maimonides understood this to be was human excellence, and there is a common human moral world united by our all having a rational nature. Of course he was talking about what is specifically required of a Jew and what is an excellent Jewish life. But his understanding of Judaism and human nature was such that Jewish excellence was human excellence, a way of actualizing and perfecting human nature. It is in this sense that the particularism of creed and tradition are not obstructions to, or contractions of ethical universality or ethical objectivity. Human excellence needs a living form, and Maimonides held that obedience to Jewish law was a manner of giving it a living form. The particularism of Judaism encourages humanly universal excellences. That particularism (of certain kinds) can make this sort of contribution to the overall character of civil society is something which is sometimes forgotten or discounted by the theory of the liberal state. To the extent that virtue is acquired and its requirements understood, this occurs in and through a particular form of life.

Judaism, as Maimonides understood it, is a way of eliminating the evils of idolatry; that is, the evils of worshipping and taking guidance from false sources of good and truth. Idolatry can take any number of forms; it can be an idolatry of the state, of the party, of the self, of money, of power, and so forth. The worship of God, the knowing love of God, is the active, effective aspiration to be guided by a true, universal, understanding of good that is loved because it is unconditionally and genuinely good. It is good that is not grounded in one's contingent interests, aims or desires, but is the good such that rational engagement with it enables one to succeed in knowing and actualizing the perfections of one's nature. The uncompromising rejection of idolatry can be expressed as a fundamental intolerance of evil, of ideals and valuations that are ethically disordered or counterfeit. This sort of intolerance is not dogma in a pejorative sense; it is not a prejudice that automatically alienates Jews from others. Rather, it is the expression of the determination not to be distracted from seeking what really is good. In that respect, it is consistent with liberty, where that involves securing the conditions for rationally informed self-realization.

In the *Guide* Maimonides says

> You know from the repeated declaration in the Law that the principal purpose of the whole Law was the removal and utter destruction of idolatry, and all that connected therewith . . .[15]

He also says

> The reason of a commandment, whether positive or
> negative, is clear, and its usefulness evident, if it directly
> tends to remove injustice, or to teach good conduct that
> furthers the well-being of society, or to impart a truth
> which ought to be believed either on its own merit or as
> being indispensable for facilitating the removal of injustice
> or the teaching of good morals.[16]

The prohibition of idolatry and his intellectualism are two
dimensions of the same basic Maimonidean commitment,
namely, that we are to be guided by reason to the fullest extent
that we are able. The prohibition of idolatry makes this possible;
the continuing project of understanding nature and the law so
that we are guided by reason is the activity of actualizing our
nature.

Maimonides' intellectualism can be a target of the same sort
of criticism as Aristotle's, namely, that it is elitist and
undemocratic. However, there is another dimension to it. The
intellectualism is an expression of the view that what is most
distinctive about the business of leading a human life is the
exercise of reason; and the more fully reason is exercised in
determining our convictions and guiding our actions, the more
effective we will be in actualizing what is genuinely good, and
the less we will be misled and distracted by what is only
apparently good. Another type of criticism that it is susceptible
to is that it takes the primary allegiance of the Jew to be not to
principles that could be universally endorsed, but to the
particularity of covenant, tradition, and community. But one of
the main points of the discussion so far is that the impartial
practical reasoner does not come to the social world committed to
universally endorsable principles and then fills in the permitted
interstices of character and aspiration with contingent aims and
interests. Every agent is such that there are certain constitutive
identifications for that person; there are values, aims, and
concerns that are part of the content of character and which are
the agent's points of valuational contact with the world.
According to Maimonides, the key point of contact is the
recognition of the requirement to seek excellence and understanding (and excellence for the sake of understanding). This
sort of view is in many ways alien to much of the modern

understanding of liberty, or at least it is thought to be. Part of that understanding is that there are no common, objective criteria of human good, and each (person or community or tradition) is to fashion its own conception, within bounds set by reason. The Jewish perspective is both more optimistic and more skeptical. It is more optimistic in the sense that it values liberty not only as freedom from tyranny and coercion, but also for its importance in securing freedom from error in the understanding of fundamental values and in the pursuit of perfection. Its aim is to facilitate understanding and excellence. Liberty has a telos in that it is not a merely formal condition for the pursuit of contingent ends. Judaism is more skeptical than secular rationalism in the sense that it does not make an idol of liberty, or of the capacity to fashion ends. It values reason as a capacity that enables human beings to understand and to do good; but reason is able to do this through engagement to a normative reality not of its own making.

The history of Judaism essentially involves the ongoing task of interpreting law and ethical requirements. It is a tradition that encourages argument, criticism, and continuous reflection. It also has involved the ongoing task of interpreting how to live in a social world that is not a Jewish world, and how to be at home in a social world in which the Jew is often not welcome. As a consequence Judaism has been tried in especially persistent and deep ways with regard to understanding its own integrity and the place of Jewish life in the world, and its relations to the non-Jewish world. In this respect Jews are well practiced at learning the value of liberty and at sustaining the integrity of ethical and cultural tradition that can socially and politically underwrite it.

An important Maimonidean idea is that the preservation of tradition is significant for its role in ethical and intellectual discipline, the discipline that enables one to perfect (or at least strive to perfect) one's nature. Observance, ritual, and the preservation of religious practice are means of sustaining a focus on the ultimate end, which is to knowingly love God. The issue of focus is central to Maimonides. Loss of focus is or creates an inclination to one or another sort of idolatry. The complete or perfect good for a human being is not a merely human or natural good. It is in that sense that moral and political good are not the most important things, though they are needed for what is most important. What is most important is not liberty or something secured by it, though the liberty to lead a life that aims at what is most important is of great value.

From the point of view of political theory, religious commitment can be regarded as just one interest or commitment among others. As I suggested above, it may be regarded as fundamentally no different from an interest in sport, or the arts or the sciences. People, after all, have many different conceptions of what makes for a good life and of what is important. On the one hand, there is virtue to this view because it is a basis for toleration. But on the other hand, there are two kinds of danger that this can involve. One is the danger of toleration being *mere* toleration, in the sense that it inevitably has a dimension of condescension: if the beliefs and practices of a group do not threaten others or destabilize the basic institutions of society, well then, it is permissible for them to persist. This is the political analogue to letting the children stay up late, as long as they don't disrupt the more rational order of the grown-ups. The other danger is that the formal notion of toleration will be just that, a sort of regulative idea without the content and criteria to enable it to be deployed effectively in the complex contingencies of the real world. I have been arguing throughout this discussion that in fact a certain type of religious seriousness (but not only that) motivates and sustains commitment to a just and decent civil society. The moral psychology of religious commitment may well be something that a liberal state is helped by.

Moreover, in Maimonides' view, what makes a person a Jew is belief; it is a matter of intellectual assent, not a matter of ancestry or possession of a distinct nature. This feature of his intellectualism offends against certain interpretations of orthodoxy, and it is not the only or the final answer to the question, 'who is a Jew?' But it is an answer that in its way is congenial to an intellectual setting very different from his own. So much modern theorizing rejects a teleological interpretation of human nature, and it relocates the position of religion with respect to ethics and politics. What motivates much of this is the aspiration to put ethics and politics on a rational basis (given a certain interpretation of rationality.) Maimonides' interpretation of religion was that religious belief and practice were modes of perfecting oneself as a rational being and that one's religiosity should express to the fullest extent possible the use of one's reason. On this sort of view, religious life is a life for an intellectual nature, and a condition for the perfection of that nature is the acquisition of the moral perfections. All of this is grounded on and given life-structuring content by the covenant with God. That is not a mere accessory to one's moral and intellectual personality.

Liberal theory would be more plausible if it were true that politics is what people take to be fundamental. But often it isn't. The political is a dimension of life that is unavoidable but, for many people, it is not foundational. It must be addressed in order for life to go on, but what should be the conditions and ideals of life in civil society are not a dispensation of thought that is exclusively political thought. Perhaps a way to put this point is to note that the political is not autonomous; it does not determine the boundaries of moral and social life from a justificatory standpoint outside of them or logically prior to them. Religiously serious individuals or communities may regard political institutions and practices as secondary in importance to the religious commitments and traditions that they take to be constitutive of who they are and what matters most. In a good deal of recent political theorizing there seems to be the assumption that politics comes first, and then in the protected sphere of pursuit of one's conception of good, individuals and groups can work out what matters to them, within the boundaries determined by considerations of political justice or right. On the Maimonidean view of both Judaism and human nature the pursuit of good just is the main business of living and is not an activity located within a social or moral order defined by the requirements of political theory. There is a way to pursue good which is accessible to the Jew regardless of the character of the political order. A state which is tolerant and which aspires to sustain just institutions is obviously preferable to one that is not that way. But again, there is something more important than the institutional conditions of civic life. Maimonides says:

What I have here pointed out to you is the object of all our religious acts. For by [carrying out] all the details of the prescribed practices, and repeating them continually, some few pious men may attain human perfection. They will be filled with respect and reverence towards God; and bearing in mind who is with them, they will perform their duty. God declares in plain words that it is the object of all religious acts to produce in man fear of God and obedience to his word – the state of mind which we have demonstrated in this chapter for those who desire to know the truth, as being our duty to seek.[17]

And '. . . for the chief aim of man should be to make himself, as far as possible, similar to God: that is to say, to make his acts similar to the acts of God, or as our Sages expressed it in explaining the verse, "Ye shall be holy" (Lev. xxi. 2): "He is gracious , so be you also gracious; He is merciful, so be you also merciful."'[18]

Notes

1 Maimonides, *Guide* III. 54: p. 395 (Friedländer)
2 Maimonides, *Guide* III. 54: p. 395 (Friedländer)
3 For example, Rawls writes, 'Liberty in adopting a conception of the good is limited only by principles that are deduced from a doctrine which imposes no prior constraints on these conceptions.' (Rawls 1971, p. 254)
4 Perry 1989, p. 479
5 Contrasting his theory to utilitarianism, Rawls writes, 'In justice as fairness, on the other hand, all agree ahead of time upon the principles by which their claims on one another are to be settled. These principles are then given absolute precedence so that they regulate social institutions without question and each frames his plans in conformity with them. Plans that happen to be out of line must be revised.' (Rawls 1971, p. 565)
6 In characterizing the original position, Rawls writes 'The description of the original position interprets the point of view of noumenal selves, of what it means to be a free and equal rational being. Our nature as such beings is displayed when we act from the principles we would choose when this nature is reflected in the conditions determining the choice. Thus men exhibit their freedom, their independence from the contingencies of nature and society, by acting in ways they would acknowledge in the original position.' (Rawls 1971, pp. 255–256)
7 'Thus, justice as fairness includes an account of certain political virtues – the virtues of fair social cooperation such as the virtues of civility and tolerance, of reasonableness and the sense of fairness' (Rawls 1993, p. 194).
8 Of the principles of justice, Rawls writes 'By acting from these principles persons express their nature as free and equal rational beings subject to the general conditions of human life. For to express one's nature as a being of a particular kind is to act on the principles that would be chosen if this nature were the decisive determining element.' (Rawls 1971, pp. 252–253)

9 Williams 1985, p. 52
10 In examining Kant's attempt to derive the fundamental principle of morality from pure practical reason, Williams raises the question of whether we can coherently conceive of an agent as 'a rational agent *and no more.*' (Williams 1985, p. 63). And he says 'Indeed, that equation is unintelligible, since there is no way of being a rational agent and no more.' (Williams 1985, p. 63). In referring to Williams I do not mean to suggest that I take his critique of the Kantian view to be conclusive; but it is an important and suggestive one.
11 Maimonides, *The Epistle to Yemen*, in Halkin and Hartman 1985, p. 104
12 Halkin and Hartman 1985, p. 162
13 Halkin and Hartman 1985, p. 163
14 See the discussion of the issue by Kellner in his *Maimonides on Judaism and the Jewish People* (1991), esp. the Introduction and chapter 7. He contrasts Maimonides' view of who is a Jew with, for example, the view of Halevi. He describes the latter's as an 'essentialist' view (p. 5). Maimonides' intellectualism enables him to give a special role to Jewish particularism without it being metaphysical particularism.
15 Maimonides, *Guide* III. 29: 317 (Friedländer)
16 Maimonides, *Guide* III. 27: 314 (Friedländer)
17 Maimonides, *Guide* III. 53: 392 (Friedländer)
18 Maimonides, *Guide* I. 54: 78 (Friedländer)

References

Halkin, A. (tr.) and D. Hartman. 1985. *Crisis and Leadership: Epistles of Maimonides*. Philadelphia: The Jewish Publication Society of America
Kellner, M. 1991. *Maimonides on Judaism and the Jewish People*. Albany: SUNY Press
Maimonides. 1956. [1904] *The Guide for the Perplexed*, translated by M. Friedländer. New York: Dover Publications, Inc.
Maimonides. 1985. *The Epistle to Yemen*. Translated by A. Halkin, in A. Halkin (tr.) and D. Hartman. *Crisis and Leadership: Epistles of Maimonides*. Philadelphia: The Jewish Publication Society of America
Perry, M. 1989. 'Neutral Politics'. *Review of Politics* 51, pp. 479–509
Rawls, J. 1971. *A Theory of Justice*. Cambridge, MA: Harvard University Press
Rawls, J. 1993. *Political Liberalism*. New York: Columbia University Press
Williams, B. 1985. *Ethics and the Limits of Philosophy*. Cambridge, MA: Harvard University Press

CHAPTER FOUR

The Communitarianism-Liberalism Debate in Jewish Perspective

Daniel H. Frank

1. The Debate

The publication of Rawls's *A Theory of Justice* in 1971 was a
turning point in contemporary political philosophy. It made
political philosophy fashionable again, at least in Anglo-Amer-
ican philosophical circles. As importantly, its blatantly normative stance, in the face of the then-regnant metatheoretical
trends in value theory, proved to be a harbinger of philosophical
sub-specialties to come. Rawls's scheme for the equitable
distribution of resources set philosophers thinking about the
utility of the program and, perhaps most importantly, its studied
neutrality about the value of the variety of goals being aimed at.

This very values neutrality concerning the desiderated social
good, a scrupulous avoidance to flesh out a notion of the good,
was of course a commitment to a particular notion of it. The good
was construed as quite general in scope, inclusive of a plurality
of values, many of which were in conflict with one another. And
this conflict of values was irreducible, in fact such incommensurability was to be welcomed as a sign of free agency, of
autonomous human beings deciding for themselves what ends
and goals to pursue.[1] Rawls's values neutrality concerning the
good depended upon a prior notion of the right, and the bearer of
rights thus emerged as the foundational source of value. So
important was the self, the autonomous agent of choice, that the
social good and its guarantor, the state, was understood as
having no function save to underwrite such autonomous action
and to step in when things got out of hand.[2] The priority of the
right over the good was paralleled by the priority of the

individual over the state. As what one chooses turns out to be less significant than *that* one chooses, so one's duties to others turn out to be less significant than one's duties to oneself.[3]

Rawls's brand of contractualism came under fire pretty soon after its appearance. Its deontological emphasis on rights was unacceptable to utilitarians, who were concerned with maximizing the aggregate happiness of all. On the other side, its positive role of the state as adjudicator of inequity was unacceptable to libertarians like Nozick, for whom Rawlsian distributive justice ill-consorted with individual rights and natural inequalities.[4] From the perspective of these opponents, Rawls's position looks pleasingly middling, straddling a position between the utilitarian consequentialist and the libertarian individualist. Rawls's position balances rights not so much with correlative duties as with a sense of fairness and decency. This is how I understand the 'difference principle,' with which Rawls attempts to square natural (and social) inequalities and inequities with universal rights. The Rawlsian brand of liberalism empowered us to create our own destiny, while simultaneously constraining us by a sense of egalitarian brotherhood.

This vision of the autonomous self, pre-social in its very being, came under fire from another quarter as well. From a neo-Aristotelian vantage point, Rawls's position seemed perverse. It seemed to presuppose a certain anthropology that was empirically flawed. The notion of the self as prior to its hopes and desires, quite disconnected from any community and historical frame, seemed to the neo-Aristotelian political theorist to be abstract to the point of empty formalism; quite specifically, the liberal notion of the self seemed incapable of accounting for our social nature and sense of belonging to and being a member of a family and a communal unit.[5] The neo-Aristotelian critique of Rawls was reminiscent of Hegel's critique of Kant. Rawlsian justice, which generated a cooperative spirit upon the twin foundations of freedom and equality, gave way to a much more 'organic' view of the relation between the individual and the community of which he was a member. For the neo-Aristotelian, liberal atomism could not begin to account for the 'political' sense. The overarching self-interestedness of the liberal self could not generate anything resembling the constitutive attachments to family and community, attachments the neo-Aristotelians held dear.

The neo-Aristotelian response to Rawls coupled a critique of
the latter's presupposed anthropology, its view of the self as
radically self-determining ('unencumbered'), with a critique of
its values pluralism. Rawls's studied neutrality with respect to
the values and goals promoted by the state was countered by a
neo-Aristotelian commitment to a small and favored set of
cultural norms postulated by any given society. Such a
commitment to cultural norms was offered as a way to defeat
the extreme subjectivism that Rawlsian liberalism was taken to
presume. Whether or not Rawls himself is so Protagorean as his
critics suppose, the debate between them set up a rather stark
contrast between a values neutral subjectivism on the one hand
and a values prescriptivism grounding a moral realism of a
benign sort on the other.[6]

The debate between liberals and neo-Aristotelian communitarians was further exacerbated by a supposed contrast
between a liberal commitment to ahistorical universalism and
a communitarian commitment to historicism. The asociality of
the autonomous self mapped on to a 'thin' view of the good,
which understood it to apply cross-culturally and atemporally.
Such a view of justice and value in general is held by liberals to
be fundamental, for it provides a clear means by which *local*
injustice can be adjudicated and remedied. In this sense, the
liberal seems to join hands with the natural law tradition, save
for the fact that the foundation of the moral and political order is
for the liberal theorist the autonomous self (and universal
reason), not the kosmos or God.[7] For the communitarian
theorist, however, such a 'thin' view of the good is abstract and
formal to the point of vacuousness. In place of such a notion of
the good, the neo-Aristotelian offers a 'thick' description of it,
embedding it and virtues generally in particular social contexts.
Analogous to the identity between the self and its values and
hopes, the communitarian identifies and defines a given social
and cultural unit by reference to the regnant virtues in it. Richly
attentive to context and history, the neo-Aristotelian evaluates
any given society not by reference to some eternal, timeless
standard, but rather in terms of some sort of coherence between
substantive value and actual social conditions.

Such a notion of value, so substantive ('thick') that it literally
defines a community, gives rise to the notion of a tradition, a
social inheritance that shapes communities and transmits

values across generations. For the communitarian, traditions are materialized norms, as it were, and stand in direct contrast to the abstract, formal evaluative framework that defines liberal society. The communitarian is fond of characterizing the liberal as a 'rootless cosmopolitan', signifying thereby the perception that the liberal and liberalism is lacking in commitment and attachment to the communally regnant norms.[8] The liberal is deemed unpatriotic. The liberal response is two-fold. The liberal denies the charge of lack of commitment. Rather, he attaches himself, as noted, to a values pluralism that makes a virtue of the very conflict of norms anathema to the communitarian.[9] Further, in response to the charge of lack of patriotism, the liberal accuses the communitarianism of a certain status-quoism, a conservative attachment to prevailing norms and values. The contest pits the rootless cosmopolitan against the traditionalist.

A very real and interesting problem is at issue in this latter debate. Upon what foundation(s) does meaningful reflection upon and critique of regnant norms reside?[10] The liberal response has generally been to ground reflection on the status quo upon transcendent, at least pre-political norms. As noted, liberalism joins hands in this regard with the natural law tradition in evaluating norms by reference to transhistorical, universal standards. The neo-Aristotelian communitarian can make no appeal to such standards for the simple reason that he denies their very existence. For the communitarian, reflection must be engendered from 'within' the very (normative) tradition it is evaluating.[11] Such 'bootstrapping' can of course only occur in communities, within traditions, that allow for free inquiry and evaluation of current practices, one practice of which is evaluation of current practices. The debate thus ramifies into the necessity of *theory* – whether or not theory must undergird practice. Liberals will affirm this, while communitarians will look hard at the notion of practice itself, reflective practice, for the sought-after foundational point. Communitarians are not ipso facto political conservatives, but I think the burden of proof is on them to account for the possibility of evaluation of existing norms and a grounded rationale for progress. After all, it is they who steadfastly support tradition and existent mores, at least in principle.

We might begin to sum up this excursion into the communitarianism-liberalism debate by noting that the debate is often presented as one between Kant and Aristotle, between the champion of ahistorical *Moralität* and the proud purveyor of *Sittlichkeit*. Never mind the historical accuracy of the characterization, due in large part to Hegel's reading of Kant. More important is that the distinction between the two is taken to be stark and irreducible. The grounds for political obligation are founded either in canons of rationality irreducible to the instrumental rationality of the empirical realm, or in the empirical nature of the human being as such. Either the right is prior to the good, or there are no rights at all. Either the community exists solely to umpire conflicting claims between its members, or the community itself has a life of its own and can play a formative role in the development of its members.

One could probably predict that in adjudicating this dispute a centrist position would begin to emerge, one that attempts to find commmon ground between classical rights-based liberalism and a virtue-based communitarianism. I think that rather recently a centrist position has indeed begun to emerge, which attempts to give good sense to seeming oxymorons like 'liberal virtue', 'liberal community,' and 'reflective practice.'[12] Indeed, liberals are forced to *materially* ground their anthropology, while communitarians are forced to look beyond or, rather, understand tradition and practice in a way that allows for the possibility of critique of the status quo. We shall return to all of this in due course.

2. The Debate in Jewish Perspective

In turning to the communitarianism-liberalism debate from the vantage point of Judaism and Jewish philosophy, let me say at once that I have no interest here in determining whether Jews should side with liberals or communitarians. First of all, I am suspicious of the very dichotomy. As suggested at the conclusion of the last section, the very dichotomy between liberalism and communitarianism is increasingly questioned, so to opt for one or the other is increasingly irrelevant. Secondly, if the question as to which side Jews should be on is in fact a political one, then such a global answer as is demanded is misplaced. Surely time, place, and historical circumstance deserve their fair share in any determination of a political affiliation. No simple answer will do.

Finally, the very issue at hand is grossly parochial, having no manifest sense if applied to Russian Jews, Moroccan Jews, and other bona fide Jewish minorities living in *illiberal* societies. One should always be suspect in speaking of Jews in universal terms. To be sure, the vast majority of Jews live in liberal democratic cultures, cultures that provide the freedom and luxury of political association and choice, but not all do, and these latter count.

Further, I am convinced, although I shall not argue the point here, that the 'tradition' is not decisive on this issue. A recent debate between Melamed and Kimelman makes clear that biblical constitutionalism is not easily decided in favor of monarchy – there is a good sense to be given to a republican tradition in the biblical texts.[13] Analogous to this 'pluralism' is the fact that in counterposition to the (communitarian) notion of individual Jews being in a very deep sense, almost without remainder, members of a collective *klal Yisrael*, there can be found (liberal) passages in which the human good is explicitly construed in transhistorical and supra-national terms.[14] Indeed, the position of the modern Jew, as we shall see, is precisely the tense one of hovering between the community and the modern liberal state.

Given that the tradition is not decisive on the issue before us, my goal in this section of the chapter will be to map the communitarianism-liberalism debate on to the rhetoric and reality of modern Jewish emancipation. The project is a descriptive one more than a normative one, although I suspect that any description will be value-laden to a degree. In any event, I am struck by the revealing parallels between the recent debate between liberals and communitarians and the classical problem of Jewish modernity, the emancipation of the Jew from his traditional past.

The modern period for Jews commences with desegregation and the gradual integration into European society in the 18th and 19th centuries. Prior to this time Jews lived as Jews and were defined as such both within and outside of their communities. Such communities were all-embracing support systems in which its members took sustenance in the variety of communal roles they played. But with the entry of Jews into civil society the problem of identity came to loom large. How was the Jew now to be defined, as a Jew or a German or Frenchman, or both?

What were his obligations to the community and to the state of which he was now a member? And what was the ordering of those obligations in case of conflict? All these questions are quintessentially modern ones, and did not, indeed could not, arise before the modern period of emancipation.

One might imagine that the transition from the pre-modern to the modern period is a transition from a communitarian sensibility, emphasizing the prominent role of the community and its normative function, to a more liberal (modern) outlook in which the (traditional) community was forced to catch up to current trends, which tended to give primacy to the autonomous individual and, as a result, demanded a studied pluralism, even neutrality, with respect to norms and goals. The transition seemed to be from granting primacy to the (communal) good to granting it to (universal) human right. Indeed, the ideology of Jewish reform is predicated on just this modern sense of the self as autonomous, as the bearer of rights and free, unfettered choice.

Jews gained much by virtue of identifying with humanity in general and a civic nationality in particular; indeed, from a certain (political) perspective, they had little to lose in breaking with their own traditional past, a past full of persecution and hatred. And in so breaking with their past, Jews began the process of engaging in modern political life, a life in which previous communal ties were (by design) attenuated. Political enfranchisement, with its demand that a private sphere be delineated and, correlatively, that a public posture of neutrality concerning the contents of the good life be adopted, enabled Jews to live at once as Jews and as citizens of the modern state. Such integration into modern society, with its privatization of religious culture, perforce brought with it a distancing from communal norms. Into this breach emerged Jewish reform, which, as noted, provided an ideology, even a theology, to account and allow for this distancing. And even non-reformed, tradi-tional Jews were forced to take note, rising to defend a (modern) life devoted to *Torah ve-derekh eretz*. Such a defense was indicative of the attractiveness of modern life.

But while Jews rushed headlong into modernity, the liberal state seems never to have dehistoricized itself to the extent that it put aside forever old prejudices and hatreds. The old prejudices hung on. The purported radical division between the public and the private, which held out the hope of overcoming the past by means of an honored commitment to a rich cultural pluralism, turned out to be an ideal unrealized. If you will, Rawls's liberalism, coupling the notion of a universal, pre-social self with that of a state catering to such selves and providing no more than the negative function of umpiring disputes between autonomous agents, never quite caught on. Historical bonds held fast and countered the liberal ideology. Jews suffered. I am not suggesting that Jews have gained nothing from modernity – that would be absurd. But I think that the history and reality of modernity and the Jewish experience of it may goad us into a reconceptualization of liberalism, at least the kind of liberalism that lays claim to being historically unencumbered. If history is to be taken seriously as providing a kind of 'proof' of human nature, a Thucydidean point, then the philosophical anthropology upon which liberalism is based must be reconsidered. This is not ipso facto a critique of Rawls, who in answering his critics is clear that his liberalism is simply political, a values neutrality concerning social and political goals.[15] But it is a critique of whoever believes that history can be sublated in the name of truth. It cannot, and this latter is a wholly *empirical* point.

For the modern Jew, the liberal state with its demand that private goals be bracketed for the sake of national, even universal ones, that religion be removed from the public sphere, and that toleration for minority rights reign supreme, held out hope. But such hope demanded a bifurcation between the private and the public self, with the result that interminable conflicts between the state and the community and, correlatively, between the community and the individual were engendered. What was needed was a way of working out the conflicts, and working them out through history, through the existing socio-political context.

This brings us to Jewish nationalism as a way to overcome the modern schizophrenia. Jewish nationalism, Zionism, was a communitarian response of the 19th century to the dilemma that liberalism posed for the modern Jew.[16] Its ideology, whether in its secular or its religious form, was designed to close the gap between the public and the private realms, between the individual and the community. Responding to both blatant anti-Semitism and the general failure of liberalism to negate history and the prejudices of the past, Jewish nationalism was an overt move to plunge Jews back into history – to take current history as a given and to address its anti-liberal features. The hope was that in a recovery of Jewish nationalism Jews would be able to 'normalize' their plight and to live as Jews, in a manner parallel to other nationalities. A new sense of community was engendered to make amends for the attenuation of the communal sense due to emancipation. There was little hope for the Jewish nationalists that a viable community could be established in the diaspora. The debate was thus joined between liberal and communitarian Jews.

It is not now being suggested that non-Zionists were lacking in a communal sense or that Jewish reform was inattentive to the history enfolding before it, but I think it undeniable that the emancipatory potential of modernity was overrated by the reformers, whose theology presupposed a cosmopolitanism almost messianic in its intension. At a pace equal to that of the later nationalists, Jewish reformers hastened to negate the galut. For them, such negation was to be accomplished by assimilation to regnant practices and cultures – praying in the vernacular, formalizing religious practices, etc. Exile was to be overcome by assimilation. Religion was driven underground, into the private sphere. What the Inquisition could not accomplish was accomplished *willingly* by Jews who rushed to the baptismal font and *spiritually* by Jews who so emancipated themselves from their past that they lived in the present as ghosts.

Unfortunately, it cannot be suggested that Jewish nationalism, in responding to the schizophrenia engendered by modernity, provided an entirely effective response. In plunging back into history it simply aped current nationalisms, romanticizing the ancient past while, unwisely, overlooking the entirety of post-exilic history. In effect, the historicity of Jewish nationalism, *its* negation of the galut, was massively ahistorical. The Zionist response to modernity, that Jews should desist from the misguided attempt to be German or French, was a quite justifiable local response; but its solution, that Jews could only flourish on their own soil, was at once reminiscent of ghetto life, and, more importantly, was grounded in the untenable belief that Jews in fact had achieved nothing in the diaspora. This was, of course, nonsense.

I hope to have shown in a brief way that Jewish reform and Jewish nationalism are each one-sided. Doubtless there are thinkers in both camps who have taken account of the aforementioned problems inherent in the respective positions. There are reformers who have a rich communal sense, and there are Jewish nationalists for whom the galut has meaning and for whom a proud nationalism is not incommensurable with a liberal outlook. In a word, there are those on both sides who have, to my mind, a sound *historical* sense, neither messianic nor romantic, fixated neither upon a future not yet here nor upon a past never to be resuscitated.

3. Some Normative Implications

We noted at the end of the first section of this chapter that a reasonable outcome of the debate between liberals and communitarians is likely to be some sort of compromise position, which, somehow, is able to square the two views. Indeed, such a hybrid view is emerging, a view that tries to make sense of such seemingly oxymoronic notions as 'liberal virtue' and 'reflective practice.'[17] And we have just noted, at the end of the second section, that an analogous compromise may be found in the Jewish arena, between reformers (universalists) and nationalists, in notions like 'liberal nationalism.' In this final section I would like to expand upon this a bit, hopefully providing a modest agenda for further thinking on the political issue before us.

First, it is important to overcome the dichotomy before us, to realize that there *is* common ground between liberals and communitarians and that the 'liberal' whom communitarians attack and, vice-versa, the 'communitarian' whom liberals attack is in large measure a caricature. Real liberals are not rootless cosmopolitans, despite what communitarians may think; and real communitarians are not fascists, despite what liberals may think. In fact, both liberals and communitarians share a passionate commitment to forms of political constitution that are democratic in nature. Both the liberal autonomous self and the communitarian 'situated' self are *political* selves, whether by nature, as the communitarian believes, or by will, as the liberal believes. To be sure, there is a real dispute between them over the grounding for political life and the consequent justification for it, but rather than fight over the foundations, it might be more profitable to reflect upon the democratic *practices* in which they both are engaged.

Whether the focus is upon the protection and enhancement of individual rights and the (merely) protectionist role of the state or upon the common good and an activist role of the state, both liberals and communitarians share a concern in the political enfranchisement and empowerment of the citizenry. Both are opposed to such exclusionary measures as would disenfranchise the less powerful members of the citizenry. Again, the grounding for such inclusionary politics will differ for the liberal and for the communitarian, but the political program is largely shared (or, in principle, can be), a program devoted to the nurturing of a liberal community (no oxymoron), one based upon equality, toleration, and respect. This is a community that has as its goal such liberal virtues (no oxymoron) as toleration and respect. The state need not be neutral with respect to the common good to be a liberal state. Indeed, as we noted at the beginning, such values neutrality with respect to the goals of civic life is itself a commitment to the value of pluralism and, correlatively, to the (liberal) virtue of toleration.[18]

Second, upon realization of the common ground between liberals and communitarians the task of reconciliation can begin. Some, like Larmore, Galston, and Gutmann, have already made a start, and we should continue their work by emphasizing and developing dialogue among disparate groups. Such dialogue is not entertained for the achievement of consensus or homogeneity, but rather for sustaining reflection and critical analysis of current norms, for clarifying a sense of the 'political,' at once attentive to private interests as well as public goals, and finally for developing institutions committed to the liberal virtues. The result would be a true liberal community, one constituted by commitment (loyalty) to reflective practices.

Paralleling such a reconciliation between liberals and communitarians one can envisage common ground between Jewish reformers (universalists) and nationalists. We have noted that both may be faulted for a certain ahistoricity, reformers too optimistically assuming that the modern, Enlightenment project would solve the Jewish problem (it did, but, alas, not as anticipated!), nationalists too pessimistically supposing that only by a negation of the diaspora could Jewish life flourish. A richer sense of Jewish history can allow us to gauge the emancipatory potential of diaspora life and the limits of nationalism. A richer sense of Jewish history can ground reconciliation between reformers and nationalists, between the diaspora and Zion.

What Jewish history teaches is a mixed story, a tale of joy and of sadness, of destruction and of creation. History teaches that Jews can live *anywhere* and flourish, or be destroyed. Given this, what is required for viable Jewish life is a realistic assessment of *local* practice. Jewish life-forms will vary and such pluralism is a weighty counter-argument against any scheme that would impose a uniform pattern. But there is unity to Jewish life, a *klal Yisrael*. Is there anything we can say about the community of Jews worldwide that is not vacuous and takes account of local differences?

Probably less rather than more. If we wish to maintain a strong sense of community and yet be attentive to differences amongst them, I think we can do worse than to look and learn from the liberalism-communitarianism debate. In adjudicating the dispute between liberals and communitarians the notion of a 'liberal community' began to emerge, a community committed to inclusiveness and enfranchisement of its members. Correlatively, we noted the need for liberal virtues such as toleration and respect to suffuse such a community. I think Israeli-diaspora relations could well be advantaged by striving to instantiate such toleration for local practices. I think religious-secular relations within Israel and within diaspora communities could do well by striving for inclusiveness. If liberal individualism militates against group loyalty and communitarian collectivism militates against personal freedom and choice, then the goal should be to strive on local, national, and international levels for what Tamir has characterized with respect to Israel as a 'liberal national-ism.'[19] This sort of nationalism attempts to create a sense of patriotism and group loyalty that will still allow for autonomy and empowerment of disparate groups. To be sure, this balancing act is modelled on the American democratic experiment. Given this, my proposal for the 'Americanization' of Jewish life is imperialistic. Further, for those who think that the Bible alone provides an adequate (eternal) constitution for Jews, my proposal will seem irrelevant. Perhaps the only response is – Yigal Amir.

Notes

1 In addition to *A Theory of Justice*, Rawls has reiterated his commitment to political neutrality in Rawls 1985, 1987; see also Kymlicka 1989
2 This corresponds to the notion of 'negative' freedom, i.e. freedom 'from', outlined in Berlin 1969 [1958], pp. 121–31.
3 Contra Rawls, Raz (1986, p. 162) points out that such a focus on autonomy (and neutrality) is self-defeating.
4 Nozick 1974
5 The founding fathers of this communitarian response to Rawls and to liberalism generally are Michael Sandel, Alasdair MacIntyre, Charles Taylor, and Michael Walzer. For brief statements of their respective positions, see the relevant articles in Sandel 1984 and in Avineri and de-Shalit 1992. For a clear summary of the debate between liberals and communitarians, see Mulhall and Swift 1992.
6 Rawls has vigorously responded to the charges of radical subjectivism and relativism brought against him by his communitarian critics, especially Sandel 1982 (Rawls 1985, 1987).
7 Kant, of course, comes readily to mind here.
8 MacIntyre 1981; Sandel 1982; Taylor 1985, vol. II, pp. 187–210; Mulhall and Swift 1992, pp. 40–126
9 Rawls 1985; Lukes 1989
10 Walzer has explicitly addressed this issue in much of his recent work; see Walzer 1987, 1988, 1994.
11 Ibid.
12 See, for example, Larmore 1987; Gutmann 1985; Galston 1991
13 Kimelman 1995; Melamed 1995
14 For a discussion of the communitarianism-liberalism debate with respect to Judaism, see Mittleman 1993.
15 See note 6 above
16 For classic historical texts on Zionism, see Hertzberg 1959. And for a fairly recent overview of the views of Zionist thinkers from Hess to ben Gurion, see Avineri 1981.
17 See notes 10–12 above
18 Raz 1988; Rawls 1985
19 Tamir 1993

References

Avineri, S. 1981. *The Making of Modern Zionism: The Intellectual Origins of the Jewish State*. New York: Basic Books
—— and A. de-Shalit (eds.). 1992. *Communitarianism and Individualism*. Oxford: Oxford University Press
Berlin, I. 1969 [1958]. 'Two Concepts of Liberty,' in I. Berlin, *Four Essays on Liberty*. Oxford and New York: Oxford University Press, pp. 118–72
Galston, W. 1991. *Liberal Purposes: Goods, Virtues, and Diversity in the Liberal State*. Cambridge: Cambridge University Press

Gutmann, A. 1985. 'Communitarian Critics of Liberalism,' *Philosophy and Public Affairs* 14, pp. 308–22

Hertzberg, A. (ed.). 1959. *The Zionist Idea*. Philadelphia: Jewish Publication Society

Kimelman, R. 1995. 'Abravanel and the Jewish Republican Tradition,' in D. H. Frank (ed.), *Commandment and Community: New Essays in Jewish Legal and Political Philosophy*. Albany: SUNY Press, pp. 195–216

Kymlicka, W. 1989. 'Liberal Individualism and Liberal Neutrality,' *Ethics* 99, pp. 883–905

Larmore, C. 1987. *Patterns of Moral Complexity*. Cambridge: Cambridge University Press

Lukes, S. 1989. 'Making Sense of Moral Conflict,' in N. Rosenblum (ed.), *Liberalism and the Moral Life*. Cambridge, MA: Harvard University Press, pp. 127–42

MacIntyre, A. 1981. *After Virtue*. Notre Dame: University of Notre Dame Press

Melamed, A. 1995. 'The Attitude Toward Democracy in Medieval Jewish Philosophy,' in D. H. Frank (ed.), *Commandment and Community: New Essays in Jewish Legal and Political Philosophy*. Albany: SUNY Press, pp. 173–94

Mittleman, A. 1993. 'From Private Rights to Public Good: The Communitarian Critique of Liberalism in Judaic Perspective.' *Jewish Political Studies Review* 5, pp. 79–93

Mulhall, S. and A. Swift. 1992. *Liberals and Communitarians*. Oxford: Blackwell

Nozick, R. 1974. *Anarchy, State and Utopia*. New York: Basic Books

Rawls, J. 1971. *A Theory of Justice*. Cambridge, MA: Harvard University Press

——. 1985. 'Justice as Fairness: Political not Metaphysical,' *Philosophy and Public Affairs* 14, pp. 223–51

——. 1987. 'The Idea of an Overlapping Consensus,' *Oxford Journal of Legal Studies* 7, pp. 1–25

Raz, J. 1986. *The Morality of Freedom*. Oxford: Clarendon Press

——. 1988. 'Autonomy, Toleration and the Harm Principle,' in Susan Mendus (ed.), *Justifying Toleration*. Cambridge: Cambridge University Press, pp. 155–75

Sandel, M. 1982. *Liberalism and the Limits of Justice*. Cambridge: Cambridge University Press

—— (ed.). 1984. *Liberalism and Its Critics*. New York: New York University Press

Tamir, Y. 1993. *Liberal Nationalism*. Princeton: Princeton University Press

Taylor, C. 1985. 'Atomism,' in C. Taylor, *Philosophy and the Human Sciences: Philosophical Papers*, volume 2. Cambridge: Cambridge University Press, pp. 187–210

Walzer, M. 1987. *Interpretation and Social Criticism*. Cambridge, MA: Harvard University Press

——. 1988. *The Company of Critics: Social Criticism and Political Commitment in the Twentieth Century*. New York: Basic Books

——. 1994. *Thick and Thin: Moral Argument at Home and Abroad*. Notre Dame: University of Notre Dame Press

CHAPTER FIVE

Can Judaism Incorporate Human Rights, Democracy, and Personal Autonomy? [1]

Ze'ev W. Falk

1. Introduction

J ewish theology confronts three ideas which have recently gained universal recognition. Unlike other rights existing by virtue of positive law, human rights (HR), democracy (D), and personal autonomy (PA) are accepted as independent, universal moral rights, informing state as well as international legal discourse. They are used to criticize existing legal arrangements as well as contemporary states, cultures, and societies. Judaism, as a legal system based on traditional culture, is therefore being questioned both by its adherents and by outsiders as to whether it can incorporate these values or not.

HR concern certain freedoms of every human being vis-à-vis society. Such freedoms allow a sphere of self-determination. The concept is related to individualism and liberalism, as well as to the biblical concept of human beings as created *betzelem elohim* (*imago Dei*). D is the rule by and for the benefit of the people through representative government, elected by universal and equal vote. Its main challenges come from an imbalance of economic power, as well as the possibility of oligarchy and dictatorship. PA is an idea prominent in Kantian ethics, making moral self-determination of the individual not only a right but also a duty. The moral behavior of a person should be determined by reason, without interference by other human beings or by non-rational factors.

Traditionally, Jewish faith, law, and culture encompassed its own versions of HR, D, and PA, which obviously could not solve all the questions of modern readers.[2] HR were seen as a divine gift and therefore formulated and limited by certain principles of the faith. D was applicable to Jewish males, without much thought about equality of gender and belief systems. PA was incorporated into the idea of free will, but not extended to recognize a right of opting out of Jewish tradition, law, and identity.

All these problems have now been put at the forefront of Israel's agenda and issue in a problem of Israel as a Jewish and democratic state. Political life in present-day Israel plays out the eternal questions of HR, D, and PA in their relations with each other and with God.

Jewish tradition and law, as incorporated in the legislation of the modern state, is now questioned by the secular majority, agnostics, and atheists, as being in conflict with HR, D, and PA. While Muslims and Christians do not, probably, feel oppressed by the Jewish religious establishment, Jewish feminists, secular humanists, and libertarians, as well as Conservative and Progressive Jews complain against the establishment and the status quo in state-religion relations.[3]

Take, for instance, the rules that Jews in Israel can marry only according to the Orthodox rite and that women do not enjoy equality in the Jewish law of divorce. Or take the official definition of 'who is a Jew?', the Sabbath laws, and other provisions of Orthodox Judaism enforced by civil authorities. All these are claimed to be in violation of HR and PA. Indeed, the Orthodox establishments, supported by the non-observant majority, represent the observant minority without granting the secular majority, or even religiously observant women, any say in their composition and on the rules imposed upon all Jews in Israel.

As a result, it is high time for a discussion of the extent to which the modern concepts of HR, D, and PA can and should be reconciled with the theonomy of Jewish faith and tradition.

2. Anthropo- and Theocentricity

HR, D, and PA are premised upon anthropocentrism, while Jewish faith and law is based on the theocentric system of the Torah. Jewish theology and religious law therefore lack motivation for incorporating these anthropocentric concepts into their system. If responsibility to God is the basis of all considerations, if he is perceived as a personal God, and if human beings are created to serve him – there is little chance that HR, D, and PA will be defended against divine norms and establishments.[4]

However, Jewish theology, despite its theocentricity and theonomy, does not disdain human thought and concern. Jewish morality is not a form of ethical voluntarism; rather it recognizes the need for reason and the existence of certain rules of natural justice. This system rejects, for instance, the equal treatment of unequals, such as the righteous with the evildoer. Indeed, it permits even pleading against God for having disregarded this aspect of justice.[5] Likewise, once God had presented himself as gracious and compassionate, he was considered to be bound by these attributes. A fundamental HR to welfare and subsistence could therefore be inferred. A person supporting the poor was seen as a defender of the divine claim of being merciful, and a proponent of theodicy.[6] Thus, while Jewish thought is theocentric, it introduces human expectations into the theological discourse.

The same pedagogical aspect, though to a lesser degree, makes Jewish thought receptive for ideas of D and PA. The central concept of Jewish faith is the covenant between God and his people,[7] which is the model of the social contract as the basis of all law and political order.[8] The people are no longer mere subjects of the divine ruler, but partners in a system of communication. They have a share in an ongoing dialogue, and their commitment is essential for the God-human relationship. Every individual is called to use reason in this relationship, rather than blindly follow authority.

Let us now consider the meaning and effect of these concepts for Judaism.

3. HR and Theonomy

The idea of purposive divine creation and of human beings as God's servants gives each human being a certain status. An Israelite must not be a slave to another human being, but must be absolutely devoted to the service of God.[9] This means that the rights of life and liberty, and probably a few other HR, are granted by God in connection with the commandments.

Creation and the common genealogy, as described in the Torah, demonstrate the unity of mankind. Every single human being bears responsibility towards God for the observance of the commandments[10] or of the law of nature.[11]

The main object of HR is the protection of individuals or minorities against state power. This protection is already given in part in the Torah, though sometimes only to kinsmen.[12] As shown by the Deuteronomic statute,[13] and by the case of Nabot's vineyard,[14] kings should be under the rule of law and bound by the HR of their citizens. Likewise, Jeremiah's trial demonstrated the freedom of speech even in a war situation.[15]

However, modern HR lawyers have found difficulty tracing HR in Jewish thought. HR presuppose the existence of rights, and not duties only, while Judaism is said to be a system of duties and commandments, rather than of rights and claims. This is especially so regarding the individual's stand in relationship to God and the community.[16]

Since HR are mentioned to criticize the religious tradition, the question arises whether HR can at all be claimed against God. In theory, God is free and no duty can be imposed upon him. This would mean that no HR could be used to support reforms of religious law. We have, however, biblical support for certain HR, even against God himself, an indication of the legitimacy of the HR in theological discourse. Even the book of Job, though describing the epistemological impossibility of human argument with God, implicitly recognizes HR. The assumption is there made that on a metaphysical level God must act according to justice, and respect at least the HR of non-discrimination.

Moreover, HR vis-à-vis other human beings follow certain legal duties which the latter have towards the person claiming the HR. The accidental manslayer, for instance, is given the right of life in the city of asylum both against the redeemer of the blood and society at large.[17] Further, the poor are given a right of support, which is even enforceable at law.[18] Legal action can be taken against a person abusing his rights against others,[19] a clear indication of the existence of a HR to benefit from the property of the owner as long as he incurs no loss by such use. A recalcitrant husband should be forced to deliver a bill of divorce, since his wife cannot be expected to suffer.[20] This is again a HR against both the husband and the rabbinical court.

115

In a system of theonomy, as represented by the Torah, any right of a human being is of divine concern and protected by divine sanction. While in medieval times divine rights were the basis of royal privileges,[21] in the Jewish tradition divine rights are the basis of the rights of the poor, the stranger, the orphan and widow, both against society and against their rich kinsmen. Divine rights therefore are the basis of social and economic HR. Moreover, sovereigns and society are unable to repeal these HR and are responsible for their violation. This makes these HR independent of any positive legislation and of any social interest.

4. Collective Responsibility

On the other hand, the concept of the covenant explains the violations of the HR of secularists by religious fundamentalists. According to biblical and rabbinical belief, Jews are responsible for one another and one may suffer vicariously for the sins of another. Any breach of the covenant falls back upon the community and is therefore of general concern.

A public desecration of God and an act of blasphemy call for protest and punishment.[22] Likewise, any act of sexual immorality committed in public is a violation of the covenant and a danger to the whole of Israel.[23] This has been interpreted to cover also immodest dress in religious neighborhoods or indecent advertisements. Even observance of the Sabbath, a central duty of all Jews, is held by fundamentalists to be a matter of public concern and not of private belief only. A secularist's claim that his or her non-observance of the Sabbath is protected by HR is therefore rejected by most religious Jews.

The same attitude prevents recognition by the chief rabbinate and by the state of Israel of non-Orthodox versions of Judaism, such as messianic Judaism, or even Karaite, Progressive, or Conservative Judaism. Likewise, recognition has been given in Israel only to the traditional Christian communities and to Sunni Islam, but not to other Christian and Muslim sects. This is seen by such minority groups as a violation of their HR and religious freedom.

A similar conflict between the HR of individuals and the spokesmen of the majority religions is the jurisdiction of ecclesiastical authorities and the application of religious law in matters of marriage and divorce. The obvious reason for this is the preservation of traditional communities and cultures, especially the wish to limit interreligious or secular marriages.

Religious Jews think that Judaism and the state of Israel should not tolerate the secularization of marriage and family. They consider marriage out of the faith as a betrayal of past and future, a grave concern for the people in general. On the other hand, secular Jews feel that private life ought to be of no concern to others, but should be left to their own discretion.

5. Limits of Democracy

The Greek concept of *demokratia*, rule of the people, is not easily reconciled with biblical *aristokratia*, the rule of the best, whether of divine kingship, of a spiritual hierarchy, or of prophetic leadership. 'As I live, says the Lord, surely with a mighty hand and an outstretched arm and with wrath poured out I will be king over you'.[24] This is a clear challenge both to the people of Israel and to the notion of popular sovereignty, as well as being a claim for the unconditional loyalty of every individual Jew to God.

This system is not at odds with contemporary notions of sovereignty. Popular sovereignty is currently challenged by concepts of international law, like HR, and by ethical principles, like PA. The will of the people has become limited by certain ideas as to what can or cannot be done.

Western democracy, moreover, imposes limitations upon the power of the state to create and protect a minimum sphere of PA for every individual. HR thereby serve as checks and balances of an otherwise absolute power. The democratic ethos of universal participation in the formulation of governmental policy demands implementation of HR, such as rights to information, free speech, and freedom of association.

These principles of Western thought are based on moral ideas, rather than on formulations of positive law. Just as the biblical prophets opposed the heads of state in the name of the divine ruler, so present-day political philosophers draw inspiration from the moral realm.

The meaning of Israel's history and existence, as well as the needs for ensuring its future, seem to impose certain limitations upon contemporary options. The Ten Commandments and biblical theonomy in general, Israel's raison d'etre, should be above any democratic argument and majority rule. Indeed, the tension between democracy and religious morality appears in the very notion, enacted in recent law, of the state of Israel as a Jewish and democratic state. It is an example of legal pluralism within the political structure of the state. Judaism and democracy function as a kind of checks and balances, restraining the absolutism of contemporary democracy by a spiritual tradition, and vice-versa.

Western thought imposed liberal principles such as HR and PA upon states and societies, thereby restraining majority rule and limiting democracy. It used techniques such as a second chamber of parliament, judicial control of the executive, and the rule of the constitution to check and balance the unfettered power of the people. Could not the principles of Israel's spiritual heritage act likewise as checks and balances to popular whims and follies?

6. Jewish Democracy

Judaism has its own concepts of HR, D, and PA. The covenant between God and the people, as well as the covenant between the king and the people, was based on the notion of consent. Though modeled after Hittite agreements between a sovereign and his vassals, the biblical idea of a divine covenant with mankind, with one people, or even with one person is unique. It rejects any kind of ethical voluntarism and grants human beings the status of partners. This, in turn, becomes a model by way of *imitatio Dei* for democratic rather than autocratic government.

The state power of ancient Israel was checked by prophets, priests, and scribes, and Israelite kings sought legitimization by acclamation.[25] The synagogue was and is a congregational institution. Spiritual leaders need the participation of a *minyan* (quorum of ten laymen), i.e. the consent of their flock, for the recital of sacred formulae. On the other hand, a majority resolution can be challenged in a rabbinical court for being oppressive to the minority or even to an individual.[26]

Personal worship takes the form of democratic participation, rather than of servile self-abnegation. Every individual should

118

participate in the establishment of the messianic era by daily prayer. The recital of the *shema*[27] means submission to divine rule and gives the person reciting the prayer a constitutive function. The presence of the individual in the *minyan* reciting sacred formulae makes clear how precious each individual is and gives him or her a say in communal affairs.

Hence, the Jewish community runs its affairs more or less in a democratic way, though the ethos of present-day democracy makes further democratization necessary.[28] Worship in the synagogue is congregational not hierarchical. Even more significant is the classical perception of Torah as a means for the physical and moral well-being of the people, rather than for the service of God. Despite their theocentrism and their reverence for the Torah, the Rabbis understood that it was created to serve Israel, not vice-versa.[29] Its object is educational, to promote spiritual values. The Rabbis rejected the utilitarianism and eudaemonism of the Epicureans[30] and submitted to the divine will, even if it was in conflict with their physical well-being.[31]

While the Rabbis considered a person's life and integrity to be non-negotiable,[32] they taught that one should give up one's life rather than commit one of the three cardinal offences: killing, sexual immorality, or idolatry.[33] The interests of the community did not permit, according to rabbinic teaching, the extradition of an individual to the Gentiles,[34] but each Jew was asked to set the commandments and the duties following from the covenant above his personal will and his HR.

Jewish democracy is therefore balanced both by a spiritual aristocracy and by the commitment of the people as well as every individual towards God.

7. Equality and Chosenness

The concepts of HR, D, and PA are connected with Kant's demand that every human being should be seen as an end in him- or herself and should never be treated only as a means to an end. In analogous fashion, Martin Buber called this relationship the *I-Thou*, as distinct from the *I-It* relationship.

The creation of mankind *imago Dei*, as well as the story of Adam and Eve, support the concepts of HR and equality.[35] The latter concept is also subsumed under the rule of justice and the equality of all before God. On the other hand, biblical historiosophy is sacral and aristocratic. It describes vocation and failure, chance and loss, universality and chosenness. Original equality of all creatures, times, and spaces gives way to a system of the chosen few, of vicarious fulfillment, of distinction between sacral and secular spheres, and the particular Torah of Israel.

The same process continues *within* the chosen people. Originally, the whole nation was called to be a 'kingdom of priests and a sacred nation,' but then the descendants of Aaron were chosen for priesthood, and after the destruction of the Second Temple the Rabbis assumed spiritual leadership. Likewise, the prophets spoke of the remnant of Israel which is to realize the original covenant in a new form.[36]

Accordingly, Jewish law distinguishes between Jews and Gentiles, between men and women, as well as between a number of other groups entitled to a rule of precedence.[37]

The question thus becomes whether this hierarchization can eventually be reconciled with the notion of human equality. While the positivist and fundamentalist interpretation of Jewish Orthodoxy replies in the negative, the attempt will now be made to show that principles of Jewish law allow the incorporation of HR and D.[38]

8. Equality of Foreigners

Originally, Jewish law recognized two categories of foreigners, namely, slaves and Gentiles. The former were either prisoners of war[39] or inhabitants of the occupied territories who had surrendered to the Israelite army.[40] The latter were either liberated slaves, laborers, tradesmen, or recent immigrants.

Although the Torah, like other ancient cultures, tolerated slavery, it abolished a small part of it, by providing for a weekly day of rest.[41] Slaves and foreign laborers were also invited, together with Israelite orphans, widows, and the poor, to participate in the meals at Jewish holidays and pilgrimages.[42]

Killing of a slave was as punishable as that of a free person, and freedom was granted to a maltreated or fugitive slave.[43] A Jew was not allowed to sell his slave to a Gentile, and if he did, the slave was thereby liberated.[44] Rules of piety and prudence were invoked to ameliorate the fate of slaves,[45] but there was no voice demanding the abolition of slavery or calling for the liberation of slaves. The nearest was a medieval opinion permitting the liberation of slaves owned by Jews by virtue of the power of expropriation vested in Jewish courts of law.[46]

Meanwhile, international law and consensus has declared slavery to be illegal and immoral, and Judaism has incorporated this view. Thus, the curse of slavery and its biblical justification[47] has finally been resolved.

A similar situation exists regarding the status of non-Jews in Jewish law. Duties and rights under Jewish law were addressed to Jews only, to those born of a Jewish mother or to converts to Judaism. Thus, the duties of solidarity and the ensuing rights of support applied only to them. The rules of *Avodah Zarah* about the various rules of non-fraternization with Gentiles reflected the Jewish reaction against the Roman oppression and the mutual hatred during the second century C.E.[48]

However, a *ger toshav* (resident alien) living in a Jewish neighborhood could appear before a Jewish court of law to make a commitment that he would observe the laws of Adam and Noah,[49] whereupon he enjoyed almost all the rights of Jewish law. Unfortunately, post medieval authorities denied the regular courts jurisdiction in this matter, so that resident aliens could no longer acquire equal status in Jewish law. Muslims, however, were granted automatic status in Jewish law.[50]

Jewish law developed also through the sense of responsibility for the reputation of God in the eyes of mankind. All people of Israel were always to behave in a way that promoted divine adoration, and to refrain from any act or omission that would desecrate God. Any rule of Jewish law that would cause such a desecration would have to give way to this rule of a higher order, viz. to the supreme duty of sanctifying the Name. R. Gamliel (c. 100 C.E.) is reported to have abolished a norm discriminating Gentiles in Jewish law, using the just-mentioned reason to do so.[51]

In this regard one also finds as basic values of Jewish law *mishum 'evah* (to prevent hatred, contentiousness) and *mishum darkhey shalom* (to promote peace).[52] 'God is good to all, and his compassion extends to all his creatures' should guide every person by way of *imitatio Dei*.[53] Charity should therefore be extended to Gentiles as to Jews.[54] Rabbinic commandments should not be observed, if Gentile neighbors are offended.[55]

Today the state of Israel has a religious obligation under Jewish law to respect the HR and equality of its minorities. Any international obligation must be observed to prevent desecration of God,[56] and to preserve the good standing of the Jewish people in the world.[57]

9. Equality of Women

Of even greater moment is the legal differentiation on the basis of gender in Jewish and in Israeli law. Although Jewish law addresses women as well as men, which reflects an egalitarian attitude,[58] it makes many exceptions to the rule and often discriminates on the basis of gender.

Women are exempt from the most important of the commandments, viz. the study of Torah, the wearing of phylacteries, and mandatory acts linked to a special time.[59] Although women have become accustomed to perform most of these commandments and to study Torah, Orthodoxy still excludes them from rabbinical and judicial office and from any public function. This prevents women from having a voice in eventual legal reform promoting HR.

Originally, Jewish marriage was polygynous and it has always been strictly monoandrous. Both marriage and divorce have to be performed by the man in the presence of two male witnesses.[60] This has always given the husband an undue advantage in marital disputes and divorce proceedings, and often results in the extortion of the wife suing for a divorce. While the husband of an insane, absentee, and recalcitrant wife is granted permission to remarry, Orthodox Judaism has no solution for the wife in the same situation.[61]

As a result of the patriarchal system, the law of husband and wife, of parental rights and duties, and of evidence[62] differentiate rights of men and women, sometimes to the detriment of the latter.

The question is how to incorporate the principle of non-discrimination and of equality into Jewish family law, without endangering its traditional and spiritual foundations. Indeed, certain forms of inequality in the procedure of sacrifices were amended either during the first century B.C.E. or the first century C.E. to 'satisfy womankind.'[63] Likewise, a husband was expected to give his wife her due, for 'she was created to enjoy her life and not to suffer.'[64]

Women today cannot be expected to consent to a double standard of rights. Both the religious and the civil authorities must make up for this deficiency in positive law by applying the concept of HR in the field of family law and in the administration of the Jewish religious establishment.

10. PA and Theonomy

Modern legal systems follow Kant's ethical theory by ascribing to human beings the capacity of self-government as a necessary condition for moral responsibility. Instead of relying on external authority, whether human or divine, human beings (persons) are called to think for themselves. Contrarily, heteronomy is deemed unworthy of human beings, indeed violating their status as moral agents.

Biblical and Jewish theonomy, on the other hand, is based on the idea of the human being being in the service of God. This cannot easily be reconciled with the Kantian point. The former is an authoritarian and paternalistic system recognizing free will, but not the right of moral self-determination.

The claim for PA before God echoes the serpent's suggestion that Adam and Eve could be 'like God knowing good and evil', if they disobeyed the divine commandment.[65] Although this insight had been put in the mouth of the seducer, humankind had been destined to achieve PA in a legitimate way, perhaps with less suffering attached to it. Jewish rationalism, too, calls upon human beings to follow the guidance of their intellect for the interpretation of Torah.

This, however, does not mean licentiousness and rejecting the divine kingdom or the divine commandments. Rather, it demands rational living under Torah and knowing one's limits and responsibility to God. It does not include full moral self-determination, moral subjectivity, and individualism, which today are often identified with autonomy. Neither does it allow arbitrary choice of values or assertion of one's ego, nor does it support the denial of God, as suggested by Feuerbach, Marx, and Nietzsche.[66]

Although Jewish theonomy does not recognize Kantian moral philosophy, it nevertheless recognizes several forms of PA. The first is the idea of observing the commandment *lishmah* (for its own sake), out of a purely deontological motivation. According to Antigonos of Sokho (c. 200 B.C.E.), we should not be like servants for reward, but like servants without any expectation, motivated solely by the awe of God.[67] This is a rather remarkable demonstration of PA by a Jewish teacher vis-à-vis the biblical authority and its emphasis on reward and punishment. A further example of this attitude is the story of R. Dov Baer Friedman, the maggid of Miedzyrzecz (18th cent.), who once complained about his fate, whereupon a voice from heaven announced the loss of his share in the future world. He then rejoiced for now being able to serve God without expectation of reward, whereupon a second voice announced the return of his future share.

Another form of Jewish PA is hermeneutical, interpretative freedom in reading Torah. Jewish rationalists, from Philo (1st cent. C.E.), through Saadia ben Joseph (10th cent.), to Hermann Cohen (20th cent.), rely on their own PA to justify their respective interpretative stands. The text is always interpreted by reference to reason, and sometimes it is consciously misinterpreted beyond the better understanding of the speaker. This was called 'silencing Scripture to prove your own point.'[68]

Jewish PA, finally, expresses itself in the selective application of *imitatio Dei*.[69] Obviously, there are some divine attributes which human beings should not imitate, e.g. vindictiveness,[70] and the distinction between the two categories follows from the use of human reason.[71]

11. Conclusion

Judaism can incorporate the concept of HR and of PA by a reformulation of covenant theology. At present the covenant is perceived as an obligation imposed willy-nilly on all ethnic Jews (by matrilineal descent or by conversion). This is de facto an invitation to the pious to act as vigilantes.

If, however, greater value would be given to the idea of 'the remnant of Israel,'[72] Judaism could accept the HR and PA of non-believers and reject religious bigotry. A voluntarist interpretation of the covenant, based on the need for a daily submission to 'the kingdom' and 'the yoke of the Commandments', would respect the individual rights of dissenters, promote tolerance, and, eventually, have greater appeal to secular Jews.

Meanwhile, certain HR have been given constitutional status in the state of Israel. This will eventually affect the interpretation of Jewish law sources by the civil courts and thereby influence also the jurisdiction of the rabbinical courts. Any norm of Jewish law should be tested by the concept of HR and be amended or repealed, if it conflicts with this concept. For instance, traditional norms permitting vigilantes and the non-recognition of Gentile interests in the Holy Land must be checked by the HR of all parties. Even if public security may impose certain limitations on HR, the life and personal integrity of all must be respected, even against long-standing law and tradition.

Jewish religious life and institutions will have to undergo a process of democratization, if the secular majority is to be attracted. Until quite recently Judaism has been quite congregational and democratic; however, mass immigration and secularization have caused a large bureaucratization of Jewish religious service and of the rabbinate. There is little chance to bring the religious message to the people without giving them a say and thereby introducing democratic procedures into Jewish law. Every rabbinic decision needs prior legitimization by the people in whose name it is made. Rabbinical authorities will have to be elected by the people or at least by representative bodies.

Some form of PA, finally, will have to be integrated into Jewish law and religious tradition. In a society cherishing individual rights and liberty, religion must respect the private sphere. Historically, this recognition of PA in matters of religion was first expressed by Moses Mendelssohn[73] in his calling for religious persuasion and education and leaving the use of compulsory norms to the state, and by Rosenzweig in his distinction between the universality of Jewish law and the PA of the individual with respect to its practicability.[74]

Notes

1 The author thanks Marie Failinger for her helpful comments and Lenn and Madeleine Goodman, may her memory be blessed, for their hospitality in Nashville.

2 There is a certain analogy between the rights conferred by the United
States Constitution vis-à-vis universal HR and the rights conferred by the
Torah upon Israelites or human beings in general vis-à-vis universal HR.
3 *Siach Mesharim*, 25
4 Falk 1981, pp. 75–89
5 Falk 1991, *passim*
6 Lev. Rabba 34:16
7 Falk 1991, pp. 65f.
8 Rawls 1971
9 Lev. 25:42, 55
10 Gen. 3; 9:1–7
11 Gen. 6:11–12; 13:13; 18:20; 20:11; 34:7; Am. 1:3–2:3
12 Falk 1981, p. 45; Jacobs 1992
13 Deut. 17:14–20
14 1 Kings 21
15 Jer. 26:7–24
16 Cohn 1984, p. 18
17 Num. 35:15; Deut. 4:42; Cohn 1984, p. 18
18 JT Pe'ah 1:1, 15c; BT Bava Batra 8b
19 BT Bava Batra 12b
20 BT Bava Batra 48a; Falk 1973, *passim*
21 Ullmann 1965
22 Lev. 24:10–23
23 Num. 25:1–18
24 Ez. 20:33
25 Falk 1964, p. 45
26 Falk 1981, pp. 43f., 58f.
27 Deut. 6:4–9
28 Hatch 1989
29 Eccl. Rabba 1; 9, ad Eccl. 1:4
30 Mishnah Avot 2:14
31 The model is Abraham's awe of God expressed in the (irrational) binding of
Isaac. The Rabbis interpreted the term *choq* (statute) as a disciplinary
norm, to be followed without rational justification (BT Yoma 67b; Num.
Rabba 19:3–4; Midrash Ps. 9).
32 Mishnah Bava Qamma 8:7
33 BT Sanhedrin 74a
34 Daube 1965
35 Mishnah Sanhedrin 4:5
36 Is. 6:11–13; 10:21; cf. Glatzer 1987, pp. 779–783
37 Mishnah Horayot 3:7–8
38 Falk 1981, p. 90
39 Num. 31:26. During the war of conquest against the Canaanites no captive
should have been taken and all bearers of arms were to be killed (Deut.
20:12–18). This was, in my opinion, a lapse from the humane standard of
the rest of the Torah. This cruel provision applied only to the most ancient
aboriginals and not to their descendants in post-exilic times (Maimonides,
Mishneh Torah, Melakhim 5:4).
40 Deut. 20:10–11

41 Ex. 20:10; Deut. 5:14–15
42 Deut. 16:11, 14
43 Ex. 21:26; Deut. 22:15
44 BT Gittin 44a; Maimonides, *Mishneh Torah*, Avadim 8:5
45 Maimonides, *Mishneh Torah*, Avadim 9:8; *Guide of the Perplexed* 3:39
46 R. Samuel ben Meir, quoted in *Tosafot* Gittin 40b, s.v. *ukhetiv*
47 Gen. 9:25
48 Mishnah Avodah Zarah 1:8; Sanhedrin 8:7; Bava Qamma 4:3; Sifre Deut. 344
49 Laws consisting of the rules of justice, idolatry, blasphemy, incest, adultery, homicide, larceny, and consumption of living creatures (or blood): Tosefta Avodah Zarah 8:4; BT Avodah Zarah 64b; JT Yevamot 8:1, 8d.
50 R. Joel Sirkis (c. 1600), *Bayit Chadash*, Tur Choshen Mishpat 249, against the earlier view of R. Joseph Karo, *loc. cit.*
51 JT Bava Qamma 4:3, 4b
52 Prov. 3:17; Mishnah Gittin 5:8–9
53 Ps. 145:9
54 Mishnah Gittin 5:8–9; Maimonides, *Mishneh Torah*, Melakhim 10:12
55 BT Taanit 27b (cf. Rabinowitz ad loc; Malter 1978, p. 424); Tosafot Avodah Zarah 26a, s.v. *savar*; R. Yomtov of Sevilla, Commentary ad Avodah Zarah 8a; Yad Sha'ul, Yoreh De'ah 152
56 The extreme demand made of King David is a case in point: Jos. 8:18; BT Gittin 46a; Yevamot 78b; JT Qiddushin 4:1, 65c; Num. Rabba 8:4, 14d
57 1 Kings 20:31; Is. 42:6
58 BT Qiddushin 35a
59 BT Qiddushin 29b, 34b
60 BT Qiddushin 5b
61 Friedman 1980 and Falk 1973
62 However, see Safrai 1983, pp. 91–106
63 BT Chagiga 16b
64 BT Ketubbot 61a
65 Gen. 3:5; cf. Fromm 1966 and Falk 1991, p.13
66 For Christian parallel tendencies, see Macken 1990.
67 Mishnah Avot 1:3
68 Sifra, Tazri a13:2, s.v. *wehabeged*
69 Gen. 18:19; Deut. 8:6; 10:12; 11:22; 19:9; 28:9; 30:16
70 Deut. 32:35, 41; Ps. 94:1; 99:8
71 Lev. 19:18
72 Jer. 23:3
73 Mendelssohn 1783
74 Rosenzweig 1924

References

Cohn, H. 1984. *Human Rights in Jewish Law*. New York: Ktav
Daube, D. 1965. *Collaboration with Tyranny in Rabbinic Law*. Oxford: Oxford University Press

Falk, Z.W. 1964. *Hebrew Law in Biblical Times*. Jerusalem: Wahrman
———. 1973. *Tevi'at Gerushin mitsad ha'Ishah*. Jerusalem: Hebrew University Institute of Legal Studies
———. 1981. *Law and Religion: The Jewish Experience*. Jerusalem: Mesharim
———. 1991. *Religious Law and Ethics: Studies in Biblical and Rabbinical Theonomy*. Jerusalem: Mesharim
Friedman, M.A. 1980. *Jewish Marriage in Palestine*. Tel Aviv: Tel Aviv University Press
Fromm, E. 1966. *You shall be as Gods*. New York: Holt, Rinehart and Winston
Glatzer, N.N. 1987. 'Remnant of Israel', in A.A. Cohen & P. Mendes-Flohr (eds.), *Contemporary Jewish Religious Thought*. New York: Scribners
Hatch, N.O. 1989. *The Democratization of American Christianity*. New Haven: Yale University Press
Jacobs, L. 1992. *Religion and the Individual: A Jewish Perspective*. Cambridge: Cambridge University Press
Macken, J. 1990. *The Autonomy Theme in the Church Dogmatics: Karl Barth and his Critics*. Cambridge: Cambridge University Press
Maimonides. *Guide of the Perplexed*
———. *Mishneh Torah*
Malter, H. 1978. *The Treatise Ta'anith*. Philadelphia: Jewish Publication Society
Mendelssohn, M. 1783. *Jerusalem oder über religiöse Macht und Judentum*. In *Gesammelte Schriften*, Jubiläumsausgabe, volume 7.
Rabinowitz, R.N. *Diqduqey Soferim*
Rawls, J. 1971. *A Theory of Justice*. Cambridge, MA: Harvard University Press
Rosenzweig, F. 1924. *The Builders (Die Bauleute)*, in *Der Jude* 8
Safrai, S. 1983. 'Pesuley 'edut,' in *Milet*. Tel Aviv: Open University
Siach Mesharim, volumes 1–25 (1986–1995). Jerusalem
Ullmann, W. 1965. *A History of Political Thought*. Harmondsworth: Penguin Books

CHAPTER SIX

Democracy and Judaism

The Current Debate

Daniel Statman

In the early 1990s, a stormy debate on the relation between democracy and Judaism erupted on the Israeli scene. It took no time before the tension between these two notions was felt everywhere. Catch expressions like 'the problem of democracy and Judaism' became code words for a whole cluster of problems concerning, *inter alia*, the Jewish character of the state of Israel, the peace process, the moral status of Zionism, and the limits of liberalism. To inquire into the relationship between democracy and Judaism sounds an embarkation on a theoretical research project, but, as I hope to demonstrate, in the current debate the issues are primarily political and ideological. The debate did not start with a publication by a political philosopher proving that the above tension exists, nor have professional philosophers played a dominant role in clarifying the terms of the debate by arguing systematically for one side or the other. Most of the written material on the debate is to be found in daily newspapers, not in academic journals, and the emotions evoked by this material are very heated indeed.

More particularly, within a very short period, not only was the problematic nature of the relation between democracy and Judaism generally accepted, but so was the notion that the two terms are incompatible, that a necessary conflict between these two notions exists. I shall refer to this view as 'The Conflict Thesis' (CT). It is supported by two opposing groups in Israeli society for different reasons: Secular liberals[1] support it because they want to minimize the role of religion in the public (legal and political) sphere, while religious[2] people support it because they wish to emphasize the absolute authority of the Torah. This common interest in CT has no doubt contributed to its wide acceptance.

A political theorist looking at this development from the outside would surely find CT quite odd. To be sure, the exact role of religion within liberal democracies is a matter of an ongoing debate in the United States and in other countries. But very rarely would we find any serious thinker in the liberal tradition saying that Christianity, for instance, and democracy necessarily conflict. In fact, for a while the opposite view was held by Christian believers, who assumed an essential connection between religion and democracy. I refer to the view on the 'religion of democracy' which was developed in early twentieth-century America and which finds expression in the quotations used by Jan Dawson in an article analyzing this view:

> 'Democracy is not merely a political theory, it is not merely a social opinion; it is a profound religious faith'; 'Democracy is at one with religion in its conception of what the full-grown and civilized man ought to be'; 'Religion is essential to democracy, and is, indeed, its foundation. It is based on the New Testament principle of the equal value of every soul in the sight of the Divine Father.'[3]

I doubt whether many Christians in the United States would accept such a sacred view of democracy today, but they would no doubt reject the opposing suggestion that there is a necessary conflict between religion and democracy. The above quotations also serve to remind us of the obvious historical fact that the idea of democracy was not developed by thinkers who were necessarily atheists or anti-religion, and the first democracies in modern times were definitely not secular in the strong sense that liberal friends of CT have in mind. In contrast to a popular view, disestablishment in American history did not mean separating the state from religion, driving religion, so to say, out of democracy. All through the 19th century and the beginning of the 20th century, state laws defend and reinforce Christian values by legislation against blasphemy, laws enjoining Sabbath closing, and other regulations.[4]

I mention these facts at the outset just to give the reader a feeling of how farfetched and exaggerated CT is from the point of view of political theory. That it is nevertheless held and argued shows that CT is not so much a conceptual or a theoretical thesis about the relation between democracy and Judaism as it is a normative position vis-à-vis fundamental questions in Israeli ideology and politics. The purpose of this chapter is to present this position and expose the real concerns of those arguing that there is a conflict between democracy and Judaism.

In the first section, I show that CT, understood as a thesis about the relation between (Jewish) religion and democracy, is unpersuasive. I then turn in section 2 to explore the concerns that really lie behind CT, concerns about the idea of Israel as a nation-state for all the Jewish people.

1. Halakha and Democracy

Supporters of CT tend to give the impression that the terms 'democracy' and 'Judaism' are clearly defined, in a way that makes it possible to speak about a conflict between them. This, however, is a misleading impression: There are different and conflicting understandings of democracy,[5] as well as different and conflicting understandings of Judaism. A fruitful discussion about CT can get off the ground only after having clarified the concepts of democracy and of Judaism one has in mind and only if the definitions chosen are such that they do not beg too many questions in advance.

An *un*successful starting point would be a definition of democracy which builds into it all of the rights recognized by some democracy, say the United States, at the end of the twentieth century, such as the right to have an abortion in the first few months of pregnancy, the right to publish pornographic material, or the equal right of women to be elected to any government job. The problem with regarding such rights as part of the *definition* of democracy is that it entails the denial of the title 'democracy' from many countries which no doubt deserve it, thereby preventing us from making crucial distinctions between different regimes. If equal rights for women and for minorities is a necessary condition for claiming to be a democracy then neither the United States nor Britain, France, or any other country in the world was democratic in the first decades of the twentieth century. But there are strong reasons to think that these countries did share some essential characteristics at that period, characteristics that made it possible to differentiate between them and countries like the Soviet Union, China, or Syria. Thus, when people object to some policy by saying that it is 'against the idea of democracy,' often they do not mean to say that if this policy is accepted the country will cease to be a democracy in the literal sense, but rather that it would be a bad democracy. The objection in such cases is a moral-political one, not a conceptual one.

Just as we should not build too much into the notion of democracy, we should not build too little into it either. In particular, we cannot be satisfied with a narrow definition of democracy as merely majority rule, which leaves everything open with regard to the other procedures, rights, and laws of the country. I suggest we start with a 'populist democracy' view, according to which the essence of democracy is 'the idea of people ruling themselves as free and equal beings rather than ruled by an external power or by a self-selected minority among themselves.'[6] The populist view recognizes substantive constraints to majority rule, such as free speech, free and open elections, but still leaves many rights and liberties outside the *definition* of democracy. A similar suggestion is made by Ruth Gavison, one of Israel's leading legal philosophers, in the context of discussion on the possibility of a state which is both Jewish and democratic.[7] According to Gavison, we should adopt a characterization of democracy that leaves most questions open to a normative-political discussion and argument, instead of stating that countries which do not include all of what we regard as desirable features of democracy are not democracies.[8]

Let me now turn to say something about the second term in the debate, 'Judaism.' While with 'democracy' I argued that only a wide definition can provide the means for an interesting discussion of CT, with 'Judaism' the opposite holds true: Only a relatively narrow understanding of this notion can serve to make sense of the thesis at hand. If 'Judaism' is understood to mean everything that Jews have thought or created, or if it is understood as no different than liberal morality, then CT simply cannot get off the ground. It is quite clear that 'Judaism' in CT refers specifically to *orthodox* Judaism, which differs from other Jewish trends by its strong commitment to Jewish law (halakha), i.e. to its traditional contents and to its methods of decision-making.[9]

With these initial characterizations in hand, we can now proceed to examine the thesis that democracy and Judaism somehow conflict. Supporters of this thesis are not always clear about their intention, though at least one of the following theses seems to be included in what they want to say:

1. Orthodox Jews cannot live in a democratic state, because, by the very act of doing so, they would be violating the halakha.
2. Orthodox Jews are allowed to live in a democratic state, but they are not allowed to play an active role in its institutions.
3. Orthodox Jews are allowed to play an active role in the political and the legal institutions of democracy, but it will necessarily be a corrupting one, because they will, of necessity, be taking advantage of their role to advance undemocratic objectives.
4. Orthodox Jews cannot acknowledge the authority of a democratic state because they regard themselves as subject only to God, and for the same reason they cannot appreciate any values that do not have their source in the Torah.
5. Orthodox Jews are a danger to democracy because ultimately they do not regard themselves as subject to its laws and institutions.
6. Orthodox Jews are a danger to democracy because they use democratic tools to advance an undemocratic regime, namely, a theocracy.
7. Democracy is not the form of government enjoined by halakha, i.e. according to halakha, an ideal Torah-State would not be a democracy.
8. Halakha is incompatible with the values of democracy.

These various theses are closely interrelated, though, as one can easily see, they do not say exactly the same thing. The basic idea that underlies CT is expressed in theses (7)–(8), namely, that the values and political aspirations of halakha are incompatible with those of democracy. This leads to most of the other theses, and to the general conclusion that the commitment of orthodox Jews to halakha prevents them from being full participants in a democracy. The most extreme version of this conclusion is (1) which draws its (very) small plausibility from the idea that if democracies are, in some sense, 'against' halakha, then a person committed to halakha cannot be part of it. Needless to say, thesis (1) is far too strong and nobody would accept it. If halakha prohibited Jews from being citizens of democracies, they would probably be obliged to emigrate from the United States, Israel and Britain to Iran, Iraq, and China – not very attractive options.

The implausibility of (1) makes (2) seem a more reasonable candidate to express CT. According to (2), Jews are not condemned for living in states with policies that do not coincide with the values and requirements of halakha, but they are not allowed to play an active role in those states, for instance, to be members of parliament or judges. To do so would imply that they support undesirable values. Yet surely (2) is also farfetched. Jews often played an active role in the political and legal systems of countries in which they resided, and although these countries encouraged (what many halakhists would regard as) idolatry, i.e. Christianity, taking on such roles – both for their personal benefit and the benefit of their people – was not considered forbidden. To put it simply, there is no ruling of halakha according to which Jews are required to refrain from all political activity unless the country in which they reside proclaims loyalty to the expectations of halakha (by Jews as well as by non-Jews).

True, a version of (2) can be found within a tiny and extreme ultra-orthodox group in Jerusalem, the *Neturei Karta*. This group refuses any co-operation with the state of Israel which they regard as a religious catastrophe. They do not take part in the elections and do not receive funds from what they see as the secular, heretic state. The *Neturei Karta*, however, are a very small group and they pose no serious threat to Israeli democracy. The rest of the *charedi* society in some way acknowledge the state of Israel; they participate in the elections and in the political institutions and take part in the democratic game. As far as halakha is concerned, the attitudes of orthodox Zionists and of *charedi* orthodox to the state of Israel are the same: 'The thinkers of religious Zionism today have no halakhic concept that enables or requires an attitude toward and a relation with the state of Israel different from the attitude toward and a relation with other states.'[10] This fact confers some support to my argument that as there is no ruling of halakha that prevents an orthodox Jew from taking part in the democratic game in the United States, there is similarly no problem for such a Jew to do so in Israel.

134

Theses (3)–(6) express in slightly different ways the fear shared by proponents of CT that Judaism is dangerous to democracy. The assumed danger stems from the fact that orthodox Jews do not really acknowledge the authority of the people through democratic decisions, because they acknowledge only the authority of God. Furthermore, they cannot truly acknowledge the value of secular-liberal-democratic morality, because 'Judaism admits only a heteronomous-theonomic approach, which views the Creator as the source of morality'.[11] This position of those committed to halakha implies that in a potential clash between halakha and democracy they would renounce democracy. Even worse, it means that they might use all possible means – including democratic ones – to weaken democracy, undermine its institutions, and ultimately destroy it.

However, this picture of the believer as unable to acknowledge any authority or any value outside halakha is incompatible with many sources, as well as with the actual history of the Jewish people. With regard to the authority of the countries in which Jews lived, there was frequent use of the talmudic principle *'dina de-malkhuta dina,'*[12] meaning that the rulings of a state are binding from the point of view of halakha. There is no reason to think that this principle should not apply to democracies too. But the problem of double loyalty has, in any case, nothing special to do with *democracy*. It concerns the general problem of clashes between religious authority and civil government, whether the nature of this government be democratic or not. That political leaders often act in ways contrary to the Torah is demonstrated in the Bible, where the prophets denounce such behavior and exhort kings and politicians to follow the ways of God. Indeed Maimonides explicitly says that if a king rules against the Torah, one ought not to obey.[13] Thus, first, halakha can acknowledge the authority of a non-Jewish or a secular state, and second, possible conflicts between such authority and halakha do not depend on the state being a democratic one.

With regard to the status of moral and other values from a religious perspective, I have shown elsewhere, with Avi Sagi, that from both a philosophical and a religious point of view we ought not to regard such values as dependent on God's will or God's legislation.[14] Theories of such dependence (known as divine command theories of morality) are also almost totally

absent in the Jewish tradition.[15] Hence, it is far from true to
assume that the orthodox Jew has no conceptual or normative
basis to acknowledge the (independent) value of justice, honesty,
freedom, or other values.

Yet, one might object, these abstract arguments do not suffice
to reject the claim that religion is a danger to democracy
because, after all, not everybody understands them or inter-
nalizes them properly. Is this danger real? Hardly. At least
outside Israel, orthodox Jews do not seem to pose any special
danger to democracies (nor do Christians or Muslims). Part of
the reason is, of course, the fact that modern democracies grant
their citizens wide freedom of worship, so that no real conflict
should arise between democracy and religious observance. As for
the fear that religious people would act to institute undemocratic
policies and laws, well, this is what democracy is all about–
having an open debate about the political morality of the
country, and allowing all citizens to argue their case and try to
advance it. Surely the fact that many believers of all religions
find the liberal attitude towards pornography or abortion too
permissive does not indicate any necessary conflict between
religion and democracy. As I suggested earlier, the conceptual
question 'what is democracy?' should be distinguished from the
moral-political question 'what are the values and policies that a
democracy ought to advance?'.

I turn now to the more theoretical versions of CT, expressed in
theses (7)–(8), according to which halakha does not, or would
not, support a democratic government for a Jewish state, but
would opt for some kind of a theocracy – having the rabbis rule
the country according to the precepts of halakha. Whether or not
this is an adequate view of halakha has no direct implication for
the versions of CT discussed earlier. It is perfectly possible that
an ideal Torah-state would not be a democracy but that in the
present social-political situation there is no significant danger
(for democracy) that those committed to halakha would take any
measures to set up such a state. In fact this possibility
represents the attitude of many orthodox Jews to the state of
Israel. The idea of a Torah-State, or a halakhic-state, is
conceived by most orthodox Jews as an ideal for some future
time, for the messianic era, and not an actual political goal to be
realized here and now. For most ultra-orthodox (*charedi*) people,
it is so because trying to realize a Torah-state would be a

violation of 'the three oaths' (shelosh ha-shevuot).[16] As Aviezer Ravitzky shows in detail, the ultra-orthodox regard their existence in Israel as being in exile (galut) and reject any attempt to take active steps (i.e. realpolitik steps) to realize the messianic ideal.[17] But even for the Zionist orthodox, the idea of a halakhic state is more an ideological phrase than a real political goal.

These comments do not release us from the need to say something about the theoretical question concerning democracy and an ideal halakhic-state. Is such a state necessarily non-democratic? Menachem Lorberbaum answers this question in the negative, arguing that the issue of the desired form of government has been left open in the Jewish tradition. The Bible itself is ambivalent about the idea of a king[18] and different views on this matter recur in the history of Jewish political thought. Of special interest is R. Isaac Abarbanel's strong objection to Maimonides' endorsement of monarchy as the desired form of government. Abarbanel had great fears of concentrated authority and considered monarchy a curse. Hence, as opposed to common belief, it is not at all obvious that halakha enjoins a particular form of government. The possibility of an ideal halakhic-democratic state cannot be ruled out a priori.[19]

This point about the sort of government halakha enjoins leads to a more general point about ascribing views to halakha. Proponents of CT often seem to presuppose that 'Judaism' or 'halakha' have more or less fixed attitudes toward questions of value or practice, attitudes than can be discovered by studying the sources. But the halakha, just like other legal systems, is essentially open-ended. We can only speak of the attitude of certain interpreters of halakha at a given time, not of what halakha necessarily says on some particular issue. The same applies to most legal systems. At the beginning of the eighteenth century, it would have been reasonable for an observer to say that the American democracy and its legal system were racist. There was ample evidence for such a claim in many laws, regulations, and court-decisions. It would not have been correct, however, to conclude that American law was necessarily racist, or that it had no resources to correct its ways and progress towards a (morally) better interpretation of the equality of human beings. The history of American law and society teaches us that such progress was indeed possible.

The same argument holds true for Jewish law too. Consider, for example, the status of women within an ideal, halakha-committed, Torah-state. The attitude towards women that one finds in talmudic sources, as well in most classical sources of Jewish law, sounds rather humiliating to a modern, egalitarian ear. By and large, women are regarded as intellectually inferior and are expected to spend their lives nursing children and taking care of their husband's needs and demands. They are not allowed to study the Torah the same way men are, and do not take any part in political or public life. Is this how a Torah-state would appear? No doubt many orthodox Jews and rabbis would say 'No.' The above negative attitude towards women, they would say, is a result of contingent historical factors and there is no justification for adhering to it today. In the past, women were treated as inferior throughout the world, and now, as their status is improving, this improvement should find its way into halakha too. As Rabbi Aaron Lichtenstein puts it: 'The question is to what extent do we want to eternalize the original situation in the halakha, or try to revise it in legitimate ways, taking into account historical developments.'[20] The status of women within an ideal Torah-state, then, cannot be determined a priori by opening the Talmud, the *Shulkhan Arukh*, or any other source. The horizons of interpretation are infinitely open, and no necessity-like claims can be defended regarding the position of the Jewish (or any other) law on some moral-political question.

What is true for the status of women is also true for the desired form of government and for what are termed 'democratic values.' In a world governed by kings and emperors with absolute sovereignty, it does not come as a surprise to find the Bible referring to monarchy as the form of government for that time and for the messianic period. Does this mean that Judaism supports monarchy? No more than it supports an unequal and unjust attitude towards women. The same goes for other democratic values that are regarded by supporters of CT as being opposed to Judaism, and there is no need to reiterate the argument.

I noted earlier that orthodox Jews do not seem to pose any significant danger to democracy. However, one might feel that I have been ignoring an essential point, namely, that CT does not concern itself with the relation between democracy and Judaism in general, but with a unique context of this relation, i.e.

democracy and Judaism within the state of Israel. And within this special context the tension between democracy and Judaism is indeed real and disturbing. To this charge I would make the following comments. First, if true, it re-emphasizes the fact that CT is not a thesis about a necessary conflict between democracy and Judaism, but rather about the (assumed) anti-democratic nature of some Jewish social-political group(s) at a given time. Second, in many cases, what CT interprets as claims against democracy are really claims about particular decisions and policies, not about democracy as such. Had the policy of the government and the supreme court been less liberal in decisions concerning homosexuality, censorship, and limiting traffic on the Sabbath, then, most probably, *charedi* society would have been quite content with Israeli democracy. And the same applies to the complaints of some right-wing orthodox Jews against democracy; the complaints are not aimed at democracy as such, but against what are regarded as wrong decisions taken by democratic institutions.

The conclusion to be drawn from this section is that theses 1–8 above cannot be the whole story behind CT. It is not orthodox Judaism as such that CT sees as a threat to democracy, but some special form of Judaism. What then is this form?

2. Nationalism and Democracy

In this section I suggest that in many cases what really fuels CT is not a concern about a tension between Judaism-conceived-as-halakha and democracy, but a tension between Judaism-conceived-as-nationalism and democracy. As a starting point, I would like to refer to the debate around the *Kastenbaum* case,[21] which reached the Supreme Court for a final ruling. An Israeli citizen, Mr. Kastenbaum, had signed a standard contract with one of the burial societies (*chevra qadisha*) in Jerusalem to purchase burial plots for himself and his wife. One of the conditions of this contract was that the inscription on the grave-stone would be carved only in Hebrew. When Mrs. Kastenbaum, an American immigrant, died, her husband wanted to have her name engraved on the stone in English. The burial society objected, and the case reached the Supreme Court, which ruled in a majority decision in favor of Kastenbaum; Justices Barak and Shamgar for Kastenbaum, and Justice Elon for the *chevra qadisha*.

On the face of it, the problem has nothing to do with democracy and Judaism. As there is no ruling of halakha according to which one is not allowed to have English letters carved on grave-stones, there is no reason to assume that halakha would necessarily support the burial society. And given that the contract is one into which Kastenbaum entered freely, there is no reason to assume that democracy, or democratic values, would necessarily support Kastenbaum's position. However, the fact that Barak, well-known for his liberal views, took one position, and Elon, the religious judge of the court,[22] took the other encouraged the thought that what was deeply at stake in this case was a conflict between democracy, or liberal-democratic values, and orthodox Judaism. In this spirit, Ilan Saban, from Haifa University Law School, writes that Elon's decision in this case 'is an example of the way in which Elon does not, and most probably cannot resolve quite a few deep contradictions and oppositions' between the liberal-democratic view and the 'orthodox view.'[23] These oppositions and contradictions 'are very essential and profoundly hard to bridge.'[24] According to Saban, because of his commitment to halakha, Elon expresses little sensitivity to individuals' autonomy, which explains his ruling against Kastenbaum, and his attitude to the violations of rights in general, especially those of Palestinians in the context of the Israeli-Palestinian conflict. Elon's orthodox view, says Saban, makes him a 'deep foe' of the liberal-democratic view.

A similar argument, in a much more hostile and aggressive style, is put forward by political theorist, Zeev Sternhal, of the Hebrew University. According to Sternhal, the opposing opinions in the *Kastenbaum* case reveal two conflicting views about the essence of nationality and about the relation between the individual and society, the liberal view and the 'organic' view. According to the liberal view, the individual comes before the collective and the nation 'is a group of individuals who have the right of self-determination.'[25] The point of departure for the liberal view is the rights of citizens as individuals. Nationality is determined by citizenship, not by race, blood, language, religion, or ethnicity. By contrast, according to the organic notion of nationality, which developed mainly in Germany and Eastern Europe, nationality is determined not by citizenship but by ethnic, religious, cultural, and linguistic identity. The liberal view of nationality is seen as democratic, humanistic, rationalist, and modern, while the organic view is considered to represent a dark nationality of 'blood and earth,' which does not acknowledge the centrality of the individual as a bearer of rights. In Sternhal's view, Barak holds the liberal view of nationality, which explains the priority he gives to the rights of Mr. Kastenbaum over religious and ethnic interests. By contrast, Elon holds the organic view of nationality and believes that the halakha is part of the identity of the Jewish state. Hence, Elon gives priority to the concerns of the nation, the collective, over the rights of the individual.

As I have shown elsewhere,[26] neither Saban nor Sternhal have established the charge that Elon's ruling is influenced by the demands of halakha. That halakha does not forbid the use of English letters or Gregorian dates on grave-stones is quite obvious to anybody who visits Jewish cemeteries around the world, and neither of the above writers refers to any halakhic sources which indicate a contrary view. Thus, it is definitely not Elon's *orthodox* commitment that (allegedly) leads him against liberal-democratic principles, but a different commitment which is shared by many non-orthodox Jews too, namely: the commitment to Zionism. Let me elaborate on this point.

One of the main concerns of the fledging Zionist movement was the revival of the Hebrew language which was to play a central role in shaping a new, 'normal,' Jewish identity. Turning Hebrew from a holy language used in religious contexts to a language used in the secular concerns of everyday life was a long, hard struggle, which finally succeeded, thanks to the efforts and commitment of institutions and individuals who decided to speak and write only in Hebrew. This is the background for the policy of the above burial society, a society that was founded by orthodox, as well as secular Zionists.[27] The reason this society forbade the use of English letters on grave-stones was not halakhic but national, i.e. a wish to strengthen the revival of the Hebrew language as the national language of the fledgling Israeli society. That Elon finds this wish reasonable and defends a contract that expresses it does not stem from the fact he is *orthodox*, but from the fact he is a *Zionist*.

In Sternhal's case this analysis is especially cogent. Though Sternhal explicitly refers to Elon's view of halakha as reflecting his dangerous opinion, Elon's view is condemned not because of its specific *religious* character, but because of its idea of nationalism, i.e. the idea that Jewish nationality is defined by culture, religion, and common history. According to Sternhal, Elon holds the view that 'the nation established a state for itself,'[28] while Barak apparently thinks otherwise, that the nation is defined by the state. Yet surely the view that Sternhal ascribes to Elon is the standard Zionist view from its early days at the end of the nineteenth century. The Zionist movement wanted to establish a state for a nation that obviously was not at that time defined by its *state*. And the state of Israel has always seen itself as the state of all Jews throughout the world, a fact clearly expressed in the Law of Return which grants an automatic right to citizenship to all Jews wishing to immigrate to Israel.

Sternhal's real target is, therefore, not orthodox Judaism, but Zionism. His analysis implies that Zionism is based on a primitive and dangerous view of nationality, which does not take seriously the idea of the individual. It is no accident, argues Sternhal, that the Zionist movement developed in Eastern Europe, 'in a world where a rationalist and individualist view of the nation was impossible.'[29] Similarly, when Saban wants to demonstrate Elon's anti-liberal views, he refers to his rulings in cases relating to the Israeli-Palestinian conflict, in which Elon allegedly shows 'very low sensitivity' to the rights of Palestinians. But this low sensitivity was typical of other judges too,[30] in fact of most judges, just as it was typical of many other Israeli institutions. Furthermore, had Elon been directed by 'the orthodox view,' he should have been insensitive to the rights of women too, but Saban believes that in this area Elon shows 'high sensitivity.' In Saban's case too, then, Elon is really attacked as representative of the Israeli-Zionist way of thought which, indeed, was not always sensitive enough to the rights of the Palestinians.

The astonishing fact is that these attacks against Zionism, especially in Sternhal's case, are carried out under the guise of an attack against *orthodoxy*, as if Zionism were an essential component of the orthodox view, and as if belief in Zionism was not held by non-orthodox Jews. It is astonishing because, historically speaking, the Zionist movement was of course mainly a non-orthodox enterprise, with most orthodox rabbis opposing it fiercely. The idea that Zionism is an essential part of the orthodox view is quite a new one, characteristic of a well-defined social and religious group. I refer to the theology and ideology inspired by Rabbi Avraham Kook and his son Rabbi Zvi Yehuda Kook, according to which Zionism marks the beginning of the period of redemption and the state of Israel is seen as 'completely sacred with no defect'[31] In the 1970s this view became dominant within orthodox-Zionist society in Israel and animated the process of settlement in what the settlers hoped would become 'greater Israel.' The settlers, together with the political and ideological groups that support them, make extensive use of Zionist symbols and rhetoric, and often argue that they are merely continuing in the paths of the early pioneers, and that they are the real – the only – Zionists of the time.[32]

This claim of (some) orthodox Jews, in ideology and in practice, for a monopoly over Zionism is insufficient, however, to explain why others would accept this claim, i.e. accept the identification of Zionism with orthodoxy. If non-orthodox Jews were strongly committed to Zionist values and ideology, as were the first generations of pioneers, then nobody could take the above claim seriously. But this is not the case. The Zionist, and indeed the Jewish identity of secular Israelis (especially young people), is constantly weakening. A cynical, or at best an indifferent attitude towards Zionist symbols and ideals, is widespread. Thus, the recent history of Zionism is characterized by two opposing trends: a very enthusiastic adoption of Zionism by orthodox Jews, and an increasing withdrawal from Zionism by non-orthodox Jews. It is sometimes said that orthodox Jews have taken over Zionist symbols and ideology, and maybe the best illustration of this is the changing attitudes towards Zion, i.e. Jerusalem. When the Israeli troops entered the Old City in 1967, a tremendous wave of excitement was felt all across Israel. There was a strong feeling of a dream being realized, a feeling shared by almost all Jews in Israel. The day of liberation, 28 Iyyar, was made a national holiday – 'Jerusalem Day' – to celebrate the reunion of the capital. However, thirty years later the only section of Israeli population that still celebrates this day in a significant way is the orthodox. Most secular Jews are either indifferent to the significance of this day or view it negatively, as the beginning of a long and bitter occupation. This decrease in the status of Jerusalem has clear demographic implications. Young secular Jews tend to leave Jerusalem for the Tel Aviv area, while religious Jews, from Israel and from abroad, prefer to settle in Jerusalem. Finally, for many secular Israelis, Jerusalem has become a symbol of religious and nationalist fanaticism, and of unnecessary bloodshed, while Tel Aviv has become a symbol of what is seen as a normal life, free of the heavy demands and false conceptions of religion, and of Zionism. In light of these developments, it is no surprise to see how claims against Zionism are easily confused with claims against orthodoxy.

Sternhal's charge that Zionism is anti-liberal and anti-democratic is part of what has acquired the name of 'post-Zionism.'[33] What is common to all post-Zionists is a strong criticism of Zionist ideology and historiography. Some are led by this criticism to the conclusion that, morally speaking, the Zionist project has been a failure, mainly because of the way the Palestinians were treated and because of the way Jews were manipulated to serve Zionist aims.[34] Others are content with making the demand that Israel become what is now termed 'a state for all its citizens,' and not specifically a Jewish state. In their view, Israel should become a pluralistic society, in which the institutions and law would bear no special Jewish character and in which Jewish citizens would enjoy no special privileges relative to other citizens. The terms 'liberal,' 'democratic,' 'rational' play a major role in the rhetoric of the post-Zionists – as features of a 'normal,' modern state, which, allegedly, are in conflict with the idea of a Jewish state.

The debate about the moral status of Zionism is thus central in understanding the debate about Judaism and democracy. But there are other factors as well that have motivated this last debate: (a) legislation of the Basic Laws, (b) the assassination of Prime Minister Rabin and other events related to the peace process.

(a) The legislation of the Basic Laws in 1992 caused what Justice Barak called 'a constitutional revolution'[35] in Israeli law.[36] Among other things, these laws refer to Israel as a Jewish and democratic state and make this idea constitutionally binding. Article 1(a) of Basic Law: Human Dignity and Freedom states that the purpose of this law is 'to protect human dignity and freedom, in order to anchor in a basic law the values of the state of Israel *as a Jewish and democratic state'* (my italics). As a result of this legislation, the issue of democracy and Judaism ceased to be a merely academic one and became at once a significant legal issue. The legal-constitutional context also shifted the question from the individual level to the political one, i.e. from the question of how an *individual* Jew can respect democracy, to the question of how a Jewish and a democratic *state* is possible.[37]

Following my previous argument, on this level too the real challenge for democracy is not the idea of a state ruled by halakha, but the idea of a Jewish state in a national context. It is very hard to find orthodox leaders who take the idea of a halakhic state seriously, i.e. as a real political goal. The ultra-orthodox explicitly oppose it, while the modern orthodox have no clear idea of what it means in practice, and make no effort to work out a plan for its implementation. The efforts of the religious parties in Israel regarding the Jewishness of Israel are directed at two objectives, taking care of the interests of the religious community in terms of education, religious services etc., and seeking to advance laws and rulings that express the Jewish character of Israel. Gavison contends that 'the intra-Jewish conflict is ultimately between those holding (not always consciously) a nation-state view of Israel and those pushing towards viewing it as a halakha-state' (1995, p. 644), and the danger for democracy comes mainly from the latter. Without denying that some people do at times 'push towards' the idea of a halakha-state, I believe that this analysis misrepresents the terms of the current debate. The deep intra-Jewish conflict, which is well manifested in the growing literature around post-Zionism, is between those who accept a nation-state view of Israel and those who reject it. And it is in this context that the notion of democracy plays its real role in the current debate, namely, as a charge against the idea of a Jewish state.

(b) Months before the assassination of Prime Minister Rabin in November 1995, a group of right-wing rabbis issued a ruling (*pesaq*) according to which soldiers who take part in the evacuation of military bases or settlements in Judea and Samaria would be violating halakha. Therefore, the rabbis stated, soldiers ought to disobey such commands if issued. This ruling raised strong opposition in Israeli public life, often expressed in the rhetoric of a clash between democracy and

Judaism. By issuing this *pesaq*, it was argued, the rabbis demonstrated that they had no real commitment to democracy and to its elected institutions. They confirmed the fear that orthodox Jews acknowledge only the authority of halakha. Then Rabin was murdered by a right-wing orthodox assassin, and the fear seemed to be re-confirmed in an overwhelmingly powerful way. This tragic event was made possible, it was argued everywhere, because the commitment to democracy among Israelis in general, and among orthodox Jews in particular, was not strong enough. In the year following the assassination, most universities held conferences on topics related to democracy and tolerance, and many established chairs and centers for the study of the values of democracy and of ways to implement them. The faculty of law at Bar-Ilan University, where the assassin had studied, has recently launched a new journal (in Hebrew) under the title *The Culture of Democracy*. There can be no doubt about the traumatic effect of Rabin's assassination on the spread of CT and the rise of the current debate on democracy and Judaism.

3. Conclusion

For the first forty years of Israeli statehood, orthodox Jews did not feel that their orthodoxy made them enemies of democracy; neither, by and large, did liberal seculars hold such a view. 'The Conflict Thesis' started to spread in the early 1990s in the context of some political events and ideological trends which I have tried to describe. That the debate about democracy and Judaism is connected to a special historical context is central to the thesis presented here. It is connected to the growing debate about Zionism vs. post-Zionism and to the debate about the Oslo Accords and their significance. I have sought to show (a) that many arguments by friends of CT do not turn on a tension between orthodox Judaism and democracy, but on a tension between Zionism and democracy, and (b) that those sections of orthodox society that are regarded as endangering democracy are really not against democracy as such, but against specific policies of the democratic government, mainly its willingness to reach a peace agreement that will give up areas in the land of Israel to the Palestinians.

146

All the above does not deny that the relation between democracy and Judaism is problematic and deserves serious philosophical analysis. From the point of view of Jewish law and philosophy, whether democracy (and what type of democracy) might be a desirable sort of government is an open question. From the point of view of democracy, the role of religion in the state is still under debate, attracting a lot of attention in the United States[38] and in other countries. I have made only a small contribution to this debate. My task here has been different: I wished to expose the underlying political and ideological concerns that fuel the current debate in Israel on democracy and Judaism. If I am right, this debate will be remembered primarily as a chapter in Israel's social and political history, rather than as a chapter in the history of Jewish philosophy.

Notes

1 I shall be generalizing about the views of 'secular' or 'religious' people, though this is often misleading. I do so for the sake of convenience only.

2 In the Israeli context, 'religious' means in most cases 'orthodox.' As is well-known, the Conservative and Reform movements are very marginal in Israel. The fundamental decision a Jew must make in Israel is one of identification with either the religious (*dati*) or the secular (*chiloni*) camp.

3 Dawson 1985, p. 48, quoting from (respectively) Abbott 1901, p. 736, Dole 1906, p. 413, and Ashworth 1918, p. 191.

4 For details, see Way 1987.

5 See, for example, Gutmann 1973.

6 Gutmann 1973, p. 413.

7 Gavison 1995, pp. 625–9.

8 Ibid., p. 627.

9 For a formulation of CT that refers to orthodox Judaism, see for instance Saban 1994 and Mautner 1993, esp. p. 128. As an illustration of the incompatibility of Judaism and democracy, Mautner quotes former chief Rabbi Shlomo Goren who said in 1991: 'I have gone through the whole of the Torah, the Talmud, *Shulkhan Arukh* and Maimonides and haven't found this *mitzvah* of democracy' (Mautner, ibid., p. 145 n. 25).

10 Achituv 1995, p. 271.

11 Twersky 1991, p. 238 n. 237.

12 This rule was laid down by the *amora* Samuel and is cited four times in the Talmud, see e.g. *Baba Batra* 54b and 55a.

13 *The Code of Maimonides*, Laws of Kings, 3:9.

14 See Sagi and Statman 1995a, part I.

15 See Sagi and Statman 1995b.
16 According to a talmudic midrash on some verses from *The Song of Songs*, the sons of Israel are not allowed to use force to capture the land of Israel and to push forward the process of redemption; see *Ketubut* 111:a. 'The Three Oaths' play a central role in the ultra-orthodox attitude towards Zionism and the state of Israel.
17 Ravitzky 1996, ch. 4.
18 See Deutoronomy 17; I Samuel 8.
19 See Lorberbaum (forthcoming). Lorberbaum makes some initial steps in trying to relate democracy to ideas we find in various halakhic sources. I shall not enter into the details here.
20 Lichtenstein 1980, p. 158.
21 Civil Appeal 294/91 *chevra qadisha Kehilat Yerushalayim vs. Kastenbaum* 46(2) p. 464.
22 Since the establishment of the Supreme Court it has been agreed that one chair will always be occupied by a religious judge.
23 Saban 1994, pp. 154–5.
24 Ibid., p. 156.
25 Sternhal 1994, p. 168.
26 Statman 1996, pp. 246–8.
27 As Elon mentions in *Kastenbaum* (*supra* note 21), p. 486.
28 Sternhal 1994, p. 171.
29 Ibid.
30 See Statman 1996, note 46.
31 Quoted by Ravitzky 1996, p. 189.
32 The nature and the danger of this messianic view of Zionism is analyzed at length by Ravitzky, ibid., chapter 3.
33 For a useful collection on post-Zionism, see Michman 1997; see also Taub 1997, ch. 4.
34 See especially Michman 1997 for the post-Zionist view of the way Zionist leaders and ideologists manipulated the Holocaust and its survivors to advance Zionist objectives.
35 Barak 1992.
36 Others, mainly Justice Elon, find this expression overstated; see Elon 1995, p. 256–7.
37 For the debate about how to interpret the 'Jewish and democratic' requirement, see the special issue of *Tel Aviv Law Review* (Hebrew) 19(3), 1995, and Elon 1995.
38 See, e.g., Greenawalt 1993; Audi 1993; Perry 1993, and the many references mentioned in these sources.

References

Achituv, Y. 1995. *On the Edge of Transition: A Reflection on Jewish Meanings for Our Time* (Hebrew). Ein Tzurim: The Yaakov Hertzog Center
Audi, R. 1993. 'The Place of Religious Argument in a Free and Democratic Society.' *San Diego Law Review* 30, pp. 677–701

Barak, A. 1992. 'The Constitutional Revolution: Protected Human Rights' (Hebrew). *Haifa University Law Review* 1, pp. 9–35

Elon, M. 1995. 'The Basic Laws: Their Enactment, Interpretation and Expectations' (Hebrew). *Bar-Ilan Law Studies* 12, pp. 253–307

Gavison, R. 1995. 'A Jewish and Democratic State: Political Identity, Ideology and Law' (Hebrew). *Tel Aviv University Law Review* 19, pp. 631–682

Greenawalt, K. 1993. 'The Role of Religion in a Liberal Democracy: Dilemmas and Possible Resolutions.' *Journal of Church and State* 35, pp. 503–519

Gutmann, A. 1973. 'Democracy,' in R. E. Goodin and P. Pettit (eds.), *A Companion to Contemporary Political Philosophy*. Oxford: Blackwell, pp. 411–21

Lichtenstein, A. 1980. 'Basic Problems in the Education of Women' (Hebrew), in B. Rosenfeld (ed.), *The Woman and Her Education*. Kfar Saba: Amanah

Lorberbaum, M. Forthcoming. 'In Favor of Democracy: The Question of the Good Regime in Halakhic and Philosophical Sources' (Hebrew), in A. Sagi and Y. Stern (eds.), *Judaism: Civil Government and Values*. Ramat-Gan: Bar-Ilan University Press

Mautner, M. 1993. *The Decline of Formalism and the Rise of Values in Israeli Law* (Hebrew). Tel-Aviv: Ma'agalay Da'at Publishing House

Michman, D. (ed.). 1997. *Post-Zionism and the Holocaust: The Role of the Holocaust in the Public Debate on Post-Zionism in Israel (1993–1996)*. Ramat-Gan: Bar-Ilan University, The Faculty of Jewish Studies

Perry, M.J. 1993. 'Religious Morality and Political Choice: Further Thoughts – and Second Thoughts – on *Love and Power.*' *San Diego Law Review* 30, pp. 703–727

Ravitzky, A. 1996. *Messianism, Zionism and Jewish Religious Radicalism*. Chicago: University of Chicago Press

Saban, I. 1994. 'Judge Menachem Elon: Law and Worldview.' *Haifa University Law Review* 2, pp. 153–8

Sagi, A. and D. Statman. 1995a. *Religion and Morality*. Amsterdam: Rodopi

——. 1995b. 'Divine Command Morality and Jewish Tradition.' *Journal of Religious Ethics* 23, pp. 39–69

Statman, D. 1996. 'On Nationality, Liberalism and What Cannot be Learned from the Kastenbaum Case' (Hebrew). *Tel Aviv University Law Review* 20, pp. 239–253

Sternhal, Z. 1994. 'Two Conceptions of Individual, Society and Nation' (Hebrew). *Haifa University Law Review* 2, pp. 167–72

Taub, G. 1997. *A Dispirited Rebellion: Essays on Contemporary Israeli Culture* (Hebrew). Tel-Aviv: Hakibbutz Hameuchad

Twersky, I. 1991. *Introduction to the Mishneh Torah of Maimonides* (Hebrew). Jerusalem: Magnes Press

Way, H. F. 1987. 'The Death of the Christian Nation: The Judiciary and Church-State Relations.' *Journal of Church and State* 29, pp. 509–529

PART TWO

LIBERTY AND AUTHORITY IN JEWISH POLITICAL THOUGHT

CHAPTER SEVEN

Is there a Concept of Political Liberty in Medieval Jewish Philosophy?

Oliver Leaman

There are certain generally-agreed propositions about medieval Jewish political philosophy. They tend to the conclusion that such philosophy is predominantly theocratic, that it gives low value to concepts like democracy and political liberty, and that political values on the whole have a relatively low priority. This is not to suggest that it was argued that social and practical life were given a low value, but rather that it was always regarded as an inferior consideration when compared with some form of the religious and/or intellectual life. One might also suggest that it is not surprising that a small and powerless community dispersed around the world should concentrate on attaining ends which are far from political, since the prospects of achieving political ends were necessarily limited. Although Jews did reach great political heights as advisors, diplomats and bankers, they were always on the periphery of society, and their very marginality contributed to their desirability as courtiers. There were no problems in chopping and changing such advisors liable to come from the main Muslim community itself, since those advisors were not part of that community, and as a result Jewish politicians were more dependent upon the good will of the rulers than was the case with their Muslim peers who perhaps could appeal to some local constituency for support.

On the other hand, we should be careful about linking marginality with political quietism. Until 1979 it was normal to see the messianic aspects of Shi'ism and the relative powerlessness of the Shi'i communities in most countries as linked, and the other-worldly aspect of Shi'ism was seen as explaining the quietism of the Shi'i world. After the Iranian Revolution, however, intellectual fashions changed, and commentators started to emphasize how politically active the basic Shi'i principles are. After 1979 it was argued that Sunnis tend to be quietist, while the Shi'i are by contrast intent on achieving political change. Nonetheless, the political philosophy of marginal groups often turns out to replicate that marginality, and medieval Jewish political philosophy as a result emphasises the distinction between Torah and nomos. While the Gentiles have laws which are capable of securing peace and justice in the state, Jews were said to have a law which is capable of perfecting both body and mind, but such a law can only really succeed perfectly in the messianic state. In the *galut* Jews will always be at the mercy of the decisions of political rulers who are not guided by the Torah. While they may be able to perfect their religious and intellectual capacities, their social lives will always be at the whim of their political rulers.

This approach to politics stems in many ways from Plato. Although within the cultural world of the Islamic empire Aristotle tended to be respected more than Plato, the former's *Politics* was not widely known in Arabic (although there is some evidence that parts of it were available) and Plato's politics were often combined with Aristotle's metaphysics, with the *Republic* being treated as the conclusion of the *Nicomachean Ethics*. It is often argued that this had a major influence on the direction of political philosophy in the Islamic world, since the *Politics* would have introduced the idea of politics as an independent system of thought, not subsumed under general metaphysical principles. The *Republic*, by contrast, sees political life entirely in terms of a overarching metaphysical system, in ways which are entirely compatible with a religious gloss. The value of political life is completely expressed in terms of its ability to enable the participant to understand the nature of reality, insofar as this is possible. There is no separate realm of political life which exists alongside one's intellectual and religious life, as is the case in Aristotle, but there is just one approach to politics which is acceptable, and that is the approach which fits in with the correct view of the nature of reality.

Aristotle was certainly not a democrat, in any sense of the word, but again he is more prepared to see some of the virtues of that system of government as compared with Plato. The latter's well-known antipathy to democracy was eagerly adopted by Jewish thinkers also. Democracy as a system of government does not fit well into a metaphysical system which regards the truth as something difficult to attain and only available to a very limited group of people. Nor does it work with a view of society which sees the majority of the population as potentially in conflict with the small group who can grasp the truth. In any case, the majority of the population are concerned with personal and petty issues such as their own well-being and improving their material lives.

The philosopher in the medieval period, by contrast, is more interested in the spiritual or intellectual aspects of life, and many Jewish thinkers were attracted to forms of asceticism and mysticism. We should recall here how the Neoplatonists took Plato in a far more other-worldly direction than one might expect given much of his thought. The Neoplatonists were not particularly interested even in the political philosophy provided by Plato. They were more interested in understanding the nature of reality, and how they were to come close to God. It is hardly surprising that their Jewish followers should share their enthusiasm for coming close to God, and also their distaste for the practical aspects of the world of generation and corruption. This is not to suggest that many Jewish philosophers advocated denial of the material world for concentration on the spiritual. That is certainly not the case. Jews shared the distaste of Muslims for what they both saw as the extremes of Christianity, with its monasticism and active hostility to the body. On the other hand, there is no doubt that in much Jewish philosophy during this period there is a concentration on the ideal in political philosophy, since the ideal leads to an understanding of the presence of God. It is as though the Jewish philosopher has to decide between working on two sorts of problems, one religious and one practical. The former is the problem of how to come closer to God. The latter is the problem of how to organize our affairs in the best way that they can be organized. The first question looks much more interesting and important than the second question, and it is hardly surprising that it received more attention. The second question, the practical problem, was explicated in terms of the first, so that the best way of organizing our practical affairs was taken to be that which would bring us closer, ultimately, to God.

Within this sort of context, the notion of political liberty seems to be a non-starter. If we use the distinction between negative and positive liberty, between freedom from and freedom to, the Jewish philosophers seem to make far more use of the positive notion. We are free to come to know God and his purposes, we are free to realize ourselves as human beings insofar as our capacities make this feasible, we are free to develop ourselves to the fullest possible extent in a variety of directions. Of course, the notion of negative freedom must also be given some significance, since it is unpleasant to be interfered with in one's plans and projects, yet this sort of interference is relatively unimportant since it cannot affect the most important direction in which we can go, to God, and other people or circumstances cannot really get in the way of this since it is something we can do by ourselves. The notion of negative liberty only comes into its own much later in history, with the development of capitalism and a particular idea of private property, when philosophers like Locke started to explore the conflict between different rights in society. The medieval period is one where a holistic view of society still prevailed, and the individual was seen as part of a larger unit, where the scope for individual action was properly part of the action of the unit itself. No doubt the notion of negative liberty was familiar to the individual when one found that something one wished to do was prevented by someone or something else, but this was too banal a concept to be worth extending into a political principle. The important feature of liberty is its links with where we as human beings ought to be trying to go and what we should be trying to do, and this is clearly positive liberty which is at issue.

This has certainly been the accepted line on the topic. For example, in his 'Two Concepts of Liberty', Isaiah Berlin says, 'Christian (and Jewish or Moslem) belief in the absolute authority of divine or natural laws, or in the equality of all men in the sight of God, is very different from belief in freedom to live as one prefers' (p.147). Yet we know from the vast corpus of halakha that the issue of how Jews are to live is not something settled from the beginning by the divinity of the law. The law has to be interpreted and understood in one as opposed to another way, and this involves choice by the believer. It should not be an arbitrary choice, of course, but one based on the strength of arguments and traditions, and yet it is still a choice. But, it will be said, this is not a good example of a real choice, because the chooser is operating from within a system of constraint, the system of halakha itself, and so while one is free *to* pick a course of action, one is not free *from* the form of life of which that action is an ingredient. Yet surely there is no negative liberty which is entirely unrelated to a form of positive liberty. Choice cannot take place within a complete vacuum. There have to be some criteria for choice to be rational, and those criteria are going to be linked to a system of beliefs and values in terms of which they are appropriate or not.

The system of beliefs and values which are relevant to this discussion is that present in Judaism, and in particular in Jewish philosophy. As far as the religion itself is concerned, there are no difficulties at all in extracting an account of negative liberty. Much of Jewish law deals with our rights and duties vis-à-vis each other, and it is clear that the notion of the individual which is at issue here is not dissimilar from the modern notion of the individual. That is why, presumably, it is possible for Jews to adhere to much the same system of legislation over huge periods of time and in very different places. But is there a corresponding notion of negative liberty in Jewish philosophy, especially in those forms of Jewish philoso-phy in the Middle Ages which pre-date the Renaissance, the Enlightenment, and the growth of capitalism? It is tempting to reply in the negative, and for all the reasons we have thus far provided. Jewish philosophers were more committed to Plato on politics than to Aristotle, they were more interested in devising routes to God than in discussing practical arrangements in this world, and they were not in any case in a position to devise a political philosophy which would apply to an existing indepen-dent polity.

But if we look closer we will find that this common assumption about the nature of medieval Jewish philosophy is questionable. It is certainly true that the use of Plato led to a rather unAristotelian political philosophy, yet the thought of Aristotle ran deep. The central Aristotelian idea which remained powerful was that of the unity of the virtues, which leads inevitably to the notion of the significance of balance in living well. We need to employ a repertoire of virtues if we are to live well, and we must respond to the vagaries of fortune through those virtues to make the best we can of it. Now, this notion of

balance became an important constituent in the medieval
Jewish (and Islamic) view of how one ought to live. One has to
bear in mind here the general acceptance of the rather Platonic
idea that matter is the source of evil. Matter, that which has not
been formed, is often treated as the form of limitation. It
prevents human beings from rising to the level of the angels, it
serves as a constant obstacle to our self-perfection being
anything more than human self-perfection. This is not an
especially unusual idea, since we are all familiar with the
myriad of ways in which our status as material creatures gets in
the way of our ability to be entirely or predominantly spiritual
beings, even to the limited extent that I may be obliged to break
off typing this by the necessity to have a cup of tea.

   We are accustomed, then, to finding that things get in our way
when we try to accomplish tasks. This can be expressed in terms
of a number of different, albeit related, dichotomies or polarities,
all of which are important in Jewish philosophy. These pairs
organize and assign values to the lives of human beings within
the context of that philosophy:

mind	body
culture	nature
reason	emotion
objectivity	subjectivity
private	public
form	matter
body	soul
nomos	Torah
awe	prayer
intellectual	practical
scarcity	plenty
wisdom	virtue

Let us examine some of these briefly. The soul is capable of
reaching great heights of perfection, it can unite with the active
intellect and even come close to knowing God. Yet while we are
embodied creatures it will be perpetually limited and restricted
by the body. There are laws which are appropriate for organizing
the body, i.e. the material and social parts of our lives. These are
the nomoi, and they involve the rational solution of problems
that arise when the varied interests of human beings have to be
reconciled. Then there is Torah, which not only sorts out our

social problems, but is also capable of placing us on a much higher spiritual level, by addressing our natures as more than just social beings. There are practical duties which are incumbent upon us, and these should not be ignored by anyone. For many people this is the only level at which they can perform, since they are unsuited or unwilling to think seriously about what the rationale for those duties is. On the other hand, if we are able to think about such deeper issues, we should, provided it does not interfere with our ability to carry out our religious obligations. We shall as a result become aware of a deeper form of understanding of the deity and indeed of ourselves, and we can perfect ourselves intellectually insofar as our capacities make this feasible. Some people can really only practice their Judaism through obeying the rituals of religion, while others can as well as this engage in conceptual investigation of the roots of their beliefs.

Many Jews find prayer to be the main route to an understanding of God, and through prayer they will establish their links with the deity. Others are able through prayer to reach a higher awareness of God, in that they express their relationship with him largely through awe. That is, prayer is indeed important for them, but what lies at the basis of their attitude to God is just awe, and they understand that the anthropomorphic aspects of prayer are really only rather misleading ways for the majority of the community to grasp that which is literally ungraspable. Most people put a value on material things which accords with the value that society gives them, so that things which are ubiquitous and vital for our very lives become of little value, while rare and relatively superfluous objects are treated as precious and eminently desirable. Everybody in society has to work within such parameters, since even the individual who despises the values of the majority is obliged to share those values in practical life. Yet while one may understand the importance of going along with such social values, one can well appreciate how far they diverge from the real values which different things have. As a result, one will come to value simple things, bread and water for instance, far above jewels and fine clothes.

Now, it will be said that these polarities may indeed define some of the features of medieval Jewish philosophy, and yet they go no way at all to establish the existence of a notion of negative liberty. Such a notion is irretrievably tied in with the concept of liberalism, and that is itself a profoundly alien idea with respect to the period in question. Liberalism has its historical origins in an atmosphere of exhaustion with the theological conflicts in sixteenth- and seventeenth-century Europe, and these led to a lack of confidence in the ability of human beings to be reconciled on religious issues. These differences came to be seen as irreconcilable, and so there was the need for a structure to contain and manage conflict, a structure within which conflicting points of view can coexist without having to be finally resolved. This is very different from the view of the world held by medieval Jewish philosophy. There certainly was an understanding that there exist conflicting points of view between religions (and where better to find these but in works like Halevi's *Kuzari*?), and even within religion itself, but the idea that these are all acceptable alternatives was absent. There was no doubt but that the Jewish religion represents the truth, and while one might respect alternative ways of understanding the nature of reality, one should not go so far as to suggest that these alternatives might be valid. Some are better than others, or more accurately, some are worse than others, but none of them is a viable alternative to Judaism, which represents the way things really are. There is a complication here, in that Judaism as a non-proselytizing religion really only applies in toto to Jews, yet if we put this aside we are still left with a very different view of how one's own faith relates to other faiths as compared with classical liberalism.

Yet is negative liberty as a political concept essentially connected to liberalism? Not necessarily. Negative liberty is the idea that there is value in being able to act without interference. As a political concept it is the principle that the individual should not, other things being equal, be prevented by the state or community from acting as he or she wishes to act. It is based on the idea that there is value in the ability of the individual being able to decide his or her own course of action, and that one attracts merit in being free to work out how one is going to proceed. Within the context of a system of religious truths, only some such choices will be correct, yet the ability to choose is itself something which Judaism recognises as valuable. Judaism takes very seriously the fact that we are embodied creatures, that we are not angels, and the polarities which result

160

form the basis of our lives. As we try to perfect ourselves intellectually we may come to regret that we are embodied, insofar as our embodiment interferes with our intellectual progress, yet the fact that we are embodied is a fact about us as human beings rather than as angels and it forms the essential parameters within which human development is possible.

It might be argued, though, that what we have here is a notion of freedom as a human characteristic, but not a notion of political liberty. For the latter to have purchase, it would need to be linked with a secular view of the state, and we know that Jewish philosophy in the Middle Ages tended to interpret the state in essentially spiritual terms. There is scope for the Jewish community to achieve a limited form of progress within the context of the Gentile state, but we need to have a Jewish state, or the arrival of the messianic age, before we can see any genuine Jewish political structure which is able to do more than preserve the Jewish community within an (at worst) hostile and (at best) indifferent political environment. Moreover, what is valuable about freedom is related to positive rather than negative liberty. We are free to follow the rules of Torah and as such we can realize ourselves as proper human beings and adequate Jews. The idea that we are surrounded by political space which gives us scope for action and independence is very foreign from the idea that there is only one direction in which we can go if we are to adhere to halakha, and that direction has been set supernaturally from the time of the beginning of the world.

This is certainly the traditional way of looking at the issue, and it has the advantage that if we adopt it we can make neat distinctions between different political attitudes finding an appropriate context at different times. Yet despite this we should be wary of such an approach. It is certainly correct to see an important difference existing between positive and negative liberty, but this difference can be exaggerated. If we are going to be free to follow a course of action, perhaps a course of action which represents the path which we ought to follow, then we must also be free from interference in following that path. We must be aware of the notion of ourselves as individuals surrounded by other individuals who are potentially allies or enemies in our pursuit of our ends. How could such a notion be historically restricted to only certain times and places? It is surely part and parcel of any life in any human (non-utopian) community. In just the same way that a human child starts to develop ideas of self and distinctness from others as it grows up, so in any society the individual is going to come to some sort of understanding of himself as an individual, and of the other as an other. This is going to lead to questions about how far the scope for action of the individual is going to be acceptable given the desires of others to act also. In other words, we see the development of a notion of negative liberty.

It might be thought that it is never going to be difficult to establish that human beings have a notion of negative liberty, since our relationships with other people are such an obvious issue for any living creature living within any sort of community. What makes this notion of liberty a political notion? The answer to this question lies precisely in its expression as an idea to help us understand life within a group. Let us take as an example here the ways in which Maimonides discusses the development of the laws of the Jewish community as a route to the growing self-understanding of that community as distinct from other similar communities and as imbued with a spiritual dimension. Maimonides acknowledges that God could have acted on us non-politically in the sense that he could have miraculously changed our dispositions so that we would reject all forms of idolatry and foreign customs all at once (*Guide* 3.32). But he decided to work with our existing nature, which is after all a nature which he himself created, and present us with laws which encourage us to change gradually our ways of thinking and operating until we acquire other and superior dispositions. We are free from direct interference from the deity, although it remains always open to him to act in this way, because he wants us to be free to change in particular ways. This freedom brings along with it the possibility of acquiring merit, so it is far from superfluous.

God is in the position of the teacher in a school who sets his children a problem, a problem which they can only solve by working together and developing appropriate communal attitudes. The teacher could solve the problem immediately, since she knows what the answer is and she knows how the children should dispose themselves to reach that answer. Yet she wants them to work it out for themselves, since only through such behavior will they more surely acquire the social and other skills which she has as her educational goal for them. The children have to learn political skills, they have to learn how to work together, whom they should support, how they should divide the task up and what amount of effort they should put into it. As a result of this they will have learned a lot about themselves as individuals and as members of a group, and if the teacher is an Aristotelian she will realize that these are two sides of the same coin. They will have learned a lot about how organizations work, how they grow and how fragile they can be, and how each individual child relates to being part of a group. This is precisely what the Jews work out as they progress from being an ordinary group of people to being special. We might take an argument of Soloveitchik here to make this point even stronger. He points out that of supreme importance in Judaism are not the times and places when God chooses the Jews, but rather when and where the Jews choose God, when they open themselves to him and to his teaching. It is an essential part of this possibility that they should be free to act in this way, since otherwise they are merely reacting to what someone is imposing on them. So it is hardly difficult to argue that there is a strong notion of political liberty within Jewish philosophy even in the Middle Ages.

Yet one might still wonder whether we have a notion of political liberty here, as opposed to a notion that there is or should be scope for human beings to act without interference from others, other things being equal. It is all too easy to transfer a concept from a context in which it really flourishes to an entirely different context, one where it seems to share some of the features it had when properly used, but which in fact lacks other features which are really quite crucial to its correct application. Often coming to such a judgment is a complex process; it is not simply a matter of deciding whether the concept is applicable or not. There will be circumstances whch make it more appropriate, and others which make it less appropriate. We do not have a full-blooded concept of political liberty in Jewish political philosophy in the period in question, the idea that the individual citizen has the basic right to non-interference in his actions, nor do we have the notion that whatever the citizen might do is valid, provided that it does not interfere with the liberty of others. There is, on the contrary, a strong notion of positive liberty, the assertion that there is a right path and that the citizen should join that path, and if he does not, then there is no value in his actions, however free they are. Of course, we should choose the right path freely, and unless we do so there is little merit in what we choose, but there is an important difference between claiming that there is a notion of negative freedom in medieval Jewish philosophy and claiming that there is a notion of free will. The latter certainly has a place, but the former seems still to be a shaky concept to apply to this period of thought. It clearly does not apply, if it applies at all, in precisely the way in which a notion of negative liberty can be described in the philosophies of liberalism. Yet there is value in medieval Jewish philosophy in going awry, not just in the possibility of going awry, and this is what we require to establish something which has many of the features of negative liberty. Individuals make mistakes, and as a result of those mistakes they are in a position to learn how not to make mistakes and how to follow the correct line of behavior. In the Jewish state such mistakes should be allowed to occur, since if this were not allowed the virtue which accrued to its citizens would be won at the expense of free choice. Once one allows that such incorrect actions have a role to play in the state, one has allowed in a notion of negative liberty, the idea that there is value in preserving the freedom of individuals from interference by the citizen, however misguided or ill-advised they are, provided that their freedom does not restrict the freedom of others.

What we should recall here is that although it is no doubt true that medieval Jewish political philosophy is heavily influenced by Plato, it is not totally dominated by him. For Plato, education is a means for the spiritual growth of the organism which is the state as a whole, while only some members of the state really succeed in achieving an awareness of true realities. In Jewish philosophy education is a means by which everyone in the state can come closer to God, both intellectually and through activity, and it can only work by guiding people to the truth, not forcing them or lying to them about some aspect of the truth. Guiding, leading, showing the way all imply that there will be some who fail to follow the correct route, and fall by the wayside in one sense or another. The individual should have the right to err, and there is value in his waywardness. Certainly it would be better if he did not err, but unless there is an alternative course of action which is allowed to take place, there is far less merit in being virtuous. The individual has a right to do what is wrong, and that right is the right of negative liberty. There is no doubt

164

that the point would hardly be put in this sort of way in the political philosophy of the time, but despite this that is the point which is being made.

We tend to divide up periods of human history and label them appropriately, as though the nature of human life were very different at different times and in different places. So we make a clear divide between the medieval and the modern, for example, although we might argue as to when precisely the divide occurs. This can be very misleading when we are considering notions which are so basic that they surely apply to any form of human life experienced in communities. As Levinas puts it in 'The Temptation of the Temptation', 'The fact that every other, my neighbour, is also a "third party" in relation to another neighbour, invites me to justice, to weighing matters, and to thought' (p. 50). All we need, that is, is three people and we immediately get into quite complex issues to do with political liberty and justice. How then could there not be a notion of political liberty in medieval Jewish philosophy? Certainly it is not discussed in precisely the same ways as is common today, but it remains part of the warp and woof of the intellectual fabric of the time. This is a very encouraging thought, for it suggests that the ideas of the past are not distant echoes from a strange and mysterious time, but they are attempts at grappling with issues and problems which still concern us today.

References

Baer, Y. 1934. 'Eretz Yisrael ve-galut be-einei ha-dorot shel yemei ha-beinayyim.' *Tzion* 6, pp. 149–71

Berlin, I. 1968. 'Two Concepts of Liberty', in A. Quinton (ed.), *Political Philosophy*. Oxford: Oxford University Press, pp. 141–52

Goodman, L. 1991. *On Justice: An Essay in Jewish Philosophy*. New Haven: Yale University Press

—— 1992. 'The Individual and the Community in the Normative Traditions of Judaism', in D.H. Frank (ed.), *Autonomy and Judaism: The Individual and the Community in Jewish Philosophical Thought*. Albany: State University of New York Press, pp. 69–120

Leaman, O. 1997. *Moses Maimonides*. Richmond: Curzon

Levinas, E. 1990. *Nine Talmudic Readings*, translated by A. Aronowicz. Bloomington: Indiana University Press

MacIntyre, A. 1981. *After Virtue: A Study in Moral Theory*. London: Duckworth

Melamed, A. 1995. 'The Attitude toward Democracy in Medieval Jewish Philosophy', in D.H. Frank (ed.), *Commandment and Community: New Essays in Jewish Legal and Political Philosophy*. Albany: State University of New York Press, pp. 173–94

Rosenthal, E. 1960. *Griechisches Erbe in der Jüdischen Religionsphilosophie des Mittelalters*. Stuttgart: Kohlhammer

Soloveitchik, J. 1983. *Halakhic Man*. Philadelphia: Jewish Publication Society

Weiler, G. 1989. *Jewish Theocracy*. Leiden: Brill

This paper was read at the seventeenth annual conference of the Academy of Jewish Philosophy conference, at Vanderbilt University, in June 1996, and I should like to thank the participants for their very helpful comments. In particular I wish to thank David Shatz for his comments, which made me think again about the main direction of the argument, although I doubt whether I have revised it enough to satisfy him on this issue.

An earlier and shorter version has been published in the *Rivista di Storia della Filosofia* LII, 1 (1997), pp. 141–51, and I am grateful for permission to reproduce parts of it here.

CHAPTER EIGHT

Liberty, Authority, and Consent in Judaism

A Maimonidean Reconstruction of the Biblical Text

Aryeh Botwinick

1. Introduction

We all know that Maimonides did not write a commentary on the Bible.[1] Or perhaps he did, under the guise of doing something else? In his commentary on the Mishnah (more specifically, in his commentary on the first mishnah of *Perek Chelek* in *Sanhedrin* [p. 140 in the Kafiah edition]) Maimonides says that he plans to write a treatise in which he will collect and explicate all of the *derashot* found in the Talmud and elsewhere and will show which are to be construed literally and which have to be understood metaphorically – and which occurred in a dream but were recorded as if they took place in a wakeful state. In the introduction to the first part of the *Guide* Maimonides alludes to his promise to write a book (or books) in which he would 'explain all the difficult passages in the *midrashim* where the external sense manifestly contradicts the truth and departs from the intelligible. They are all parables' (*Guide* I: introduction:9 [Pines]). He says that even though he began writing books of this sort and actually 'composed a part of them,' his project became impaled on the horns of a dilemma. If he followed the Rabbis' model of concealing 'what ought to be concealed,' his purpose in writing the book would have been defeated because he would merely 'have replaced one individual by another of the same species.' 'If, on the other hand,' he says, 'we explained what ought to be explained, it would be unsuitable for the vulgar among the people.' He intimates in the conclusion of the paragraph from which I have been quoting that the project of elucidating the biblical exegeses of the Rabbis was not really

167

abandoned, but was reconceived and continued at least in part in the *Guide* in accordance with a revised set of ground rules that he now summarizes: 'We have confined ourselves to mentioning briefly the foundations of belief and general truths, while dropping hints that approach a clear exposition' (*Guide* I: introduction:10).

James Joyce in *Ulysses* calls Averroes and Moses Maimonides 'dark men in mien and movement, flashing in their mocking mirrors the obscure soul of the world, a darkness shining in brightness which brightness could not comprehend.'[2] Perhaps the 'darkness shining in brightness which brightness could not comprehend' refers not only to the ways in which negative theology both presupposes and links up with a vast anti-realist metaphysics, but also the ways in which that metaphysics yields a hermeneutical key for reconstructing the biblical text as being preoccupied with a dramatic Absence, rather than literally detailing the communications of an overwhelming Presence. Maimonides makes his argument for negative theology both analytically and exegetically by reinterpreting one term and text in the Bible after another as reflecting his understanding of the nature of God.[3] The exegetical passages work to reinforce the coherence of the argument of the *Guide* because if the argument for negative theology is a largely skeptical one, then the materials out of which it is constructed have to be mainly skeptical, too. This is to say that on grounds of consistency Maimonides cannot transcend a rhetorical defense – a persuasive manipulation of the biblical texts to support his theological and philosophical arguments – of his negative theological vision. It is thus the exegetical passages with which the *Guide* abounds that constitute Maimonides' implicit commentary on the Bible. Unlike many other medieval Jewish commentaries on the biblical text, Maimonides' commentary is informed by a systematic philosophical understanding that moves beyond local context to grapple with issues of larger philosophical import.

In order to piece together a distinctly Maimonidean, negative theological reading of the Bible, we begin with a discussion of how he analyzes the Garden of Eden story. The disenchantment of literalism and embrace of skepticism which he expresses there set the tone for nearly all subsequent interpretations which he provides of the biblical text. What emerges from his construal of the expulsion from Eden is a conception of radical human liberty that has distinct political overtones. I next try to illustrate how the thematics of the Garden of Eden story get duplicated in the Joseph story. Proceeding from Genesis to Exodus, I show how Maimonides' reconstruction of the events surrounding divine revelation on Sinai issue forth in a distinctive conception of the relationship between authority and consent that is a harbinger of modern liberalism. Next I explicate the relationship between Sinaitic revelation and the Exodus story in ways that more fully highlight the liberal, contractarian political import of the latter. Then I will try to theorize the relationship between the Jethro story and Sinaitic revelation in a Maimonidean vein that effects some variations on his central theme of negative theology. I then juxtapose to the Maimonidean readings of the central events of the Exodus a pivotal dispute between Rabbi Akiva and Simeon Imsoni that can be most appropriately interpreted as a controversy centering around the political and structural implications stemming from negative theological doctrine. I also discuss from a Maimonidean perspective how one theologically distinguishes between the sin of the golden calf and the building of the *mishkan*. Finally, I conclude my discussion of the Exodus with an analysis of how Maimonides' conception of the messianic age casts a retrospective gloss on the hermeneutics he applied to Moses' role in the Exodus story.

In the next section I show how Maimonides' historicism, structural-functionalism, and philosophy of law redound upon his conception of authority as being grounded in consent. In a concluding section that considers Maimonides' interpretation of the book of Job I explore further the implications of Maimonides' philosophy of law.

2. The Garden of Eden and Joseph Stories

Maimonides' interpretation of the Garden of Eden story in the Bible in *Guide* I:2 is entirely in conformity with his convention-alist philosophy of language (*Guide* II:30:357–58). According to Maimonides, the pre-expulsion state was defined by Adam's ability to distinguish between truth and falsehood:

Through the intellect one distinguishes between truth and falsehood, and that was found in [Adam] in its perfection and integrity. Fine and bad, on the other hand, belong to the things generally accepted as known, not to those cognized by the intellect. . . . However, when he disobeyed and inclined toward his desires of the imagination and the pleasures of his corporeal senses – inasmuch as it is said: that the tree was good for food and that it was a delight to the eyes (Genesis 3:5) – he was punished by being deprived of that intellectual apprehension. He therefore disobeyed the commandment that was imposed upon him on account of his intellect and, becoming endowed with the faculty of apprehending generally accepted things, he became absorbed in judging things to be bad or fine. . . . With regard to what is of necessity, there is no good and evil at all, but only the false and the true. (*Guide* I:2:24–25)

Thus, the story of the expulsion from the Garden of Eden amounts to convention being substituted for truth. Man can no longer know anything beyond what convention sanctions and decrees. 'Good' and 'bad' which are conventionalist terms are substituted for 'true' and 'false' which are essentialist terms.[4]

In his interpretation of the Garden of Eden story, there is an important point of affinity with Hobbes. With the expulsion from Eden, truth is placed beyond the realm of human inquiry and discourse. Truth is what Adam and Eve could utter before they were thrown out of the Garden of Eden. After the expulsion, truth remains beyond the metaphysical and semantic pale. The sort of commentary that Maimonides provides upon the Garden of Eden story is suggestive of the skeptical idealism developed by Hobbes. Debarred from a neutral objectivist verbal currency to access natural, psychological, and social phenomena, we are reduced to a conception of truth that is limited to 'the right ordering of names in our affirmations.'[5] If after the expulsion from Eden we cannot aspire to a truth beyond convention, then there is never a point in our theoretical imaginings and projections and the practical and technological translations of the same where we safely drop anchor upon a reality beyond our verbal constructions. Hobbes charts in a systematic way the freedoms and limitations – and the freedoms afforded by our new limitations – of our post-expulsion human estate.

In his paraphrase of the Garden of Eden story, Maimonides provides us with an utterly subversive hermeneutical code for unraveling the teaching of the Bible. The Bible and consequently Judaism become for Maimonides a series of object lessons not about belief in God and the attainment of a secure truth about the human condition, but about the impossibility of belief as ordinarily conceived and the unavailability of a secure truth about human beings and the world. Through his reading of the Garden of Eden story, Maimonides converts the Bible into a skeptical text, a skeptical scripture. The Garden of Eden story in Maimonides' interpretation of it epitomizes the impossibility of a religious life as mass consciousness has generally understood it with its reassurances and cosmically-emanating importunings that confer certainty and direction upon an ordinary human life. Negative theology is already presaged in the emblematic tale that sets the human story in motion. The Bible in Maimonides' decoding of it is about the self-consuming and self-erasing character of its own content. The Bible as a religious and historical text is about the receding and ultimate absence of religion outside the sphere of the sociological experience of humankind.

The biblical text of the Joseph story seems to corroborate and reinforce Maimonides' reading of the expulsion from Eden story. In the biography of Joseph, his self-aggrandizing dreams become an instrumentality for their own realization. The very jealousy which his dreams arouse in his brothers leads them to wrench him away from their ancestral home and to sell him to a caravan of Ishmaelites who sell him to Midianites who in turn sell him into bondage in Egypt. (Rashi on Genesis 37:28) His brothers' very large-scale spurning of him provoked by his dreams becomes in a Machiavellian sense Joseph's opportunity for making his dreams come true. A sequence of events is engendered whereby he becomes the second-in-command in Egypt and they turn to him in a spirit of complete subservience to sustain them in a period of great famine. By resisting and rejecting Joseph's dreams, his brothers ensure their ultimate actualization. Joseph, in turn, by having, harboring, and announcing these dreams in the first place inserts enough hard-core data and elements into the world to trigger a causal chain that facilitates their realization.

The Joseph story taken as a whole seems to underscore Maimonides' point that after Eden we are no longer capable of formulating and sustaining judgments of 'true' and 'false,' but only more conventional judgments of 'fine' and 'bad.' Joseph's personality is defined not in terms of some rational essence, but is rather constituted by some colossal assertion of will that ends up re-making reality in its own image. The Joseph story appears to be insinuating to us a skeptical idealist metaphysics and epistemology as the basis for the belief system and sets of practices which it seeks to foster. 'Theory' and 'self' – indeed most of the stable categories through which we strive to organize and orient our lives – are underdetermined by facts. The facts of Joseph's life get formed in relation to the theories which he propounds about them rather than the other way around. The 'true' and 'false' of Joseph's life are fashioned and made – rather than simply found and affirmed. The 'human taint' extends to the outward theoretical parameters that give shape and content to a human life.

This reading of the Joseph story receives additional reinforce-ment from one of Maimonides' numerous philological-theological exercises in the *Guide*. In *Guide* II:48 he says that 'when speaking of things the cause of which lies with human free choice – such as the war waged by a ruling people upon another people or an individual's setting out to harm another individual, even if he only insults him,' the name of God is invoked because 'intermediate causes are sometimes omitted in the dicta of the prophets.' Since God's 'willing' on a literal level is as incompre-hensible to us as any other attribute we might ascribe to him, the relevant causal frame of reference for Maimonides becomes human willing and free choice. As an example of an event whose cause lies 'with human free choice' Maimonides cites the sentence which Joseph proclaims to his brothers, 'It was not you that sent me hither, but God' (Genesis 45:8). Likewise, another key sentence which Joseph announces to his brothers (which occurs immediately before the one just cited) Maimonides subsumes under the rubric of 'accidental things due to pure chance': 'And God sent me before you' (Genesis 45:7). The key words that occur in both sentences are grammatical variants of the verb 'to send.' In the conclusion of II:48, Maimonides summarizes his conception of the role of this verb (among a family of four other terms) in the biblical narrative: 'Accordingly it has become clear to you that in order to designate the shaping of the causes in whatever way they are shaped, whether they are causes by essence or by accident or by free choice or by volition, these five terms are used – namely, *to command, to say, to speak, to send, to call'* (italics in original).

There is a remarkable midrashic formulation that encapsulates how skeptical idealism might be envisioned as the key to the theological system propounded by Judaism. The midrash says that 'The Torah was not given except to those who ate manna' (*Mechilta, Beshalach*, parsha 17; *Tanchuma, Beshalach*, Ot 20).[6] What is the connection between the reception of the Torah and the eating of manna? The Jewish community that ate manna in the desert on a regular basis for a period close to forty years formed different habits of thought association from those that prevailed among their more prosaic contemporaries. Because they enjoyed food that they did not have to toil for in any of the accustomed ways they immediately connected nature with God. They identified the natural with the miraculous and associated the merged category of nature-miracle with God. The author of this midrashic statement wants us to take our cue from the generation of Jewish nomads in the desert. We who need to till the soil and go through a whole rigorous agricultural regimen before the earth will yield up to us her fruits can also through a redirection of our mental outlook and energies come up with the same thought association as the generation in the desert. If there reside no intrinsic connections or rational essences in nature – if perception and causality are largely a function of habitual association – then if we were to train ourselves as a matter of course to link so-called natural processes with God, then we would collectively inhabit a God-suffused universe where the boundaries between nature and miracle would have been eroded through our new mental orientations. How do we choose between one mapping of reality and the other – the God-suffused one and the God-disenchanted one? The implicit answer of the author of this midrashic statement is that on the basis of the so-called facts there is no basis for choosing between them. The facts are what they are (what we take them to be) because of our antecedent theoretical commitments and understandings. The strongest case for those standing on the religion side of the religion-science dichotomy is that those standing on the other side cannot do any better in terms of validating and justifying their position than those standing on the religion side. The Torah in its full philosophic sense was only given to those who could appreciate the inescapability of merely negative justification that is under-written by a skeptical idealist metaphysics.

3. Revelation: Authority and Consent

There are three references in the eighth chapter of the *Laws concerning the Basic Principles of the Torah* to a plural, communal affirmation of the prophetic mission of Moses: 'We saw with our own eyes, and heard with our own ears.' Moses enjoys a special sanctity – plays a pivotal role – within the monotheistic religious tradition. He sets the whole tradition in motion. The legitimating revelation that validates a whole tradition occurs with him. On what basis is Moses believed? What authenticates revelation? The approach that Maimonides adopts both in the *Guide* and in the *Laws concerning the Basic Principles of the Torah* in his *Code* is duplicated by Hobbes in parts three and four of *Leviathan*. First, Maimonides empha-sizes the primacy of the auditory over the visual. Revelation – even the grand foundational revelation at Sinai – is mainly an auditory experience, not a visual one. 'And the voice speaks to him and we listen.'[7] Revelation is more a function of voice – of speech – than of spectacle – what is seen. Auditory verbs and images predominate over visual ones in Maimonides' and Hobbes's accounts of revelation. Speech requires an addressee. The addressee in all instances is one person, namely, Moses. The rest of the Jewish nation are collective eavesdroppers upon that personal auditory encounter. Before the advent of modern technology, auditory experiences are much more private, much less subject to mutual verification, than visual ones. The relevant actors at revelation are God and Moses. Given the primarily auditory character of the experience, the rest of the Jewish nation are spectators for whom the content of revelation is a matter of interpretation. On what basis can the biblical interpretation of revelation be validated? Maimonides' implicit answer to this question is entirely in keeping with his skeptical reading of the tenets of monotheism. The interpretation of 'revelation' as revelation – its construal in these terms – is validated by the consensual judgment of the Jewish people: '*We* saw . . . *we* heard' (emphasis added). There is even an intimation of a more audacious extension of this line of approach. In the third paragraph of the eighth chapter of the *Laws concerning the Basic Principles of the Torah*, Maimonides says: 'But with our eyes we saw and with our ears we heard the divine voice, even as he also heard it.' Moses' hearing is ontologically leveled to the hearing of the rest of the Jewish community. Just as for them it was a matter of interpretation what transpired, so too for the direct recipient of revelation it was a matter of interpretation what was indeed taking place. The radical human freedom to fix the sense and pin down the reference of a current experience in relation to endlessly receding verbal and theoretical contexts was present for the direct addressee of revelation himself, namely, Moses. Moses chose to read the Sinaitic events in a certain way, and his reading was corroborated by the rest of the Jewish people.

Maimonides follows the Rabbis in restricting God's direct address to the people to only two of the rabbinically-sanctioned six hundred and thirteen commandments of the Torah, namely, the first two commandments of the Decalogue (affirming 'the existence of the deity and his being one') (*Guide* II:33:364). With regard to these, Maimonides develops an astoundingly negative hermeneutical approach which emphasizes that the role of the term 'God' in this context of direct revelation is merely to rule out dependence on a special intermediary such as a prophet in order to become aware of these two focal points of revelation, but not to suggest that God literally spoke. Since God's existence and his being one are speculative truths (truths of reason alone), they can be appropriated through a proper and sufficient cultivation of reason without recourse to a special set of charismatic powers attributed by the masses to the prophet.

Maimonides invokes additional strategies to qualify and limit the efficacy of prophecy understood on a literal level even with regard to the first two commandments of the Decalogue. He says concerning these primary commandments, 'As for the voice of the Lord, I mean the created voice from which the *speech* [of God] was understood' (*Guide* II:33:365). Given the premises of negative theology, if a voice was heard at all even in relation to the first two commandments, it could not have been God's voice (since God does not speak in the way human beings speak), but only 'the created voice' which required interpretation and ultimately the backing of consensus in order to be attributed to God.

175

'Know with regard to that voice too,' Maimonides adds, 'their rank was not equal to the rank of Moses our Master. I shall draw your attention to this secret, and I shall let you know that this is a matter that is transmitted by tradition in the religious community and that is known to its men of knowledge. Thus in all the passages in which you will find, And the Lord spoke [va-yedabber] to Moses saying, Onqelos translates: And the Lord spoke (u-mallel]. Thus: And God spoke [va-yedabber] all [these] words [Exodus 20:1], is translated: And the Lord spoke [u-mallel] all [these] words. On the other hand, the words of Israel to Moses: But let not God speak [yedabber] with us [Exodus 20:16], he translates: [Speech] should not be spoken [yitmallel] with us on the part of the Lord. Thus he, peace be on him, has made clear to you the proposition that we have set forth in detail' (Guide II:33:365). Apparently, given Moses' philosophical dis-countings of the literalness of God's appearances, it is theologi-cally permissible to translate God's speech to him in a literal way, since, given the nature of the addressee, *he* will transpose it to the theologically and metaphysically correct register. In the case of the masses of the Jewish community, however, who are likely to be beguiled into thinking that they heard the voice of God, the de-literalizing of the biblical text has to be undertaken by the biblical translator in order to restore the negative theological integrity of the narrative. In relation to the community of Israel, it is 'speech' rather than 'God' that speaks.

In order to heighten his account of the mystification of the people, Maimonides adds: 'All that you find mentioned about hearing many *voices* – as for instance the dictum: And all the people saw the voices, and so on [Exodus 20:15] – refers only to the voice of the trumpet, the thunderings, and the like' (Guide II:33:365).

Maimonides reinforces his naturalistic construal of Moses' prophetic mission when he glosses a key sentence in the Torah's eulogy for Moses at the end of the book of Deuteronomy: 'This is the meaning of the dictum: And there hath not arisen a prophet since, and so on, in all the signs and wonders, and so on, in the sight of all Israel [Deuteronomy 34:10–12]. For here it estab-lishes a connection and a tie between the two notions, namely, that there will not arise either someone who will have apprehensions similar to his or one who will perform actions similar to his' (Guide II:35:368). In this passage, Maimonides establishes an equivalence between Moses' apprehensions and his actions, as if to suggest that the key for unraveling one must be invoked to make sense of the other. Just like the actions (in the light of Maimonides' discussion of miracles (at *Guide* II:29:345–46) need to be understood with the naturalistic factors predominating, so too the apprehensions need to be assessed with the naturalistic factors predominating. With this textual gloss as a backdrop, in the next paragraph Maimonides goes on to state even more boldly and simply: 'The extraordinary character of his apprehension is similar to the extraordinary character of his actions' (*Guide* II:35:369).

At the conclusion of II:38 Maimonides emphasizes once again the equation between prophecy and cultivation of the intellect: 'Therefore one ought not to pay attention to one whose rational faculty has not become perfect and who has not attained the ultimate term of speculative perfection. For only one who achieves speculative perfection is able to apprehend other objects of knowledge when there is an overflow of the divine intellect toward him. It is he who is in true reality a prophet. This is explicitly stated: And the prophet [possesseth] a heart of wisdom [Psalms 90:12]. It says here that one who is a prophet in true reality has a heart of wisdom. This too ought to be known' (*Guide* II:38:378). In order for this passage to come fully into focus, we need to pin down what Maimonides means by 'divine overflow.' At II:12:279, Maimonides defines 'divine overflow' negatively as 'the action of one who is not a body.' In terms of what I am describing as Maimonides' negative hermeneutics, overflow needs to be grasped in relation to what it rules out, something that can be directly, materially, physically, palpably perceived, not in terms of what it ostensibly affirms, some metaphoric substance called 'overflow.' Viewed in this light, the larger passage that I have cited argues for the conceptual equivalence of 'speculative perfection' with 'prophecy.' The second term almost without remainder is subsumable by the first.

At II:39 Maimonides also relates Moses' uniqueness as a prophet to the fact that he is the sole lawgiver among the prophets: 'After we have spoken of the quiddity of prophecy, have made known its true reality, and have made it clear that the prophecy of Moses our Master is different from that of the others, we shall say that the call to the Law followed necessarily from that apprehension alone [i.e., that of Moses]. For nothing similar to the call addressed to us by Moses our Master had been made before him by any one of those we know who lived in the time between Adam and him; nor was a call similar to that one made by one of our prophets after him' (*Guide* II:39:378–79). Apparently, according to Maimonides, the superiority of Moses' prophecy resides in the fact that unlike earlier and later prophets, he was never for one instant distracted by the possibility that there was anything beyond the projections triggered by moments of ecstatic transport to latch on to by way of identifying an external source for prophecy. For Moses, the coincidence between speculative perfection and 'prophecy' is more fully achieved than for any other prophet, and he realizes that without deliberate human intervention the fate of rationality itself (and our rational deliberations upon and delimitation of revelation) remain precarious. For Moses (according to Maimonides' reading of him), speculative insight leads to a recognition of the centrality of law (a systematic engendering and allocation of structures of authority) in regulating human affairs. The limitations of reason that the rationally-cultivated person becomes privy to suggest that there is no piercing beyond structures of authority for framing and organizing human life. Reason and revelation rest upon authority, rather than authority being dependent on reason or revelation. These salient features of Hobbesian political thought are prefigured in Maimonidean teaching.

According to both Maimonides and Hobbes, after Sinai revelation plays a distinctively secondary role in the development of monotheistic religion to the scheme of authority relations introduced and sanctioned by Moses. 'Hence,' Maimonides says, 'one may conclude with regard to every prophet after Moses, that we do not believe in such a prophet because of the signs he shows, as much as to say that only if he shows a sign, we shall pay heed to him in all that he says, but we believe in him, because of the charge laid down by Moses in the Torah that if the prophet gives a sign, 'Ye shall listen to him' (Deuteronomy 18, 22); just as the lawgiver directed that a case is to be decided on the evidence of two witnesses even if we have no certainty as to whether they are testifying to the truth or to a falsehood. Similarly, it is our duty to listen to the prophet though we do not know if the sign he shows is genuine or has been performed with the aid of sorcery and by secret arts.'[8] Thus, the source of our obligation to future prophets is the political command of Moses, rather than the indubitableness of the sign provided by the prophet, which can never be rendered invulnerable to skeptical questioning.

Maimonides and Hobbes follow an identical strategy in squaring their interpretation of monotheistic teaching with the phenomena of revelation and prophecy. First, they restrict the scope of direct revelation (mouth-to-mouth or, in Onqelos' phrase, 'speech to speech') to the furthest extent possible – with Moses for both philosophers being the prime recipient. Second, aside from the pivotal figure(s), all subsequent manifestations of prophecy are a function of the scheme of authority relations introduced by the key figures (especially Moses), rather than purely religious phenomena that can be validated out of their own resources. Obedience to prophetic authority is ultimately analyzable in the same tautologous terms as obedience to God: they and he are accepted because they are accepted.

The central tenet of classical liberalism as articulated by Hobbes is prefigured and encapsulated in the Maimonidean passage where he says, 'and the voice speaks to him [namely, Moses].' The source of our obligations is that they stem from the appropriate and legitimate political authority. What is the ultimate sanction for political authority? In our justificatory quest, how far might we legitimately press? Hobbes's answer to this question is presaged by Maimonides: *'Our* eyes saw . . . *our* ears heard' (emphasis added). The interpretation that is consensually arrived at grounds political authority. In the last analysis, political authority rests upon consent. The ultimate move in the authority-game – invoking God's literal will or presence – breaks down according to both theorists of monotheism and what we are left with is human management and construal of the materials that from a rigorous philosophical perspective resist cooptation into a strictly God-ordained discourse. The ultimate symbol of authority – God – according to Maimonides' and Hobbes's monotheistic theorizing is a humanly-acquiesced-in symbol. Its coerciveness stems from below, not from above. Monotheistic theorizing – negative theology – in the hands of both Maimonides and Hobbes prefigures the liberal equation of political authority with consent.

179

Given the primacy assigned to the idea of authority in the foregoing account, one way to conceive the relationship between the textual accounts of slavery and bondage in Egypt and the exodus therefrom and the entry into the covenant with the monotheistic God at Sinai is to view the latter series of events as an implicit response to (an implicit) problem posed by the former. This problem has a logical-legal character. The recurring pattern manifested by Pharaoh's behavior was that the plagues were sufficient to jar Pharaoh from his complacency, but not enough to get him to comply with the word of God as transmitted by Moses. Each time witnessing the horrors that his recalcitrance unleashes he vows to let the Israelites go, but once the plague is removed through Moses' intervention he reneges on his commitment. As a formal logical-legal problem we could say that the dilemma posed for divine authority by Pharaoh's behavior is how to get the penalties for transgression of divine mandates (or threats thereof) to fully match the rewards and incentives attached for compliance with them. In Pharaoh's case, the two are pronouncedly asymmetrical. The rewards for even a promise to comport with God's word are immediate: Moses in his beseeching gets God to withdraw the particular plague. Once the status quo ante is restored (the plague is rescinded) and Pharaoh refuses to follow through on his promise, the visiting of additional plagues upon Pharaoh only initiates further rounds of the same asymmetry (the incentives are powerful enough to get Pharaoh to commit himself to compliance; the punishments are too tardy and too unthreatening to deflect him from a course of failing to follow through on his promises) without resolving the fundamental problem of authority of evoking timely compliance with its decrees.

The scheme of authority relations introduced at Sinai constitutes a veiled response to the problematics of Pharaonic disobedience manifested in Egypt. It accomplishes this on a dual level. Firstly, the monotheistic God reaffirmed at Sinai against whom the cardinal sin is idolatry (premature concre-tizations and reifications) insinuates a doctrine of radical human equality by his very conceptual remoteness and inaccessibility, and thus deflates temptations to transgression stemming from one's superior social position. In relation to the unmitigated transcendence of God, all human beings, no matter how exalted their lineage or magnificent their prowess, pale into insignificance and equality (or are leveled by their insignificance in relation to the monotheistic God into a condition of equality with other human beings). In comparison to the quasi-human gods of animistic religion who are themselves intensely competitive and who instill a spirit of competitiveness and inequality among their adherents, the monotheistic God by his august remoteness trivializes all human differences and distinctions and restores all of human-kind to a condition of de-divinized equality.

Secondly, the inscrutability of rewards and punishments that flows from the utter transcendence and hiddenness of the monotheistic God also works to tame a lone defier like Pharaoh. From a monotheistic perspective, rewards and punishments are humanly incalculable and a believer is defined precisely by his refusal to establish immediate palpable connections between success with virtue and failure with sin or corruption.[9] Timely compliance with divine edicts becomes a means for managing the tension engendered by a totally non-present God.

For analogous reasons the inscrutability of rewards and punishments stipulated by monotheistic doctrine helps to resolve the starter-up problem endemic to social contract theorizing, and this affords us an additional perspective as to why Hobbes in *Leviathan* devotes so much space and energy to setting forth his negative theological construal of monotheism. The game-theoretic, rational-choice mentality of the parties to the social contract can only be translated into a set of working arrangements for a whole society if at least some members of the society act as if this rationality were already in place, even though in accordance with the tenets of this conception of rationality it is not rational for anyone to be rational unless everyone else is as well. Negative theology offers a theological resolution to this dilemma. The inscrutability of rewards and punishments gives people an incentive to act justly even before the assurance of compliance by the other members of the community. In a society suffused by a monotheistic ethos, there can be a collective assumption of the yoke of political obligation even before there is complete assurance of the mutual compliance of all the members, so that the starter-up problem can be resolved when game-theoretic rationality is accompanied by monotheistic theology.

4. The Jethro Story and the Machloqet between Simeon Imsoni and R. Akiva

The biblical text in parshat Jethro in Exodus seems to register the linkage between theological creedal vacuum and the need for an ordered system of authority relations that emerges as central from Maimonides' reading of the Bible. The structure of parshat Jethro is extremely puzzling. The conclusion of the parsha contains the great revelation at Sinai, the promulgation of the Ten Commandments. The beginning of this section of the Torah, however, is devoted to the comparatively much more mundane topic of appointing local and more remote magistrates. While Rashi in effect tells us in his commentary on this parsha, *'Ein Mukdam U'Meuchar B'Torah'*, that Jethro's advice and its implementation followed rather than preceded the revelation at Sinai, nevertheless the literary structuring of events in contrast to their actual sequence invites independent elucidation. It seems to me that the passages detailing the routinization of charisma at the beginning of the parsha precede the account of the most charismatically charged moment in Jewish tradition – the revelation at Sinai – as a way of instructing us how to assimilate and respond to the Sinaitic events. The revelation needs to be mediated and channeled through a series of authority structures that dilute its content suitably to the exigencies of daily life. There is a beginning before the beginning in Jewish life which consists in a recognition of authority as a precondition for and facilitator of religious truth.

While Michael Walzer in *Exodus and Revolution* (Walzer 1985, p. 127) cites Rashi again on this parsha to the effect that assuming 600,000 adult males, following the principles of judicial organization laid down in the parsha would yield 82,600 magistrates, the largeness of the number of leaders should not obscure from view the fact that notions of hierarchy and bureaucratic elaboration are being introduced in the biblical text which limit the sheerly consensual elements of covenant which participatory theorists might wish to emphasize.

The ambiguity surrounding the appropriate political response to monotheism, whether a voluntarism culminating in an accentuation of the values of participation and community or a voluntarism giving rise to counter-structures of organization and hierarchy, is reflected in a famous but perplexing division of opinion that is mentioned several times in the Talmud between Rabbi Akiva and Simeon Imsoni:

Simeon Imsoni – others state, Nehemiah Imsoni – interpreted every ETH in the Torah; but as soon as he came to, Thou shall fear [ETH] the Lord thy God, he desisted. Said his disciples to him, 'Master, what is to happen with all the ETHIN which you have interpreted?' 'Just as I received reward for interpreting them,' he replied, 'so will I receive reward for retracting.' Subsequently R. Akiva came and taught: Thou shalt fear [ETH] the Lord thy God is to include scholars. [T.B., *Pesachim* 22b and *passim*; Soncino trans.]

Simeon Imsoni's position seems to be predicated on the notion that given God's majestic otherness – that all our human vocabularies pale into meaninglessness in relation to him – then the most fitting response to God is one of mystical solitariness and contemplation. There is absolutely nothing to be conjoined to the monotheistic conception of God – not even a hierarchy of expositors and interpreters of the divine will. The religiously-driven individual can only contemplate in abject humility and aloneness the unfathomable otherness of God. The talmid chakham (the scholar), for all his intellectual development and spiritual sensitivity, is from the divine perspective posited by negative theology no better off in this regard than anyone else. He only has more sophisticated ways for registering his ignorance, but he is metaphysically debarred by the concept of negative theology from developing a successful strategy for overcoming it. Given this situation, Simeon Imsoni feels he has no choice but to say – 'Just as I received reward for interpreting the ETHIN so will I receive reward for retracting.' To strive for authenticity, boundlessness, and non-transferability seems to be the appropriate ethical and theological implication to be drawn from the metaphysical content of negative theology.

Rabbi Akiva, by contrast, sees the voluntarism implicit in negative theology as a basis for not only creating spontaneous individual order through the attainment of insight and possible spontaneous interaction with other similarly motivated individuals, but also extends the voluntarism to include a collectively-ordered response to God's presence through the introduction of systems of authority and hierarchy. The idea of negative theology for Rabbi Akiva contains an implied legitimacy for rabbinic authority. In this sense, Maimonides follows in the footsteps of Rabbi Akiva in drawing out the political implications of negative theology.

5. Idolatry, the Golden Calf, and the Sanctuary

Yosef Duber, the grandson of Reb Chaim Wolozhoner, and the author of a commentary on halakhic themes and Torah texts called the *Beit Halevi*, confronts a question that should be most disturbing from the perspective of negative theology: If *Klal Lo Yasiguhu*, if our ostensibly referential God-talk and all attempts at material concretization of God's presence are to be construed metaphorically, then in what sense is the building of the mishkan, the sanctuary in the desert, less a sacrilegious act than the fashioning of the golden calf? Don't they both constitute forms of idolatry, an inability to live with the extraordinary tension that monotheism imposes which leads to a reification and sanctification of human handiwork? The *Beit Halevi* answers in a spirit that both Maimonides and Hobbes would have instinctively understood.

> Since their essential transgression with the golden calf was that they wanted to rely on their own wisdom – to do in accordance with their own understanding something concerning which they were not commanded – therefore in the building of the sanctuary which came to atone for the golden calf the Biblical text states concerning each aspect of their work, 'in accordance with God's command.' The import of this recurring phrase is that even though Bezalel knew how to combine the words through which heaven and earth were created and knew secrets and hidden meanings in his work, nevertheless his whole intention in his work was only to fulfill the command of God. They [Bezalel and his co-workers] only intended to fulfill God's will and commands, not because their own reason dictated that they should do what they did. It was this that atoned for the sin of the golden calf. [*Beit Halevi*, Exodus, p. 54; my translation]

6. Moses as the Model of the Future Messiah

Maimonides' conception of the messianic age as being continuous with historical time can be read as surreptitiously encoding an interpretation of the Exodus story. Maimonides' major criterion for certifying to the authenticity of a would-be messiah is political success. This means unification of the Jewish people in their national homeland in Israel in a political climate characterized by undisturbed peace and prosperity. What is the textual warrant for Maimonides' projection of the messianic age in this radically voluntaristic and worldly manner? Most commentators are baffled on this point. It seems to me that Walzer is right when he claims that the Exodus events provide a model for central Jewish and secular imaginings of redemption (Walzer 1985, pp. 16–17). The ancient redemption from Egyptian bondage was initiated by Moses, whose highest biblical accolade is that he is an *Eved Hashem*, a servant of God. Moses is resolutely not deified in the biblical account of the Exodus events, and he is nearly omitted altogether from the Passover Haggadah's recounting of the Exodus story. Maimonides would probably agree with Rashi that Moses' elevated status among the prophets – 'All the prophets looked into a dim glass, but Moses looked through a clear glass' (T.B., *Yevamot*, 49b) – has paradoxically to do with Moses' unwavering understanding that all his prophetic visions did not yield a direct glimpse of God.

The future Messiah is envisioned by Maimonides after the manner of Moses. He is a successful political revolutionary who accomplishes the goals of collective consciousness-raising and political unification appropriate to post-Exilic times. Negative theology forecloses resort to any other criterion for validating the advent of the messianic age except worldly success achieved by a political and religious reformer. To invoke exclusively a more narrowly religious set of preconditions (although some of these are included in Maimonides' account) would be a form of blasphemy, a claim of access to knowledge of God which negative theology forecloses. The implicit textual model for Maimonides' conception of the messianic age might therefore be the role assigned to Moses in the exodus from Egypt. Exodus and revolution might thus be conceptually indissolubly linked, serving as a permanent invitation to Jews to remake themselves and their history to bring them closer to the ideals inspiring their founding.

7. Maimonides' Historicism, Structural-Functionalism, and Formalistic Philosophy of Law

Maimonides' historicism, structural-functionalism, and philosophy of law converge upon a dissociation of the word of God from God, thereby contributing toward a reconceptualization of authority as being grounded in consent. First I would like to discuss these notions in their own right and then in a concluding section that considers how Maimonides decodes the teaching of the book of Job I explore further the ramifications of his philosophy of law. A remarkable thing to notice about the *ta'ame ha-mitzvot* (the reasons or rationales for the commandments) that Maimonides adduces in the *Guide* is their deliberate lopping-off of the rabbinic extensions and elaborations of the mitzvot (commandments) and issurim (prohibitions) stated in the Torah and their willful recircumscribing of the biblical text within its original, pre-rabbinic context.[10] This very search for a return to the original biblical setting of Jewish law appears to be theologically motivated. The tenets of negative theology after all debar Maimonides from attributing a literal content to the ubiquitous statements found in the Torah setting forth God's commands. Anthropological investigation and structural-functional analyses fill in the space created by the de-literalization of God's word. In some passages such as at III:45:575, Maimonides integrates his historical account of a biblical passage with a talmudic citation which he claims is inspired by the same historicizing urge:

It is known that idolaters sought to build their temples and to set up their idols in the highest places they could find there: Upon the high mountains [Deuteronomy 12:2]. Therefore Abraham our Father singled out Mount Moriah, because of its being the highest mountain there, proclaimed upon it the unity [of God], and determined and defined the direction toward which one would turn in prayer, fixing it exactly in the West. For the Holy of Holies is in the West. This is the meaning of the dictum of [the Sages]: The Indwelling is in the West [T.B., *Baba Bathra*, 25a]. They, may their memory be blessed, have made clear in the Gemara of the Tractate *Yoma* [Pines in a footnote says that he is not able to trace the exact source of this citation but the passages on pages 28b and 54b 'may be interpreted in the way suggested in the text'] that Abraham our Father fixed the direction toward which one should turn in prayer, I mean the Temple of the Holy of Holies. In my opinion, the reason for this is as follows: Inasmuch as at that time the opinion generally accepted in the world was to the effect that the sun should be worshipped and that it is the deity, there is no doubt that all men turned when praying to the East. Therefore Abraham our Father turned, when praying on Mount Moriah – I mean in the Sanctuary – toward the West, so as to turn his back upon the sun.

Maimonides' strategy of reinserting biblical law in its original context is manifested in two ways. The first consists in Maimonides attempting to show how much of both the grand design and the detailed application of biblical law are responsive to the need to deflect the Jewish community of believers away from the pagan practices of the surrounding nations. For example, the priests are commanded 'to cover the flesh of their nakedness' (Exodus 28:42) in order to counteract the worship of Pe'or which 'consisted in the uncovering of the nakedness' (*Guide* III:45:578). The abstraction from rabbinic context and restoration of original biblical context also leads to a structural-functional preoccupation with how the architectonic and detail of biblical law promote obedience and loyalty to the monotheistic God. For example, the priests were commanded to wear 'Holy garments . . . for splendor and for beauty' (Exodus 28:2), and those with blemishes and deformities were debarred from the Temple service because 'to the multitude an individual is not rendered great by his true form, but by the perfection of his limbs and the beauty of his clothes; and what is aimed at is that the Temple and its servants should be regarded as great by all' (*Guide* III:45:579).

Both the historicizing of the biblical text and a structural-functional analysis of it are grounded in the principles of negative theology. The human self viewed in a historicist vein duplicates many of the same features of God underscored by negative theology. The monotheistic God projected by negative theology is thoroughly de-essentialized, stripped of any literal set of attributes that we can rationally penetrate and describe, and historicized and contextualized solely on the basis of his actions as conceived by the fundamental tenets of the faith, e.g., his creation of the world in time, his continual providential ordering and management of the world. Since we can never approach the 'whatness' of the monotheistic God, his 'thatness' becomes manifest to us only through the actions attributed to him by the texts and traditions of the faith. With regard to the nature of the monotheistic God, there is no text without context. The settings in which he moves – the interactions and actions ascribed to him – become the dominant basis for determining identity and fixing the outward boundaries of a 'self.' The monotheistic God becomes a significant precursor of a 'self' primarily disclosed by its actions, which is the image of the self presupposed in historicism.

The relationship between an historicized reading of the Bible and a structural-functional analysis of it might be stronger in Maimonides even than I have so far suggested. An unavoidable circularity links an unfathomable God with the moral and legal mechanisms regulating human action. Just as Maimonides regards enforcement of the *idea* of reward and punishment as much a part of the law of the Torah as any concrete instance of behavior grouped under either heading, so too does he distinguish between biblical monotheism and the pagan religion of the surrounding nations classically exemplified for him by the Sabians by the relationship that each religion articulates between the prophet and God. For biblical religion, 'belief in the existence of angels precedes the belief in prophecy, and the belief in prophecy precedes the belief in the Law' (*Guide* III:45:576). While pagan religion converges with biblical mono-theism in assigning a central role to the prophet in spelling out the content of the law, it differs from it in one crucial respect. In pagan polytheism the prophet enjoys an unmediated relation-ship with the deity: 'As the Sabians [Maimonides' chief exemplars and spokesmen for ancient polytheism] were ignorant of the existence of the deity, may He be exalted and glorified, and thought that the Sphere with its stars is the being that is eternal and to which nonbeing can never come, and that forces flow over from the Sphere toward idols and certain trees – I mean the *asheroth* – they thought that the idols and trees give prophetic revelation to the prophets ... and make known to them what is useful and what is harmful' (*Guide* III:45:576). Monotheism transforms this picture not only by teasing God out of all natural phenomena and consigning him to the remotest conceptual reaches, but also by introducing intervening layers between God and 'the Sphere and its stars' : 'When the truth became clear to the men of knowledge and it became known by demonstration that there is a being that is neither a body nor a force in a body, who is the true deity, and that he is one; and that there are also other beings that are separate from matter and are not bodies, beings toward whom His being, may He be exalted, overflows – namely, the angels, as we have explained; and that all these beings are beyond the Sphere and its stars; – it became known with certainty that true prophetic revelation is given to the prophets by the angels, not by the idols and the *asheroth*. Thus it has become clear through what we have stated before that the belief in the existence of angels is consequent upon the belief in the existence of the deity and that thereby prophecy and the Law are established as valid' (*Guide* III:45:577).

For Maimonides, it is not only the mechanism of rewards and punishments, but the very content of the law itself that is predicated upon an irredeemably circular process. The monotheistic God cannot be transposed into an idiom that establishes him as the direct legal commander and issuer of directives. Maimonides postulates an additional metaphysical stratum between God and human beings, namely, the angels, by way of dramatically highlighting the unbreachable distance of the monotheistic God and ruling out the polytheistic alternative. However, the problem of establishing the existence of angels and specifying their mode of communication with the loftiest of human beings, namely, the prophets, is qualitatively continuous with the problem of proving the existence of God and delineating the ways in which he communicates with the most superior human type. Problems of provability and communication with individuals in the sublunar spheres loom almost as significant with regard to angels as they do in relation to God himself. The prophet therefore must play the strategic role of not only legitimating himself as a human being by showing that he is the appropriate occupant of the role of prophet, but of validating the background categories of 'God' and 'angel' which form the monotheistic categorial presuppositions for the notion of a prophet. The system of ancient biblical belief and practice is set in motion by institutionalizing a certain circular moment where the prophet affirms all the categories that affirm him and having that serve as the initiating phase of a new history – the history of a new beginning. In the passage from which I have been quoting, Maimonides goes on to discuss in effect how the resplendent symbolism of the ark in the Holy of Holies deflects away from – or compensates for – the issue of circularity: 'In order to fortify belief in this fundamental principle, He, may He be exalted, has commanded that the image of two angels be made over the ark, so that the belief of the multitude in the existence of angels be consolidated; this correct opinion, coming in the second place after the belief in the existence of the deity, constituting the originative principle of the belief in prophecy and the Law and refuting idolatry, as we have explained. If there had been one image, I mean the image of one cherub, this might have been misleading. For it might have been thought that this was the image of the deity who was to be worshipped – such things being done by idolaters – or that there was only one individual angel, a belief that would have led to a certain dualism. As, however, two cherubim were made and the explicit statement enounced: The Lord is our God, the Lord is One, the validity of the opinion affirming the existence of angels was established and also the fact that they are many. Thus measures were taken against the error that they are the deity – the deity being one and having created this multiplicity' (*Guide* III:45:577).

The way Maimonides presents the picture polytheists are incorrigible realists whose insatiable urge for a divine grounding can only be satisfied by a direct (unmetaphoric) overflow of divinity to their prophet and thence to them. Monotheists by contrast are unswerving nominalists, forever scrupulous about extending a human naming process to some putatively incontestable reality beyond itself. The pivotal role that circularity plays for Maimonides in the structure of monotheistic argument suggests that both in the elaboration and decoding of monotheistic metaphor we never leave a human plane. In his explication of the rationales for the performance of mitzvot in the *Guide* Maimonides both reads the Bible historically as a response to its own immediate religious and cultural context and engages in structural-functional analysis of the points of particular commandments. The upshot of both sorts of analyses is that while the Bible is ostensibly a story or series of stories about God's intervention in the world, it is on a more authentic level a story or series of stories about how a particular human community was able to cultivate a critical vantage point with regard to the symbolic systems that helped to organize the social and personal existences of their neighbors and managed to evolve a counter-system of symbols that helped to nurture new possibilities of selfhood and new visions of collective life that engendered new values of autonomy and freedom. Maimonides' recourse to varieties of historicism and structural-functionalism as tools of biblical textual analysis registers his awareness of how the irresolvable presence of circularity in his delineation of mono-theistic argument forces a turning away from God-centered to man-centered narratives in providing translations and para-phrases of the canonical texts of divine revelation.

The upshot of Maimonides' approach to mitzvot in the *Guide* is that it is only the idea of mitzvah that can lay any claim to being rational, not the content of any particular mitzvah (except those having universal application such as the injunction against killing; these are codified in the seven Noahide laws), let alone the details of their application. Maimonides states this position very broadly at II:33:364: 'As for the other command-ments [aside from the first two of the Decalogue, relating to God's existence and his unity], they belong to the class of generally accepted opinions and those adopted in virtue of tradition, not to the class of the intellecta.' In this sense, Maimonides strikingly prefigures Hobbes. It is only the idea of order itself, of political obligation, that enjoys a limited, pragmatically-ordained rationality. Most of what lies beyond this, most of the actual content of law, is sheerly arbitrary and adventitious in character, a fit subject matter for history, not for philosophy.

A formalistic conception of law is reinforced from the later sections of the *Guide*. Maimonides' analysis of biblical law in terms of its role in its immediate historical context (how its many provisions work to deflect its adherents away from the religious practices of the surrounding nations) and from a structural-functional perspective (how particular rituals and symbols contribute toward establishing and strengthening a certain belief system, whose very difference from the adjacent cultures facilitates the achievement of Jewish autonomy) already suggest how for Maimonides there is no intrinsic correctness to the content of Jewish law, only instrumentalized precepts designed to effect renovations in collective outlook, attitudes, and patterns of behavior. The highest human vocation for Maimonides consists in contemplation and apprehension of God. This apprehension, however, does not consist in coming into substantive contact with God so that his essence is in some way grasped. Maimonides equates apprehension of God with 'knowledge of the Name' (*Guide* III:51:627). Since the Name refers to what transcends 'an individual or group of individuals,' it evokes the most general sort of category to which innumerable ranges of phenomena must be related, the Name must be conceived as a 'mental notion' originating with the human individuals and communities who find its invocation congenial and useful (*Guide* III:18:474–75). Apprehension of God for Maimonides therefore translates into preoccupation with the sources and limits of our knowledge, where direct knowledge begins and ends and where organizing frameworks and categories take over.

Maimonides conceives of reason almost entirely in proceduralist terms: 'It is possible that the meaning of *wisdom* in Hebrew indicates aptitude for stratagems and the application of thought in such a way that the stratagems and ruses may be used in achieving either rational or moral virtues, or in achieving skill in a practical art, or in working evil and wickedness' (*Guide* III:54:632–33). Maimonides in this passage theorizes reason in thoroughly neutral terms, as a capacity or power, not linked with any particular end or vocation. If reason considered as a search for ultimate explanatory factors ends up, when it postulates the existence of the monotheistic God, in engendering conundrums that prove well-nigh insurmountable, then what is at stake in the operations of reason needs to be rearticulated. The totally singular, unified, and unique monotheistic God can function as the ultimate explanatory factor of events and phenomena in the world only at the cost of being so completely drained of literal content that he serves as a metaphoric expression or reflection of the limitations of human reason, rather than embodying a satisfactory consummation or transcendence of it. Reason's inability to negotiate its end, as manifested most dramatically in the explanatory failure of the God-hypothesis, forces us to reconceive the nature and role of reason in the economies of human life and the human person. If the performance of reason fails to match the pretensions of reason, then, as Maimonides says in the passage quoted, reason has to be re-diagnosed as a matter of 'stratagems and ruses' that playfully evokes and playfully eludes certain targets, thereby directing our attention to the idea that its resources and energies reside in the playfulness. In a universe where there are no fully rationally validated ends, reason discloses a continuum between itself and morality (the requirements of truth and the requirements of right action), between theory and practice, and between good and evil. In each of these cases, we do not find the rigid bifurcations associated with the inexorable flow of rational argument, but indications that the first in each of these three sets of paired categories partakes much more of the content of its opposite number than most of us are wont to acknowledge. From a Maimonidean perspective, chains of successive reasoning whose literal import and patterns of interconnection soon get aborted are suggestive of the need to reclassify thinking as a form of doing, whose overarching norms stem from morality rather than from some autonomous domain labeled 'rationality.' The unanchored character of our judgments also evokes the specter of how in many instances our epithets 'good' and 'evil' get transmuted into one another, with often hairline differences in intention and circumstance being responsible for our assigning an action to the one category or the other.

Maimonides identifies 'reason' with 'stratagem' and 'ruse' because the multiple ways in which the reach of rational argument exceeds its grasp constrain an incessant preoccupation with the tools and methods of argument and the relegation of the ends of argument to a secondary status. Extended patterns of reasoning dissolve substance into stratagem in the sense that they transform preoccupation with their official objects into an enlarged grappling with the sentential and logical materials composing them.

Philosophy dissolves the ends of argument into a series of endlessly protracted means. This is most apparent when Maimonides theorizes the nature of the monotheistic God. It is also manifested in Maimonides' analysis of the structure of commandments and prohibitions upon which the monotheistic God gets displaced in the texts and traditions of Judaism. Maimonides says that 'the law as a whole aims at two things: the welfare of the soul and the welfare of the body' (*Guide* III:27:510). He emphasizes that 'the first aim can only be achieved after achieving this second one' (*ibid.*). The 'welfare of the soul' which as we have seen consists in apprehension of God (*Guide* III:54:636) requires the establishment of a physical infrastructure that nurtures and supports this activity at its apex. 'Corporeal preservation,' unlike rational cultivation, is not an end that can be achieved in isolation. It 'can only be well ordered through political association' (*Guide* III:27:512). There is thus a premium placed on the ordering mechanisms integral to political association as affording an indispensable means for nurturing the rational contemplation engaged in by the few. The content of law for Maimonides remains subordinate to the formal institutionalization of legal mechanisms. The 'thatness' of law supersedes its 'whatness.' Of the twin emotional poles that regulate relations between God and human beings, fear cements the relationship of the intellectually less-endowed strata to the political community and love is symptomatic of what binds the intellectually more-cultivated elite to the political community: 'For these two ends, namely, love and fear, are achieved through two things: love through the opinions taught by the law, which include the apprehension of His being as He, may He be exalted, is in truth; while fear is achieved by means of all actions prescribed by the law' (*Guide* III:52:630). Maimonides spells out his concept of actions in the following way: 'For it is by all the particulars of the actions and through their repetition that some excellent men obtain such training that they achieve human perfection, so that they fear, and are in dread and awe of God, may He be exalted, and know who it is that is with them and as a result act subsequently as they ought to. . . . It says: If thou wilt not take care to observe all the words of this law that are written in this book, that thou mayest fear this glorious and fearful Name, the Lord thy God [Deuteronomy 28:58]. Consider how it is explicitly stated for your benefit that the intention of all the words of this law is one end, namely, that thou mayest fear the Name, and so on. The fact that this end is achieved through actions, you can learn from its dictum in this verse: If thou wilt not take care to observe. For it has already been made clear that this refers to actions prescribed by commandments and prohibitions' (*Guide* III:52:630). In this passage, Maimonides emphasizes the role of actions and their repetition in engendering fear of God and thereby promoting the basis for civic order. Maimonides even mentions an elite sub-group within the larger class of those who fear God, for whom the fear has become so thoroughly internalized that it suffuses everything they do 'and as a result [they] act subsequently as they ought to' (*ibid.*). This elite needs to be distinguished from the rational elite within the Jewish community who have moved beyond the ambit of fear altogether and for whom love is commensurate with rational understanding. For the Jewish masses, however, for whom the relationship with God is governed by fear, monotheistic doctrine yields a double displacement: We are debarred from ascribing on a literal level any attribute to God, so that doctrinal belief and creedal affirmation are displaced onto conformity with biblically-ordained commandments and prohibitions. However, given the sheerly instrumentalized role of a vast number of biblical commandments and prohibitions in discrediting and blocking continuing allegiance to the religious practices and beliefs of the surrounding polytheistic cultures – and their role over time in fashioning a close structural-functional fit between those commandments and prohibitions and the promotion of an alternative collective lifestyle that affirms the value of Jewish difference – the content of Jewish law for Maimonides consists in a celebration of the idea of law itself with its scheme of formalized inducements and constraints rendering the achieve-ment of political order possible, rather than a set of intrinsically compelling categories and principles that fill in the space created by an irredeemably metaphoric theology.

8. Interpretation of the Book of Job

Maimonides interprets the book of Job in such a way that the character of Job emerges as a proto-Maimonidean. He construes the periagoge (the reversal) that takes place in the book of Job to consist in a shift in Job's grasp of the God-human being relationship from the way the masses understand it to the way the philosophically-undeceived comprehend it: 'While he had known God only through the traditional stories and not by the way of speculation, Job had imagined that the things thought to be happiness, such as health, wealth, and children, are the ultimate goal. For this reason he fell into such perplexity and said such things as he did. This is the meaning of his dictum: "I had heard of thee by the hearing of the ear; but now mine eye seeth thee; wherefore I abhor myself and repent of dust and ashes" (Job 42:5–6). This dictum may be supposed to mean, "Wherefore I abhor all that I used to desire and repent of my being in dust and ashes" – this being the position that he was supposed to be in: And he sat among the ashes (Job 2:8). It is because of this final discourse indicative of correct apprehension that it is said of him after this: "For ye have not spoken of me the thing that is right, as my servant Job hath"' (Job 42:7) (*Guide* III:23:493). According to this reading, Job's error consists in his having believed that there was direct, literal, conceptual and moral commerce between the vocabularies that we invoke to make sense of our lives and those that we employ to make sense of the nature of God and his relationship to us. Until the end of the biblical book that bears his name, Job is not able to fathom the unlimited extent of human freedom and of how convention-ally unsupporting the whole panoply of divine categories are: 'But the notion of his providence is not the same as the notion of our providence; nor is the notion of His governance of the things created by Him the same as the notion of the governance of that which we govern. The two notions are not comprised in one definition, contrary to what is thought by all those who are confused, and there is nothing in common between the two except the name alone. In the same way, our act does not resemble His act; and the two are not comprised in one and the same definition. Just as natural acts differ from those of craftsmanship, so do the divine governance of, the divine providence for, and the divine purpose with regard to, those natural matters differ from our human governance of, provi-dence for, and purpose with regard to, the things we govern, we provide for, and we purpose. This is the object of the Book of Job as a whole' (*Guide* III:23:496–97). In harmony with this notion of the utter untranslatability of the category of divine providence into that of human providence, Maimonides emphasizes earlier in part three of the *Guide* that 'providence is consequent upon the intellect. Accordingly divine providence does not watch in an equal manner over all the individuals of the human species, but providence is graded as their human perfection is graded' (*Guide* III:18:475). By making providence dependent upon the intellect Maimonides does not mean that as we cultivate our reason more fully we are able to grasp more clearly the nature of God's providence. If anything, he means the reverse: The more we develop our reason, the sooner we confront its limits and the more we shy away from direct imputation to divine providence of actions and outcomes in this world. Paradoxically, it is this coming to grips with human limitation that I believe restores for Maimonides some semblance of continuity between the conventional understanding of divine providence and the philosophically-enlightened conception of it. The humility engendered by our philosophical insight into the nature of our rational limitations is the closest we come to an existential guarantee that our actions are in harmony with some kind of divine plan, that they are faithful to the scruples of Heaven.

If my reading of Maimonides' theology of mitzvot is correct, then Job's strictures concerning the untranslatability of divine providence needs to be extended to the 613 commandments and prohibitions comprising the laws of the Torah. The content of these laws as binding rules regulating in perpetuity the life of the Jewish community remains fundamentally irrational. As Maimonides' extensive analyses in part three of the *Guide* underscore, the rational content of a vast number of these laws was exhausted in their historical utility in negating pagan practices and in their structural-functional point of reinforcing the value and belief differences of Judaism. This is equivalent to saying that their rationality is instrumental, not intrinsic. Why then should these laws be obeyed beyond the early generations when they were instituted and took root? Are they valuable beyond their role as mechanisms for triggering assent to a Jewish constellation of values? I think as with most other areas of his thought Maimonides is willing to go the distance in transforming a troublesome inference of his thinking into a new premise for comprehending Judaism. For Maimonides, what makes Judaism a historically viable religion is its structuring of a scheme of authority relations that maps out areas of permissible, prohibited, and mandated behavior. The content of the norms evoking compliance and interiorization – and setting the stage for the emergence, reinforcement, and transmission of collective identity – is almost secondary to the formal existence of the norms themselves. The emasculation of the categories affecting God's relationship to the world, e.g., divine providence and divine action, is extended by Maimonides to encompass

successor categories within the structure of biblical law where
Maimonides effects a dissociation between formal mechanisms of
institutionalization and perpetuation of laws and practices and
the content of what is being institutionalized and perpetuated.

In chapter 53 of part III of the *Guide*, Maimonides defines
'*chesed*' ('loving-kindness') as 'excess in whatever matter excess
is practiced' (*Guide* III:53:630). 'This reality as a whole – I mean
that He, may He be exalted, has brought it into being – is
chesed.' Since we have no right to claim creation of the world
from God, creation as well as 'every benefit that comes from
Him, may He be exalted, is called *chesed*' (*Guide* III:53:631). I
think that in his philosophy of law Maimonides is modeling
patterns of human behavior that center around an appropriation
of the divine attribute of *chesed*. Maimonides' philosophy of law
is dependent for its internalization upon the cultivation and
nurturance of the attribute of *chesed*. In the end, for Maimonides
the simultaneous necessity and excess of God (he is both
required to bring the explanatory quest to a halt and this very
niche which he occupies makes him in a literal vein unassimil-
able and therefore redundant as an explanatory factor) is
matched on a human level by the simultaneous necessity and
excess of law (without mechanisms of entrenchment all
philosophical insights would remain transient, unable to shape
the lives of human communities, but the insights themselves
might have to do with human rational limitation, thereby
inhibiting their direct use as legal principles organizing the life
of society). Correspondingly, the compliance to law manifested
by the Jewish community of believers represents *chesed* in the
sense that it is in excess of the substantive rational warrant of
the law.[11] Maimonides' dialectic of *chesed* as excess which
transfers from God's behavior to the content of law to human
compliance with law[12] yields new registers in terms of which to
assess the ramifications of the Psalmist's understanding that
'Olam Chesed Yibaneh' – 'The world is built up in loving-
kindness (Psalms 89:3).'[13]

Notes

1 A possible exception to this might be the book of Esther. An Arabic edition
   of such a commentary was published in Livorno in 1760. A Hebrew

translation of it by Ben-Zion Krinpis was published in Jerusalem in 1952, and reprinted in Brooklyn in 1994.

2   James Joyce, *Ulysses*, Gabler edition[1986], p. 23.

3   As Zev Harvey once put it to me in personal conversation, 'The *Guide* is part philosophy – part midrash.'

4   A similar interpretation of the Garden of Eden story is in fact found in Hobbes, *Leviathan*, chapters 20, 29, and 35; see Zev Harvey 1981, pp. 27–38 (in Hebrew; English summary, pp. 68–70).

5   Hobbes, *Leviathan*, chapter 4.

6   There is a variant reading of this midrash which states that the Torah was given only to those who interpret the eating of the manna; compare the discussion of this midrash in Dessler 1973, pp. 185, 205. Rav Dessler interprets the midrash to mean that the concept of Torah is antithetical to the idea of nature. Only when daily occurrences were subsumed under the category of miracle (when the boundary demarcating 'nature' and 'miracle' had been effaced) did the Jews become ready to receive the Torah.

7   Maimonides, *Mishneh Torah, The Book of Knowledge*, Laws concerning the Basic Principles of the Torah, chapter 8, paragraph 1, 43b (translation amended on my part).

8   Maimonides, *Mishneh Torah, The Book of Knowledge*, Laws concerning the Basic Principles of the Torah, chapter 8, paragraph 2, 44a.

9   Compare the famous mishnah of Antigonous of Socho in *Avot* I:3, in which he says that we should not be like servants who serve the master in the expectation of receiving a reward.

10   Compare *Guide* III:41:558 where Maimonides states very forthrightly that 'At present my purpose is to give reasons for the [biblical] texts and not for the pronouncements of the legal science.' In note 4 on that page Pines states that the phrase 'the legal science' refers to 'the Talmudic legal code.'

11   The seven Noahide laws constitute the major exception to this as yielding a minimal natural law content.

12   *Chesed* is also a relevant category for metaphorically encoding the ways in which formulations of extreme skepticism and relativism and the tenets of negative theology remain sustainable despite their flouting of the protocols of reflexivity. The virtue of *chesed* symbolically softens the dilemmas associated with issues of reflexivity – how, for example, statements of unmitigated skepticism and relativism refute themselves. These statements violate protocols of consistency and are therefore strictly speaking unwarranted; they are logically speaking useless and super-fluous. A metaphysical category like *chesed* normalizes these excesses by reconceiving 'excess' in the senses described in the text as a guiding norm of the human condition.

13   Maimonides at III:53:631 glosses this phrase to mean 'the building-up of the world is loving-kindness.' This syntactical revision of the phrase from the way that I cited it in the text coheres entirely with the interpretation of *chesed* developed in the text as the conceptual counterpoint to foundationalism. Given Maimonides' nominalism, conventionalism, and phenomenalistic philosophy of science, our everyday practical and scientific judgments through which the world is improved and built-up exceed a warrant of strict assertability. It is only on the basis of a principle

of *chesed* that the world, and the multiple worlds within it that go to compose it, are established.

References

Dessler, E. E. 1973. *Michtav M'Eliyahu*, volume 1. Bnei Brak

Duber, Y. 1884. *Beit Halevi*. Warsaw

Harvey, Z. 1981. 'The Israelite Kingdom of God according to Hobbes.' *Iyyun* 30, pp. 27–38

Hobbes, T. 1946. *Leviathan*, edited by M. Oakeshott. Oxford: Basil Blackwell

Joyce, J. 1986. *Ulysses*, edited by H. W. Gabler. New York: Random House

Maimonides. 1994. *Commentary on Megilat Esther*, trans. Ben-Zion Krinpis. Brooklyn

——. 1965. *Commentary on the Mishnah*, translated by J. Kafiah. Jerusalem: Mosad Harav Kook.

——. 1974. *Mishneh Torah: The Book of Knowledge*, translated by M. Hyamson. Jerusalem: Feldheim Publishers

—— . 1963. *The Guide of the Perplexed*, 2 volumes, translated by S. Pines. Chicago: University of Chicago Press

Walzer, M. 1985. *Exodus and Revolution*. New York: Basic Books

CHAPTER NINE

Political Liberty

The Rhetoric of the Responsa

Peter J. Haas

1. Introduction

Probing the relationship between personal liberty and communal authority in Judaism raises a host of methodological problems. The most basic is that the very terms of the question are modern. This means that any answer has to be adduced from documents which never address the issue directly in the terms in which the question is posed. Finding an answer is made even more complicated by the fact that there is no one single text which contains a comprehensive articulation of 'Judaism' or 'the Jewish tradition'. There are, quite to the contrary, numerous texts and documents – of diverse genres and from a variety of times and places – each of which gives its own characteristic view of what Judaism means to its authorship. Given the length, diversity, and complexity of the Jewish historical experience, it is hardly surprising that finding a single answer to any philosophically sophisticated question is fraught with methodological minefields. Several strategies have evolved, nonetheless, to deal with such questions. One has been to choose a widely-recognized classic articulation of 'Judaism' – the writings of Philo, Maimonides, Spinoza, or Mendelssohn, for example – and use that text as the basis for adducing the Jewish view of the issue at hand. Another strategy is to frame a statement of the (or a) Jewish view by bringing together in some logical relationship citations from one or more of the classical pieces of Jewish literature: Tanach, Talmud, Shulkhan Arukh and the like. A third, and related, approach, finds an acceptable articulation by a non-Jewish philosopher such as John Locke, John Stuart Mill, or John Rawls and then shows that this statement of matters is implicitly compatible with Judaism by adducing supportive or parallel passages from authoritative Jewish texts.

None of these alternatives is without its difficulties, however. I see two problems in particular. One I have already alluded to, namely, the inadequacy of the assertion that any one document can be taken to be reflective of all of Judaism. The other is the assumption that one can arrive at the content of Judaism, even at some time and place, by looking at philosophical or doctrinal discourse. The operative assumption in what follows is that one must look also, as best as one can, at the actual life as lived by the community. I will take it to be my task in what follows, then, to try to take a preliminary look at how Jews in the formative period of post-Geonic Judaism actually proposed to deal with conflicts between personal liberty and communal authority. An examination of the extent to which actually lived Jewish life is compatible with contemporary or classical philosophical descriptions goes beyond the boundaries of this paper.

In my view, then, the way to get at the Jewish understanding of such concepts as personal liberty is to examine how these are given shape and substance in the lives of Jews. The best source we have for this kind of information is in the concrete give and take of rabbinic legal discourse. The primary body of data for this kind of analysis, it seems to me, is the responsa literature, the answers that rabbis give to specific questions put to them. In this paper, then, I will examine the concept of personal liberty as it is taken up and articulated in the responsa literature. I then want to use the result of this investigation to speculate on what this means today for those who want to shape normative Jewish behavior in light of halakhic precedents. The problem, as we shall see, is that the traditional halakhic attitude is that personal liberty may be limited by communal authority. Given the emphasis on individual liberty in modern Western society, as well as the voluntary nature of the Jewish community today, the deployment of such authority must obviously take on a different character today than was true in pre-modern Jewish society.

2. Methodological Considerations

Before proceeding, it must be said at the outset that there is no one timeless and definitive statement of personal liberty in the halakha. This is so because the responsa literature represents over a thousand years of legal decision-making emanating from

Jewish communities throughout Europe, North Africa, and the Middle East. This means that any legal concept we might choose to study will have an intricate and variegated history. We are dealing here with a long and complex legal tradition which takes up here and there issues which touch upon personal liberty and the extent to which it is permitted or delimited. Thus, while the halakha is at least in theory an internally consistent legal tradition, it is on another level an historical construct that reflects the times and places in which it received articulation.

Because of the complexity and detail of the literature, it will be impossible for me to sketch out the unfolding of the rabbinic notion of personal liberty here. Instead, I will limit my search in two ways. First, I propose to illuminate only one aspect of personal liberty in the halakha, in this case, the intersection between individual liberty and the community's power to coerce the individual in the name of the public good. While not addressing the full concept of personal liberty, this angle of approach does reveal some of its definitional parameters. In addition, and this is my second limit, I propose to look at only a small number of responsa by well-regarded poskim on this topic. With these criteria in mind, I have chosen texts which, I believe, lay the halakhic foundation for all subsequent discussions.

For my test cases I propose to focus on the responsa of two of the most definitive responsa-writers of the thirteenth century: Meir of Rothenburg (1215–93) and Solomon ben Adreth of Barcelona (1235–1310). I have chosen these poskim for a number of reasons. For one, this was a crucial time for the formation of classical Judaic halakha, especially in the area of political theory. The thirteenth century was a critical time for the development of political theory in the halakha because the institutional basis for Jewish communal life in Spain and the Christian West was then undergoing a profound structural change. I shall return to this theme in a moment.

For now let me say that in this context, both Meir and Solomon ben Adreth played significant, even seminal, roles. Both men not only addressed such issues, but both were regarded by their peers, as well as by subsequent generations of halakhists, as seminal and defining figures in the conceptualization of Jewish law. In fact, so influential were they that in some sense their different convictions and styles stand at the head of what was to become the major bifurcation in medieval

Jewish halakha: that between the Ashkenazic and the Sephardic. A comparison and contrast of their rulings on the issue of personal liberty can thus give us good insight into the early stages of the elucidation of this principle in medieval rabbinic Judaism.

As we shall see, both men agreed that personal liberty can be overridden at times by the needs of what was perceived to be the more common good. They do, however, have slightly different understandings on why this should be so. Roughly speaking, Meir of Rothenburg, living in a community that was socially and legally distinct from the surrounding host culture, wanted to protect the autonomy of the Jewish community and so its authority to govern its own affairs. His stance as worked out in numerous responsa relating to this subject can be roughly characterized as follows. Jews are first and foremost servants of God, and the community they comprise is founded on principles communicated by God through Torah. Consequently, it was entirely proper for the community to limit the liberty of individuals living under its jurisdiction. On the other hand, Rabbi Solomon ben Adreth was a member of a Jewish community that was more integrated into the surrounding Islamic civilization, and so more ready to limit the exclusivity of rabbinic power in the Spanish Jewish community. Yet, although he did not share the suspicion of Gentile government that was part of his Ashkenazi colleagues' mental baggage, he does agree that the Jewish communal authorities do have the right to impose bans on individuals in the interest of 'law and order.' In their respective responsa, Meir and Solomon ben Adreth thus defined along strikingly similar lines the conceptual and legal framework within which the discussion of individual liberty has taken place in rabbinic halakhic discourse. As we shall see, their major difference lies in what they conceive to be the legal foundation of communal authority.

Before turning to the texts themselves, I need to say a few words about the responsa as a literary form, especially as this form took shape at the time that Meir and Solomon ben Adreth were writing. The responsa genre, as best we can tell, had its beginning in about the eighth century or so of the Common Era. These early responsa were little more than brief questions over halakha or talmudic or biblical exegesis that were addressed to the heads of the Academies in Sassanian Babylonia. These questions were taken up either by the administration of the Academies or at semi-annual sessions and an answer dispatched to the petitioner. Hundreds of such responses survive in collections put together in the twelfth and thirteenth centuries. These consist of a restatement of the question and a brief reply, often only a word or sentence.[1] What is important for our purposes here is that the responsa of the eighth through the eleventh century, when the Academies began their decline, were generally short rescripts emanating from a more or less universally recognized center of authority.

The style and substance of responsa changed significantly and dramatically in about the twelfth century. This change coincides with a major organizational shift in rabbinic Judaism. The Geonic Academies in Babylonia had declined to the point of irrelevancy. This was due in part to internal developments in the Abbasid empire, and in part due to the dislocations consequent to the Crusades, which disrupted communications between centers of Jewish life in Europe and the Academies in the Islamic world. In all events, we find the authoritative rescripts from the Babylonian academies being replaced with responsa written by local experts. That is, Torah no longer went forth from Sura and Pumbedita, but from Mainz, Rothenburg, and Barcelona.

This realignment of authority is important for our purposes because it was accompanied by perhaps an even more dramatic shift in the literary style, or rhetoric, of the resulting rescripts. No longer will a brief one-sentence answer do. Rather, we find that responsa now have suddenly become rather long and detailed essays in which the answer is not merely given, but justified.[2] It is really at this time that responsa, as we know them, come into being. This change in turn bears two significant implications for our understanding of the texts at hand. One is that the halakha will become more localized. This can be seen in two different ways. First, there is, I think, a discernable and consistent difference between responsa written in the Islamic sphere (Spain and North Africa) on the one hand, and Ashkenaz (Southern France and the Rhine valley) on the other. Second, the issues that are addressed become much more immediate and concrete. Writing to the Academies of Babylonia could take a year or so until the query arrived, the semi-annual meeting was held and an answer composed, dispatched, and delivered. This would serve for general questions of interpretation or inquiries of say holiday customs, but would hardly serve issues of more immediate concerns or civil disputes. Responsa from more local authorities thus develop *halakha le-ma'aseh* in a way that was relatively unusual for the Geonic responsa.

A second implication of the shift in responsa writing is bound up with the whole question of rabbinic authority. Although the term 'rabbi' is very old, going back at least to the second century of the Common Era, the office of the rabbi as we know it really emerges in the eleventh and twelfth centuries. It evolved partially as a response to the collapse of the centralized Geonic authority of the Academies, partially in response to the counter-claims to authority put forward by the Karaites and partially to the particular social and legal position of Jewish communities as these developed in the late Middle Ages. The problem, I submit, was that the deployment of authority as proposed by rabbis freed from the supervision of the Academies, was without precedent and was not self-evident. It is for this reason, I think, that we see the rather dramatic shift in responsal rhetoric of this time toward more full articulation and argumentation. The discourse reflects an attempt to ground rulings in logic or talmudic precedent. The Geonim did not have to do this because their authority to render decisions was implicitly accepted; the local 'free-lancing' rabbis of the eleventh and twelfth centuries, had to make the case for accepting their readings of Judaism.

These internal realignments of authority within the Jewish community corresponded with a deep shift in the social and political worlds in which the Jewish communities found themselves. The older forms of community incorporation, as developed especially under the Carolingians, was giving way in the face of increasing anti-Jewish sentiment, to the legal status known as *servi camerae*. In essence, Jews were being made the personal servants of the ruler. This arrangement gave the Jews a certain amount of status and protection that they did not have (and really by and large did not need) under the older system. But it also removed any 'constitutional' guarantees or rights they might have; they were subject to the whims of the ruler. This meant that the whole question of political liberty and personal freedom had to be rethought from the Jewish perspective, in a community that was in the midst of making the transition from Geonic leadership to regional rabbinic leadership. In short, the need to reconsider the shape and substance of Jewish political theory was occurring just as the character of Jewish communal authority was being reconsidered. It is to this rediscursivization of the Jews' political status in terms of rabbinic (in distinction to Geonic) halakha that I now wish to turn.

3. Rabbi Solomon ben Adreth V:220

The two texts which I present for your consideration come, as noted, from the thirteenth century. I have chosen texts which address a similar situation. A tax is placed on the community. In order to insure that each member will pay his fair share, the leaders of the community have sworn to place a ban on anyone who refuses to pay. Now such a ban is causing hardship in some case or another. May the individual have the ban lifted?. The answer, in both cases, as we shall now see, is no. The community ban is not retractable. There may be legal fictions that the community can use to offer relief to certain individuals, but the community can impose a ban on an individual and that ban is not revocable.

The first text we shall consider is by Solomon ben Adreth of Barcelona. He was a member of a prominent family in Barcelona and remained in that city all of his life. One of his teachers was Moses ben Nachman, also known as Nachmanides, a leading Spanish philosopher, kabbalist, biblical exegete, and poet. Solomon ben Adreth was highly respected by Spanish Jews as an authority before he reached the age of forty. Even Pedro III of Aragon is said to have submitted a number of cases to him for arbitration. Nor was his influence restricted to Spanish Jewry. Questions are recorded to have come to him from all over the world, including Germany, France, Crete, Morocco, and even Palestine. He wrote over a thousand responsa, all of them reflecting a knowledge of Roman and Spanish law. He drew on this background in establishing the basis for Spanish Jewish halakha in the thirteenth century.

Rasba Part V: 220

You asked: all matters of *niddui* (ban) and *cherem* (quarantine) in this book apply only in lands in which *niddui* and *cherem* are permitted by the regulations of the sovereign.[3] But in our land, and so also in many foreign lands, they are prohibited by royal decree and so by *'dina d'malkhuta dina'*.

We have proclaimed a *cherem* in conjunction with the tax – a complete *cherem* [made on the basis] of majority consensus with no opening for release or recantation for ever – that it is to be paid at some known time in accordance with what is written in our regulations (*taqqanot*). Now there remains until that time some two years and now the final collection has become burdensome. It occurred to us to correct the matter and to aid the poor because of the weight of the tax. Let us know: is there release to this or not?

Answer: You already know that *cherems* and oaths (*shvu'ot*) and vows (*ndryn*) have by law no release except by complete recantations and absolute annulments; vacated from the beginning [*htrh dmqr*]. Further, it is possible to release [such vows] only through others [i.e. a third party], not through the agency of the one sworn against or the vower, even if he were like Moshe Rabbenu a'h, for so is it written, 'he shall not break his word' [Numbers 30:3]. This comes explicitly as received at Sinai [Chagiga 10], 'he does not forgive, but others forgive.' And as regards an oath imposed on the many, it is impossible to find a release for it except with great difficulty, since the pretext for [releasing] one is not the pretext for [releasing] another. Do we not in fact say, 'for this reason we have not sworn oaths and we have not made vows.' However, it has been the practice in all of the places in Israel regarding the community *cherem* that each [community] releases itself without pretext or recantation. The assertion on which we base this practice is that [we assume] that everyone who is accustomed to imposing and releasing *cherems*, everyone who imposes a *cherem* – lo, he has done so on the following condition, 'this *cherem* will only be in practice at such time as we want; and anytime we want, it will be null.' Even if they do not make this condition explicitly it is as if they made this condition [implicitly]. This is like what is written as regards the annulment of vows by the husband, 'whoever makes a vow with the knowledge of her husband has made a [valid] vow [with the implicit stipulation that the husband approve; if it turns out later that he does not offer approval, then the vow is null and void].'[4]

However, if they made the *cherem* with the approval of the majority – lo, they have made clear that their intention was not to proclaim the *cherem* according to the custom observed in Jewish communities [that is, as contingent], but rather to proclaim the *cherem* according to the laws of Torah like all private *cherems* and vows [and these can not be annulled by the parties involved].

Therefore, I find no pretext for release from this *cherem* . . . On the other hand, it is possible to find a remedy for the poor . . . Even though I do not see or know on what matter the question falls, I can give the particulars for some cases and from these it may be possible to learn about others. Lo, the communities in a few places are accustomed to impose a fixed, known amount on each person or a fixed amount on every artisan or the like. Now if you want to give them relief, make a rule that the trustees will return to them after the debt-payment what you raised from them, thus it turns out that this one pays [and so satisfies the stipulations of the ban] but his money is returned. Or the community can give a general sum from which the community then pays off the entire sum on behalf of all of the poor of the city. And thus what you want, and this, all come to the same point. But as for release from a *cherem*, it is completely impossible from this angle.

Solomon ben Adreth finds these kinds of communal oaths to be equivalent to personal oaths. Once they are uttered they become valid and cannot be undone *ex post facto*, even by Moses himself. The only hope for remedy is if the oath can be annulled *ab initio*. This can occur, for example, if a wife makes a vow because such a vow is made with the implicit (if not explicit) condition that the husband must approve it. If the husband renounces the vow it is deemed to have been void from the beginning. On this model, a community ban can be declared null and void *ab initio* if it is made at the beginning with the stipulation that the community can renounce it later. If this was not the case, then the ban must stand.

Interestingly, at this point the Solomon suggests some legal fictions to offer relief to the poor. His concern here is clearly to give some relief to the poor or others hurt by the ban, but to do so in a way that does not compromise the power of the community to issue irrevocable bans against its individual members. There is for him, then, a sort of flexibility in the halakha that allows for tailoring the law to individual needs. But the larger issue, the right of the community to impose its will on individuals, is maintained.

4. Meir of Rothenburg IV:1022

My second text is by Meir of Rothenburg. He was the scion of a long established rabbinic family in Worms, a city associated with one of the primary founding intellectual figures of Ashkenazi rabbinic Judaism, Rabbi Solomon ben Isaac (Rashi). After spending some time in Mainz, where he studied under the two famous Tosaphists Samuel b. Solomon and Jehiel of Paris, Meir settled in Rothenburg in 1240. He gradually became one of the most respected authorities on Jewish law of this period, receiving inquiries from all over Europe and even North Africa. He was considered one of the greatest judges in Europe of the time and was even asked to settle a dispute that had broken out between the Jews of Bohemia and Moravia. He was part of a small group of scholars, with their many bonds of family and discipleship, established the beginnings of a European tradition of Jewish responsa discourse that continues to influence Jewish life in our own century.

Meir of Rothenburg IV:1022

A rule is received from the three communities of Mainz, Worms, and Speyer that one will be under *niddui* (ban) in all [three] communities until his failure shall be made good as the officers of the city [*tobei hair*] instruct him. That is, one who is banned (*mnudh*) in his community is banned in all places.

Further, if one has books deposited with him, the community has no authority to take a pledge from him for any tax the owner of the book owes.

If one swears to his community that he has nothing except such-and-such out of which to give his tax and it is known to the community that he has more – that he swore to a lie – this man is disqualified from oaths. Thus if any one demands money of him, let this one swear against him and take [what he claims]. And one can not exempt himself from the tax because he rides in the royal court . . . .

If the community demands tax from an individual or anything that the individual has of the community, let the individual give to the community whatever it asks. Otherwise the community can go to judgment with him in their place before whoever has no part in the testimony and [even though] the individual is like one who is holding on to what is his, the rule of 'one does not go and take from his fellow' does not apply [that is, the community has the right of eminent domain]. Whoever shall transgress these regulations shall be under ban in all communities [kehillot] and if he should persist in his rebellion for a full month his money shall be permitted to be given over to the king or ruler. And whoever transgresses our regulations, we have the power to punish according to our opinion and we may curse the informers each Sabbath.

. . . One can not make one a leader (prns) in secret nor release a cherem without the consent of the entire community nor may a rabbi in his official capacity [hrv brbnuto] impose a cherem on any one nor release a community cherem except in public convocation.

The opening situation here bears some similarity to the one assumed in Solomon ben Adreth's responsum. The community must raise taxes and has agreed to place a ban on anyone who withholds his fair share. Now however, the tone of the law is even more stringent. There is no hint that the communal ban can be declared null ab initio. Rather the ban is assumed to remain in effect once it is pronounced, and has effect even in other communities. On the other hand, a ban, can be lifted by the issuing authority, something that Solomon ben Adreth apparently would not allow. That is, Meir argues that if the community as a whole decides a person or persons are to be released it can do so. The implicit assumption here is that this kind of communal ban is not analogous to personal vows. For

211

Meir they function as tools of community policy and so can be revoked (NB: not annulled) by the same power that imposed them.

5. Conclusions

In the end, these two authorities have different theories about the nature of individual liberty vis-a-vis what we would call the state. For Solomon ben Adreth, the community is something like a corporate individual. Its bans have the same legal character-istics as the vows of an individual. Made properly they can only be annulled, never revoked. On the other hand, there may be ways of getting around the vow without violating its letter. Meir is working with a different assumption. For him, the community is a corporate body that has the power to impose and revoke bans on its members willy nilly. It is in this regard not like an individual but is *sui generis* For this reason, of course, no subterfuge is needed to get around it; the community can simply declare it null and void.

What these two poskim agree upon is that in rabbinic Judaism as it was taking shape in the thirteenth century, individual liberty could be subordinated to the needs and power of the community. They disagree merely on what the basis for this power of the community might be. Let me stress here that at issue is not merely the fact that people must obey the law. What is at issue here is the right and power of communal authorities to apply social pressure on an individual so as to force that person to conform to policies created by the ruling authorities. Despite their differences, both Meir and the Rashba agree that for Judaism as they understood it, the individual's right to autonomy can definitely be limited by government decision. At the very foundations of post-Geonic halakha, then, is a strong sense that individual liberty is not absolute vis-a-vis communal authority. This perspective is in fact carried forward in the halakha and is encoded in the codes, such as the *Shulkhan Arukh*. There can be no question, then, that this is the halakhic perspective on matters.

The only question remaining is what this means in the contemporary context and how, if at all, such bans can be implemented given today's realities. Jewish communities do not have anything like the authority they had in medieval times to enforce obedience to their rules. Leaving aside Orthodox communities, within which the traditional halakha as received can still function by and large, how can modern American, European or Israeli Jewish institutions enforce this halakhic principle in the absence of power to impose meaningful *niddui* and *cherem*?

The question can be answered in two possible ways. One is simply to declare the halakha in this case to be of theoretical interest, but of no practical weight (in non-traditional community settings). The other is to find some way to maintain the integrity of the halakhic position even while shaping it in light of the modern situation.

To my mind, one usable approach along this second line is exemplified in Solomon Freehof's *Modern Reform Responsa* #32.[5] In the case at hand, a congregation had passed a resolution that would bar from worship services and religious school any one who was able to pay dues but was unwilling to do so. The rabbi of the congregation wants to know whether or not this is right. Freehof's answer begins with the assertion, in line with what we have seen, that 'in general one may say that the authorities of a community or a congregation have the right to exercise a considerable degree of compulsion with regard to the establishment and the maintenance of a synagogue.' Freehof goes on to discuss *niddui* and *cherem*. His conclusion is basically that while the congregation has the right to impose a ban (whether of limited duration, a *niddui*, or of unlimited duration, a *cherem*), this power should be exercised with caution. After all, the effect may be merely to drive the person to another synagogue, or may result in alienating the person and his or her children from Jewish communal life altogether. So for Freehof, the right of a Jewish communal organization, specifically a synagogue, to impose a *niddui* or a *cherem* is still in effect; the only question is the pragmatic one of how best to exercise this right. It is the use of *niddui* and *cherem* that is more difficult nowadays.

I submit that Freehof offers a model (whatever one may think of the argument and content) of how to carry forward the halakhic tradition into the modern world. In all events, if we propose to stay within the bounds of traditional rabbinic thinking about personal liberty, it seems to me that we must be committed to the proposition that such personal liberty is limited, specifically by the right of the community to impose *niddui* and *cherem*. What is open to us is the task of thinking through how that communal power might be brought into modern or even post-modern Jewish life.

Notes

1 There is some debate in the scholarly literature as to whether or not these answers are the full answers as given by the Academies, or are only précis meant for the record. There is some evidence that the answers preserved from later Geonim are longer than answers from earlier centuries, suggesting that what is preserved is in fact authentic; otherwise we would expect an equal distribution of styles across collections. At any rate, the evidence is too meager at this point to arrive at a definitive conclusion.

2 This shift in legal rhetoric in the Jewish community coincides with a revival of Roman law and jurisprudential thinking in Europe. There in fact may be some influence from the larger European context onto Jewish legal rhetoric. The shift in European legal rhetoric at this time is discussed in Cantor 1969, pp. 337ff.; see also Kisch 1948, pp. 208ff.

3 'Niddui' and 'cherem' are biblical terms that took on specific meaning in the halakhic literature. Roughly speaking, *niddui* was the imposition of a ban on an individual for a period of 30 days. This usually meant isolation from the community and a sort of enforced contempt. The *cherem* came to be a more serious form of *niddui* in which the victim was isolated even more completely and usually for an indefinite period of time. These matters are more fully spelled out in *Shulkhan Arukh*, YD 334.

4 Bavli Shabbat 46b, Yeb. 29b, Ned. 73b *et al.*

5 Freehof 1971, pp. 179–183.

References

Cantor, N. 1969. *Medieval History: The Life and Death of a Civilization*, 2nd ed. London: Macmillan

Freehof, S. 1971. *Modern Reform Responsa*. Cincinnati: HUC Press

Kisch, G. 1948. *The Jews in Medieval Germany*. Chicago: University of Chicago Press

R. Meir b. Baruch of Rothenburg. Bar-Ilan's Torah Educational Software 3.0 [CD-ROM: 1994]

R. Solomon b. Abraham ibn Aderet. Bar-Ilan's Torah Educational Software 3.0 [CD-ROM: 1994]

Index

Abarbanel, R. Isaac 137
absolutism 21
Akiva, Rabbi 169, 182–4
anthropocentrism 113–14
Antigonos of Sokho 124
Aristotle 15, 23, 56, 65–6, 69, 85, 102, 154–5, 157
Ashkenazi 204
authority 135; communal 212; and consent xiii, 174–81; realignment of 205–6
Averroes (Ibn Rushd) 168
Avineri, S. 79

Basic Laws (of Israel) 144–5
Bentham, J. 4, 57
Bergson, H. 3
Berlin, I. 156
biblical texts, Maimonidean reconstruction 167–9; authority and consent 174–81; Garden of Eden 169–71; historicism, structural-functionalism, formalism 186–95; idolatry, Golden Calf, sanctuary 184; Jethro story 182–4; Job, book of 195–8; Joseph story 171–3; Moses as future messiah 185
Buber, M. 66, 119

Chasidism 66
chesed (loving-kindness) 198, 199–200

choice xiii, 156–7, 160, 172; and the individual 70–1, 76
Chumash (prayer book) 64, 65–6
church/state separation xi–xii
Cicero 20
classical liberalism xi, 73, 179
Cohen, H. 124
Collins, R.K.L. and Skover, D.M. 27, 30
colonialism 58
communal ends 64–7
communitarian/liberal debate 98–102; and compromise/ reconciliation 107–9; Jewish perspective 102–7; normative implications 107–9
communitarians x–xi, xii, 65, 75–6, 80
community: and Judaism 63–71; particularism of 88; *see also* individual/communal intersection
Comte, A. 24
Conflict Thesis (CT) 129–31, 146–7; and concepts of democracy 131–3; nationalism and democracy 139–46; theses concerning 133–9
consent xiii, 174–81
contractualism 98–9
covenant 16, 87, 92, 116, 118, 119, 120

215

Dawson, J. 130
democracy 112–13, 124–5,
130–1, 155; anthropocentric
and theocentric 113–14;
definition of 131–2; and
equality of foreigners 120–2;
and equality of women 122–3;
and equality/chosenness
119–20; and halakha 131–9;
Jewish 118–19; limits of
117–18; and nationalism
139–46; populist view 132
deserts 38, 40–1, 51–2
difference principle (Rawls) 99
Duber, Y. 184
Duran, Simeon ben Tzemach 19
Durham, P. 60

education 50–1, 55–6, 77
Elon, M. 140, 141–2
Epicurus 12, 13, 38
equality: and chosenness 119–20;
and foreigners 120–2; and
women 122–3, 131
Erasmus 22
Exodus story 169, 180, 182, 185

First Amendment 27–8, 30
Frankel, C. 80
Frankel, S.H. 7
free will 6–7, 9, 164
freedom from/freedom to 156–7
Freehof, S. 213
Friedman, R. Dov Baer 124
Friedman, M. 73, 80

Galston, W. 108
Gamliel, R. 121
Garden of Eden 71, 168–71
Garver, E. 22–3
Gavison, R. 132, 145
Geonim 206–7
Gitlin, T. 25
God 16–17, 19, 52, 87, 89, 93,
114, 135, 155, 172; existence of
175; and human rights
114–16; and nature 173; and
personal autonomy 123–4; as
teacher 162–3

Golden Calf 184
good life 86, 94
good/s 82, 83, 84–5, 95, 98, 102,
108
Goodman, L.E. and Goodman,
M.J. 58
Gutmann, A. 108

halakha 131–9, 141, 145–6, 156,
157, 203–4, 207, 210, 212,
213–14
Halevi, J. 160
Hammett, D. 48–9, 60
happiness 64, 65, 66, 69–70, 99
Hegel, G.W.F. 102
Himmelfarb, G. 23, 24, 58, 60
historicism 186–95
Hobbes, T. 52, 170, 174, 178, 181,
184, 191
holiness 64–5, 66, 71, 77
human rights (HR) 112–13,
124–5; anthropocentric and
theocentric 113–14; and
collective responsibility
116–17; and equality of
foreigners 120–2; and equality
of women 122–3; and equality/
chosenness 119–20; and
Jewish democracy 118–19; and
limits of democracy 117–18;
and theonomy 114–16
humanism 34, 38–9
Humboldt, W. von 38–9
Hume, D. 29
Huxley, A. 30

'I-Thou' relation 66, 119
identity 73, 79–80, 90, 94, 103–4,
143
idolatry 91–2, 119, 184, 190
Imsoni, Simeon 169, 182–4
individual ends: as dependent on
the state 67–8, 69–70; and free
choice 70–1; undermining of
66–7, 71, 72–3
individual/communal
intersection 203, 204; and
enforcement of law 207–14; see
also community

216